FIFTY-FIVE YEARS OF MY ERA
OF THE TWENTIETH CENTURY

Jan. 19. 2002

To Connie,

All four of us thank you
for taking care of our dear
father, "E.C.", during the
last 3 months of his life.
You made him feel cared for
and not alone.

Gratefully,

Betsy

Nancy
E. Hope

Mary
His daughters

Jane

FIFTY-FIVE YEARS OF MY ERA OF THE TWENTIETH CENTURY

Elden C. Weckesser, M.D.

VANTAGE PRESS
New York

Permission has been granted from the following for the use of illustrations/photographs in the photo section:

Weckesser, *Treatment of Hand Injuries,* 1974, from Mosby Year Book Inc., St. Louis, MO;
"Journal of Bone and Joint Surgery" (JBJS), from Managing Editor Emeritus Stephen Tilton.
"Journal of Trauma," from Williams and Wilkins, Baltimore, MD; and
The Plain Dealer, © 1939 (formerly the *Cleveland News*), Cleveland, OH.

FIRST EDITION

Published by Vantage Press, Inc.
516 West 34th Street, New York, New York 10001

Manufactured in the United States of America
ISBN: 0533-12583-9

Library of Congress Catalog Card No.: 97-91193

9 8 7 6 5 4 3 2 1

To my lovely devoted partner in marriage of sixty-one years, Kathryn Tuttle Weckesser, and to our daughters, Jane W. Tuteur of Chicago, Elizabeth W. Leshner of Richmond, Nancy W. Andersen of Atlanta, Mary W. Oas of Erie, Pa., and their families.

Mrs. Kathryn Tuttle Weckesser sadly passed away on April 2, 1998.

Contents

Franklin
Delano
Roosevelt
1933–45
(d. 4/12/45)

Harry S.
Truman
1945–53

Prefatory Note

Dr. Elden C. Weckesser has written a fine dissertation on the profound changes of the twentieth century, as they have affected his life and particularly his medical and surgical experiences.

"Nineteen-ten was the year that Halley's Comet appeared as a beautiful array of light and color in the night sky. . . ." Elden Weckesser and I were both born in this same year. I have had the pleasure of associating with Elden as a longtime friend and colleague, beginning with our student years in medical school at Case Western Reserve University. This was followed by four years of service in the army with the 4th General Hospital Unit from Cleveland's University Hospital. During World War II, this was the first medical unit to be activated and serve overseas. We were stationed in Australia, New Guinea, and the Philippines. Framed within the historical perspective of this period, Elden's documentation of his experiences is a particularly valuable record.

Elden recounts the events of his personal life and a remarkable medical career against a backdrop of many significant historical events and scientific discoveries. Professionally, Dr. Weckesser has made a significant contribution to medicine through his splendid career as a surgeon and in research. To use his own expression, Elden is "a survivor". He looks back over a lifetime with both awe and optimism for the future: "it has been an exciting and good life. . . ."

Webb P. Chamberlain, M.D.
Clinical Professor Emeritus
Case Western Reserve University,
Medical School
Cleveland, Ohio
October 1997

FIFTY-FIVE YEARS OF MY ERA OF THE TWENTIETH CENTURY

Introduction

These pages contain recollections from memory aided by recorded compilations of events, discoveries and developments that have occurred during my lifetime in this twentieth century. It is hoped that these recollections and comments on discoveries and developments are of interest and kindle memories for you.

On the good side, perhaps more things have happened in this period to make life more comfortable, interesting and meaningful than ever before. But not everything was upbeat—it never was or is, in my experience. On the down side, the worst economic depression of all time descended upon us in the 1930s. Five wars have cast shadows across our paths and affected all of us, and taken an untimely toll on many lives. In addition, a Cold War (1945–1992) although undeclared, caused much worry and defensive preparation. Fortunately the awesome, no-win consequences of atomic energy destruction prevailed and made this a period of standoff for all countries in the world.

During high school I became fascinated with learning and increasing my knowledge. I can particularly remember a general science experiment in my freshman year. Mr. Garver, our principal, produced water from dry ingredients by chemical reaction. It intrigued me tremendously. It seemed like magic, which I still think it is, although it follows natural law. I found learning a great satisfaction and became determined to learn as much as I could.

My older brother Ethan was experimenting with making static shocking machines and electrical motors—and many interesting things. Mother had died four years earlier and I was alternately living with my older sisters who lived nearby and who were in the early stages of raising their own families. My sister Ruth lived in Doylestown, Ohio (population 1200). She and her husband, Eldon Cleckner, had taken over the family home at 136 Marion Street after Mother died. My sister Esther married Harry Galehouse and lived two miles south of town near Father's apple orchard. Both were in the Doylestown school district, where I attended school. My oldest sister Louisa was earning a Ph.D. in botany at the University of Chicago and was away with her husband, Dr. Joseph Banks Rhine, doing interesting things at the University of West Virginia, and then at Duke University.

Mother, a wonderful person, had been greatly in favor of education for all of her children. She was a good academic influence in the family,

1

in addition to Father who operated apple orchards and greenhouses as described later. Three years after he married Mother, he had financial reverses in the panic of 1893 in New York state and had never fully recovered from his losses. His kind, gentle nature was not meant for cold business dealings. He should have been a professor in a university—he would have made a good one—but his frugal, rural, early life did not provide that possibility.

We had little money to spare when I was growing up and each of us had to finance his and her own education. Though Father and Mother could not finance our education, they instilled in us the desire to do it ourselves. Louisa, the eldest, did it first and set the stage for the rest of a family of nine to follow.

Having grown up under austere circumstances and seen my father struggle to meet mortgage payments on his orchards, I decided to avoid the burden of debt.

My father's youngest brother, Uncle Ray, was a dentist in Sandusky, Ohio. He liked his work and was quite successful. My own personal dentist, Dr. H. M. Peters, in Barberton, Ohio also had influence on me. He told me that I should learn to do something that not everyone else could do. This made good sense, I thought. Dr. Vern Sharp, an Akron surgeon also from Doylestown, encouraged me and took me under his wing by allowing me to visit Akron City Hospital, make rounds to his patients with him and watch him operate. His friendship and interest was very encouraging. With my brothers, sisters, and Father in agreement, I set my goal on a medical degree knowing I would need to finance it myself. I would find out later there were many medical doctors among my ancestors, particularly among those of my mother.

When I became a college student, like many young people in the late 1920s, I had to work to support myself and earn my own tuition. Scholarships in 1928 had barely come onto the scene. I tried for one at Duke but was not successful. Later, I did have a Crile fellowship during the summer of 1935 between my junior and senior year in medical school. I will tell you about that later.

Events of 1910
William Howard Taft,
President of the U.S., 1908–12

William Howard Taft, a large conscientious man, son of a Cincinnati judge, was president of the United States. He had been Secretary of War

2

in Theodore Roosevelt's cabinet and had been nominated by Theodore Roosevelt to be his successor. His greatest interest, however, was in law rather than politics. He was noted for doing what he thought was right rather than expedient or self-advancing (Freidel 1968, 161). His father, Alfonso Taft, of Townsend, Vermont (later he moved to Cincinnati), had been a delegate to the National Convention in 1856, which led to the formation of the Republican Political Party. President McKinley had made William Howard Taft civil governor of the Philippine Islands (1901–1904) where he became very popular among the natives by improving the economy, building roads and schools and giving local people limited participation in their government. He had also been Secretary of War in the Roosevelt cabinet, in charge of construction of the Panama Canal.

Soon after his election as president, President Taft initiated antitrust suits, dissolved giant oil and tobacco trusts, encouraged irrigation projects and reserved oil and coal deposits in federal lands. He also initiated the Postal Savings System which later was a great help to me as a student in the 1930s. Mrs. Helen Herron Taft was responsible for the gift and planting of 3000 Japanese cherry trees about the Tidal Basin in Washington, D.C. (Degregorio, 396). Taft ran on Roosevelt's record but his methods in office were different. Soon there was dissatisfaction among some Roosevelt followers that led to a break between Taft and his former mentor leading to unfriendly relations and unhappiness for President Taft. This became so severe that in the election of 1912 Roosevelt ran against Taft in the Bull Moose Party, leading to the election of the Democratic candidate, Woodrow Wilson (Freidel, 165). In 1921, President Harding appointed William Howard Taft to the Supreme Court making him the only person ever to hold the offices of President of the United States and Chief Justice of the Supreme Court.

The population of the United States nearly doubled from 1910 to 1960 from 92.2 to 179.3 million and has continued to rise rapidly to 248.7 million in 1990 (World Almanac, 378). Crime has increased, we can no longer leave our doors unlocked, we have a serious drug abuse problem in our communities, morality has declined, teen-age pregnancy is high, divorce is common, many are unemployed and it seems that there is a greater emphasis on monetary things and that selfishness and greed have increased.

Neon lighting was discovered by the French chemist George Claude who first showed that light was produced when electricity was passed through a noble gas in a sealed tube (Asimov, 447). These tubes could be shaped into lettering on an electric sign leading to the popular development of neon sign advertising. Eugene Ely flew his airplane from the deck of the U.S. cruiser *Birmingham* November 14, 1910. This was the first launch of an aircraft from a ship (Encyclopedia America, 8:411). Abraham Flexner made a report of his study of medical education in the United States and Canada which he had carried out over the previous year now known as the Flexner Report. He reported on 155 medical institutions.

Halley's Comet

1910 was the year that Halley's comet appeared as a beautiful array of light and color in the night sky, according to my father. There was little artificial lighting in those days and its brilliance was beautiful. In addition, the brilliance caused consternation in the minds of many people. It had been predicted that the Earth might pass through the tail of the comet with dire results. Many people stayed home to spend the last day of their life with their family (Carruth, 421).

On May 18, 1910 I was seven weeks old and it was no concern of mine. Father spoke only of the comet's beauty to my recollection. Halley's comet on its return visit in 1986 had sadly lost its luster and its beauty as seen in Ohio and caused no consternation and little admiration.

In 1682 an observer of the heavens by the name of Edmund Halley observed a beautiful comet in the sky and from historical recordings of previous comets noted that such a comet had appeared in the past with a striking regularity every seventy-five to seventy-six years. Copernicus, from personal observations of heavenly bodies, had published a book just prior to his death in 1543, one hundred and thirty-nine years earlier, in which he gave reasons that indicated that the Earth rotated about the sun and gave mathematical computations to substantiate his view (Asimov, 206). His death fortunately prevented persecution by the church, which did not accept the heliocentric system in which our sun is the center of our universe with the planets rotating about it. Halley, in 1682, accepted the heliocentric system and postulated that the periodically recurring comet was one and the same in elliptical orbit about our sun. He rightly postulated its return in the year 1758. Little attention was paid to his postulation until the latter year when it did, indeed, reappear proving his theory. The regular subsequent reappearances in 1834, 1910 and 1986 have substantiated his view making the name Comet Halley appropriate.

Shoemaker-Levy 9 Comet

In July 1994 a new Shoemaker-Levy 9 comet struck and was destroyed in Jupiter's atmosphere with results less severe than conjectured. The collision of a comet somewhere in the universe has been postulated as one possible explanation for the disappearance of dinosaurs on earth.

Faith, Dr. Millis

In the medical field we have been favorably influenced by the great medical advances of the era. I shall comment on many of these advances in medical care, their cost and distribution, which are important problems at present. For survivors such as myself, overall, it has been an exciting and good life and I have faith that the future will be similar. My definition of faith is that of my friend, the late president of Case Western Reserve University, Dr. John Schoff Millis, who said: "Faith is the belief that things will turn out well due to combinations of unforeseen forces, factors and circumstances."

Energy

Mechanical, physical, chemical and electrical energy has been developed to drive machines to perform work for the human race to a tremendous degree. The great advances of the era are related to increased learning, understanding of physical phenomena, and the development and control of energy. As referred to later, the development of energy to work for us is largely responsible for the great material developments that we enjoy. Modern methods of travel reflect this. Now electronic methods of recording, storing and transmitting information are making that type of change also.

Thought to Electrical Charges, Computerization

Conversion of thought and data to electrical impulses within the computer has revolutionized life as much as the printing press did in the fifteenth century. All sorts of data, although fragile, can be compactly stored, transmitted at the speed of light, or converted to printed words here or around the world. More on the computer and its electronic aspects later.

Personal Responsibilities

In spite of these marvels, we must all continue to realize our responsibilities and the necessity for good will among one another and not let selfishness and greed tear us apart, which is an increasing danger as our numbers increase and we know less about our neighbors. We must remember the need for empathy and concern for our fellow beings here on Earth so that we can live together in peace. We must all remember that, under democracy, the control of selfishness and greed is a personal responsibility of the individual. We must realize this especially in our present age of what seems to be "aggressive individualism."

In our present period of available power and electronics, beasts of burden have given way to modern machines including robots that are now replacing human muscular effort to the greatest extent ever. This makes it harder and harder for the unskilled laborer to find work, the only salvation for him or her being education and special training to operate the complicated machines and electronic equipment of today and the future.

In China, in 1983, I witnessed projects designed to create manual labor—something that has not been done in our country, where emphasis has been on the development of machinery to replace it. For example, in Beijing, China, where labor was very cheap, I saw a crew of men excavating a river bank to widen a river channel. They had dug out shelves one above the other in the river bank and each worker shoveled to the level above him. It was a shovel brigade, similar to a bucket brigade, but using shovels with each worker keeping his own. It was getting the dirt to the top of the bank slowly but effectively and employing many people. The wages I'm sure were not high, which is the catch of course, but work was being provided and people were kept busy. Projects of this nature could be considered for emergency employment if necessary. I hope they never are.

Early Days

My earliest childhood memory is the sale of household and farm belongings at Williamsville, New York in December 1912, before my family returned to Ohio when I was nearly three years old. I remember it particularly because I saw tears in my father's eyes and knew he was upset by it. Other childhood memories were supplemented by family tales handed down by Father and older members of the family. "Current Events" are from memory and publications of each period.

When I was a boy, the usual way of getting about locally other than walking—and we did plenty of that—was by horse and buggy. The beast of burden was the main form of energy available beyond human effort for most undertakings, although the scene was beginning to change. I remember going to the dentist in Wadsworth, Ohio, seven miles away, by horse and buggy with my older sister, Esther. She was having a tooth filled and I was along to have the fine gentleman, Dr. Baldwin, look at mine. Little did I suspect what I was getting into. He found a bad one. It needed to be pulled and that took place right then and there much to my surprise. In my boyish mind, I thought the roots went clear down to my feet because when he pulled that tooth, my feet came right up into the dental chair! After it was over, Bucy, our white horse, faithfully took us home. On the way I didn't get much sympathy from my sister who said, "Wait till you have to have one filled!" I pondered that.

That first trip to the dentist by horse and buggy was about 1915, but already it was a period of change and "horseless carriages" were coming onto the scene. Father had bought a truck to replace his horse and wagon. There was skepticism about "these new-fangled things," which frightened horses on the road, but they traveled faster than a horse could trot! This truck was quite an innovation in the little village of Doylestown where I was growing up. Automobiles were not common and airplanes were rare. When you saw one of the latter you called out so that others could see it too.

Lighting inside the home was usually by oil lamp or candle until natural gas was piped in. There was no electricity in town. It was before radio and television. (I was in the fourth grade at school when radio first became available and television did not arrive until after World War II when Kate and I had our first home on Coleridge Road, Cleveland Heights when our children were small.) Longer trips during my childhood were usually by train over land or by boat if a navigable waterway existed.

Mother was from Williamsville, New York and the family made trips back and forth there on the C. B. (Cleveland–Buffalo Steamship Line) taking an overnight boat from Cleveland, arriving next morning at Buffalo. In the summer when it operated, one usually had a pleasant journey over Lake Erie.

Family Backgrounds

My mother, Ella Elizabeth Long (1870–1920), was born in Williamsville, New York, a suburb of Buffalo. She was a Long family descendant of John Long upon whose farm much of the village of Williamsville developed. That John Long and his wife, Mary Hershey Long, had migrated there in 1808 from Mannheim, Pennsylvania (just north of Lancaster). His great-grandfather, John Lang, had migrated to Pennsylvania from Switzerland in 1716. He *anglicized* his name to Long after arrival in the United States.

Another of Mother's ancestors was the Reverend Hans Herr, a Mennonite minister who in 1709 came from Switzerland in his seventies bringing two hundred and seventy-two of his congregation with him because of religious intolerance and persecution. Rev. Hans Herr made arrangements with William Penn to purchase land in what was to become Lancaster County, Pennsylvania. After arrival in Philadelphia, the group walked the sixty plus miles to the area of their land purchase and became the first, or some of the very first, settlers in Lancaster County, Pennsylvania.

The Longs in the Williamsville area were farmers, teachers, businessmen and doctors. Many continued to embrace the Reformed Mennonite faith after that branch of the Mennonite Church was formed in 1812 in Lancaster, Pennsylvania by one of the Herr descendants. Mother's father, Emanuel Clifton Long (1845–1932) was a farmer, teacher and businessman. He and Grandmother Anna Bishop Secrist Long joined the Reformed Mennonite Church, on the main street of Williamsville, about five years after they were married, which would have been about 1874. Grandfather became one of the lay ministers (all were this type) in the church but evidently maintained a rather broad view of religion in that he did not take church dogma too seriously. When he was called on to preach a funeral service for a friend who had left the church, instead of condemning his friend, as was expected of him, he dwelt on the man's good points of character. He was castigated for this by the church hierarchy and asked to repent. This he refused to do. He had spoken his sentiments and stood by them. Eventually, as a consequence of this dispute, he left the church. This happened in the 1920s, several years after Ella, my mother, had died. The nice little limestone church still stands on the main street of Williamsville, New York. To me, it is a reminder of

9

Grandfather Long's opinion of a friend, which he would not change to conform to church doctrine.

Ella, Emanuel Long's eldest daughter, my mother, grew up on his farm about one and a half miles east of Williamsville on the road to Albany. The Williamsville village portion of the original "John Long" farm had been passed on to other descendants previously. Emanuel's farm had been inherited from his father, Daniel Long, who had purchased it in 1832. On this farm, Mother passed the first nineteen years of her life until my father, Christian Weckesser, came to Williamsville in 1889 in search of queen honey bees for his orchards. He and Emanuel Long were both bee keepers. In my mother, Father obtained the greatest queen of all, much more than he anticipated, but whom he and the entire family greatly appreciated.

Weckesser Family

My father, Christian Weckesser (1865–1945), was born on a farm one mile north of Marshallville, Ohio. His father Henry Jacob Weckesser had emigrated to America from Germany in 1854 at eighteen years of age. Grandfather's ship, the New Era, coming from Bremen, Germany, ran aground in fog followed by a storm off Deal Beach, New Jersey, about seventeen miles south of the New York harbor, the intended destination. The weather had been rainy and windy and the last reading on the ship's position had been taken on Friday, November 10, three days before running aground. *The Ambrose Lightship* I do not think was stationed at the harbor entrance in those days, at least there is no account of it in the records.

Wreck of *New Era*
November 13, 1854

The tragic shipwreck in which Heinrick Jacob Weckesser narrowly escaped death at Deal Beach, New Jersey, during a more than twenty-four-hour ordeal in which 230 passengers perished, is described in detail by many on shore and other vessel observers in the accounts of *The New York Daily Times*. This article was kindly supplied to me and to Cousin Fern Weckesser in 1953 during our planning of an observance at our

10

Wayne County Cottage July 4, 1954 in remembrance of the one hundredth year following Grandfather Weckesser's arrival in America. It gives a complete account of what happened and the confusion that existed after the vessel ran aground. We are very appreciative of this account and are very indebted to the *New York Times* for supplying photostatic copies of it. The ship's physician and steward did not survive. The captain and the rest of the crew came safely ashore on the first ship's boats Monday November 13! Pay particular attention to the account by Mr. Abner Allen, who opened his home on shore to the survivors. He describes seeing the *New Era* come aground in the fog about 250 yards off shore about six o'clock on the morning of the 13th. Fog is a very treacherous thing that obscures landmarks and can vary rapidly, but if Mr. Allen could see the vessel from shore, the shore should have been visible from the vessel.

The *New Era*, a sailing vessel of 1326 tons displacement was built and launched at Bath, Maine earlier in 1854. It was returning from its first voyage abroad having taken on 600 tons of chalk in London, additional hardware and dry goods at Bremen, Germany plus 396 cabin and steerage passengers. Twenty-nine of the ship's company made a total of 425 people on board. We do not know precisely how heavily the vessel was laden during its voyage home, but it was probably riding deeply in the water.

According to my father, quoting Grandfather, there was an outbreak of cholera on board soon after leaving port. Many people died. The account of the captain lists forty lives lost in passage, many of which were probably due to that cause. With all these sad events, there was still more to come. The passage was very rough. On October 20, the twenty-second day out, the sea became extremely high so that waves broke over the deck killing three people and sweeping everything on deck overboard including the passengers' cooking range. The sea was so rough that it strained the vessel, according to the captain, causing it to take on water, which became quite severe as the voyage proceeded. The passage, which usually required thirty-five days, had taken forty-six up to the day of grounding.

There is a grave marker for *New Era* victims in the cemetery of the Old First Methodist Church at West Long Branch, New Jersey, which my wife Kathryn and I with two of our daughters, Betsy and Mary, were able to locate in 1967. The inscription reads, "In Memory of the 240 German passengers of the ship *New Era* who lost their lives November

11

13, 1854." The marker was erected by The *New Era* Monument Association in 1892. Ship records were all lost and many bodies were probably not recovered from the sea.

Henry Jacob Weckesser, a strong vigorous eighteen-year-young man did survive by climbing and clinging to the mast rigging, all that night, while those below him were swept away by the strong cold ocean waves. He, in later life wrote a poem entitled *A True Tragic Story of a Journey, Which Happened to Heinrich Weckesser in the Year 1854.* In view of his close and prolonged brush with death over an entire stormy day and night while he clung to the rigging of the *New Era* while those about him were washed away in the storm, it was in his words "an earnest admonition and call to his Lutheran friends and relatives in Germany, and to all sinners, who are led astray by false teaching."

Losing all his possessions and miraculously escaping with his life, when he reached shore, he was given warm dry clothing, some of which was odd fitting, including a frock coat. He was thankful for all this but his appearance was not the best. When he arrived in Philadelphia, a relative slammed her door in his face thinking him a tramp. She did let him in when he explained who he was and what had happened. In this way his life in the New World began.

He was a farm boy and soon found work among the Mennonites of Lancaster County, Pennsylvania. These people were good to him. He greatly appreciated their kindness after his terrible experiences and joined the Reformed Mennonite Church in 1860.

A few years later after working and accumulating some money, Grandfather began travelling westward, stopping among members of the Mennonite Faith on the way, as was customary at that time, planning to go to Iowa where new fertile land was available at low prices.

En route to Iowa he stopped with the Christian Zimmermann Mennonite family in Marshallville, Ohio and met the eldest daughter Catherine. Though he continued on his journey, he eventually thought that he had overshot his mark and returned to Ohio. He proposed to Catherine in 1864 but she did not want to go to Iowa. This was a dilemma. Christian Zimmermann, his father-in-law to be, would sell the Zimmermann farm to him, but the price was high—$45 an acre, post war inflation, compared to the $3 to $4 per acre—without buildings, in Iowa. It was said that he may have had to take the farm in order to get the bride. At any rate he took the bride and bought the farm. Father was born the next year and named Christian for his grandfather, Christian Zimmermann. This also accounts for my middle name.

Father's Early Life

Father's early life was spent on his father's farm. He attended a nearby rural school (#8) for eight years and absorbed every bit of learning possible from that source. He became an excellent penman. His handwriting was beautiful. Higher education, unfortunately, was not available or economically feasible and the need for labor on the farm was great in the period following "The War between the States." He was a dutiful son and did what was expected of him.

He soon became interested in the propagation of plants and trees by seed, cutting and grafting, and pollination with honey bees. I often think what a wonderful professor he would have made. Instead, his interest in growing things developed into his becoming a seedsman, advertising seeds and plants for sale. In order to do this, his father helped him buy a printing press. He began to publish a bimonthly rural paper in 1885, at age twenty, which he named *Rural Life.* In this he not only advertised his seeds and plants but also published advertisements for others. One of his customers was E. C. Long of Williamsville, New York. It was in this way that he came in contact with the man who became his father-in-law. Mr. Long advertised queen honey bees for sale in Father's journal and Father himself made a trip to Williamsville, New York to see them as told elsewhere.

Christian and Ella

Model City, Love Canal

After their marriage in Williamsville, New York, on February 16, 1890, there was a brief period spent in Ohio. Mother wished to remain near her own family. After all, by people living in New York state, Ohio was considered a frontier land in those days. Through Mother's cousin, David Long, a young entrepreneur, inventor and developer who was interested in harnessing the mighty power of Niagara Falls, father was able to buy property on Cayuga Island. This island was in the Niagara River a few

13

miles above the falls. Father transferred his seed business there. On November 9, 1891 my oldest sister, Louisa, was born there. Two years later, needing more land, the family moved inland about ten miles to Sanborn, New York where two more of my older sisters and my oldest brother Ernest were born. At this point the economic panic of 1893 intervened and the Cayuga Island property reverted to father when the people could not carry their commitment. This was a heavy burden but finally a sale of it was arranged. In the transaction, father obtained two lots in Model City (essentially worthless by that time), which was being promoted by William Love. Love was building a canal to bring water from the Niagara River to the Niagara escarpment at a more eastern location, about seven miles from the river where a new waterfall was to be built with water diverted from the Niagara River. This would supply power for a new Model City. This was just before the discovery of alternating current and high-tension transmission of electricity, prior to which electrical direct current could only be transmitted short distances without heavy loss. Love's idea was to bring the water to his new city and have it flow over the ledge there turning the generators at the city where it was needed. It seemed and was a very good idea, except, first he did not adequately determine the amount of rock that had to be dug through to make the new seven mile canal to his city and secondly he had bad luck. A Croatian by the name of Nikola Tesla discovered alternating current, leading to induction motors and transformers while Love was digging his canal. This eclipsed the undertaking. The discovery that alternating current could be converted to high voltages which then could be transmitted with very little loss made Love's idea obsolete. It was much cheaper to transmit high-tension electrical current than to divert part of a river for a water-fall at a new location. High-tension transmission of power is the method still used today.

The subsequent use of the never-completed Love Canal for toxic waste disposal is another story which came to light in the 1970s.

Because of all these financial problems, Father returned to Ohio in 1899 with his wife and four children. Grandfather Weckesser gave him an option on forty acres of the north portion of his farm at Marshallville, Ohio.

Here, Father built a small house near a spring in a hollow on a back part of the farm and the family moved there. This was adequate but not fancy. About 1905 an adjoining piece of property with frontage on what is now State Route 94 was purchased from an Aunt Lizzie, who had a small log house next to the road. This log house had been covered with siding over its logs. I think a room had been added to it also. I was born in that house in 1910 bringing the living family to four girls and four boys.

There were two ways of keeping time in 1910: Eastern Standard Time and Sun Time, which was an hour faster. I was born about midnight according to my sisters. Mother chose Eastern Standard Time, which made my birth date March thirty-first.

A sister, born six years before me, died of whopping cough at the age of three weeks. She was the only child not to reach adulthood.

In January 1911, Grandmother Long, Anna B. Secrist, died on the Erie County farm near Williamsville, New York, where Mother had been raised. I think mother felt sad and very much needed to help her father, even though he now had four daughters and four sons there to help him. Her family at this time numbered eight, I the youngest, being ten months old. All the factors are not known but it is a reasonable assumption that Mother was still having difficulty adjusting to rural life in Ohio. People in New York State considered Ohio the Western frontier. At any rate, a decision was made for the Weckesser Family to return to the Williamsville farm with Grandfather Long. This, it turned out, was a mistake.

Father advertised in the *Rural New Yorker,* a farm magazine of that time, for a family to live on his Marshallville property. The Rhine family answered and accepted.

Louisa, my eldest sister, did not accompany the family to New York state. She, twenty years old, had graduated from high school and had a teaching certificate. She taught school in Marshallville, lived in one room at the Henry Weckesser farm, one mile north of town, and cooked her own meals over a small stove in her room. It was during that year that Louisa met young Joseph Banks Rhine.

The stay at the Williamsville farm in New York state lasted less than two years. In Ohio, the Rhines did not stay on Dad's property and, during the second year, sisters Louisa and Esther lived there and took care of it. Things apparently came under control in Williamsville, at least the emergency aspect of it did. Grandmother Long's death became accepted and Mother's younger brothers and sisters were adults by then. It was never mentioned in my family, but I presume the large Weckesser family did not fit in too well when the emergency was over. At any rate, Mother told Father that she would go with him anywhere. Previously she had missed her family in New York but now, with her own growing large family, she was ready to return to the "wilds of Ohio."

Grandfather Weckesser had died in Ohio in November 1911, another unsettling family factor. At the end of 1912 the Weckesser family returned to Ohio for the last time. Brother Ernest, age fifteen, drove a horse and buggy from Williamsville, New York to Marshallville, Ohio, alone, during the move. Father soon bought a forty-acre, apple-bearing orchard one mile south of Doylestown, Ohio. This was on the opposite (northeast) side of the beautiful, broad Chippewa Valley. The orchard could be seen across the valley from Grandfather Weckesser's farm. (In the 1950s, Grandfather's farm was readily visible from our weekend cottage on the east side of the Chippewa valley. The forty-acre apple orchard south of Doylestown fulfilled Father's dream of having a bearing fruit orchard. Father, in the same transaction through Dr. E. A. Stepfield, president of the Doylestown Bank, obtained a ten-room house at 136 Marion Street, Doylestown. The owner, Mr. Beal, had died during construction and the bank had taken it over. We lived in a rented house on High Street for several months until construction was completed before moving into it in early 1913, the year of a severe spring flood. The 1913 flood of the entire Ohio Valley was quite a memorable event. I remember it as a child with water in the basement and apples floating at the new house on Marion Street.

For the first time, mother had sufficient room for her eight living children plus one more to be born at Doylestown: sister Miriam, three years later. The three eldest daughters, Louisa, Esther and Ruth were soon to be away teaching school and in just a few years Louisa would be away to college with the funds she was accumulating from her teaching plus money she could earn while in school. This was the pattern set for all of us.

Events of 1911

September 17 to November 5 entailed the first transcontinental air flight with many stops en route; it was a harbinger of things of the future. (World Almanac, 520). Rutherford put forth his theory of the nuclear atom, (Asimov, 448–50), which would eventually prove correct and which would lead to the development of the atom bomb thirty-one years later. Cosmic rays were observed in the atmosphere not arising from the earth. The first automobile is said to have been built in 1896. Charles Kettering invented the electrical self-starter for the automobile engine in

1911 (Asimov, 452). This device was not present on many automobiles until about ten years later. The early ones of my boyhood all had to be cranked.

Events of 1912
Thomas Woodrow Wilson
President 1912–20

The British ocean liner *Titanic* struck an iceberg off Newfoundland on her maiden voyage to the U.S. and sank with loss of 1500 lives (Carruth, 424). "The Great Ship Went Down." The parcel Post system was established. The Florida East Coast Railroad was completed to Key West. Elmer McCollum discovered vitamins A and B (Carruth, 425). The Nobel Prize in medicine was awarded to Alexis Carrell for vascular reconstruction and organ transplantation in animals. Common drinking cups were prohibited on all interstate railroad trains (Carruth, 427). The communal tin drinking cup on the pump at the well at my school was taken away when I was in the first grade (1916). This was replaced by collapsible metal drinking cups for each student.

Events of 1913

A wireless message was sent from Arlington, Maryland, to the Eiffel Tower in Paris (Carruth, 429) demonstrating the long distance capabilities of the method which had been seriously doubted. It was previously thought that these signals would travel outward into space rather than follow the surface of the earth. This was later shown to be due to a layer of ions in the outer atmosphere.

John D. Rockefeller donated one hundred million dollars and the New York State legislature chartered the Rockefeller Foundation. Henry Ford set up the first automobile assembly line to produce the Model T Ford. In 1930, I would work on one in Cleveland. The fiftieth anniversary of the Battle of Gettysburg was celebrated in that city on June 30th by both Blue and Grey veterans (Carruth, 429).

The 16th Amendment to the Constitution granted power to Congress to collect income taxes without allocation to the states (Carruth, 428).

This could have made "States Righters" turn over in their graves! Woodrow Wilson was inaugurated as the twenty-eighth president of the United States. The Ohio Valley Flood of March 21–26, 1913, caused losses of 100 million dollars and 400 lives (Carruth, 428).

Conrad Roentgen had shown in 1895 that penetrating rays, which he named X-rays, emerged when cathode rays (electrons) struck a tungsten anode in a vacuum tube. These rays he observed penetrated solid objects and exposed photographic film. The Coolidge X-ray tube introduced in 1913 made the production of X-rays *readily available* for use in medicine, dentistry and industry (Asimov, 457). The Federal Reserve Banking System was established (Carruth, 431) and culminated many important events of that year.

Boyhood in Doylestown, Ohio, 1913–28

It's interesting to realize that the period of my life in Doylestown consisted of only fifteen years, 1913 to 1928. Events of one's young life are so vivid that it seems much longer. My earliest childhood memory is of the sale of the farm and equipment as the family was leaving New York state in 1912. I remember my father being very upset by this event when a farm wagon was driven out of the lane by a new owner. I, at my young age, did not understand the reason for the sale or for his feelings but was very sensitive to the event and the sad situation it produced.

I do not recall the trip to Ohio from Williamsville, New York, but remember events soon after our arrival in Ohio. I recall the house on High Street, where we lived while the new house on Marion Street was being completed. My brother Ethan, eight years older than I, made a mechanical voice transmitter with string and two tin cans that he strung up between the upstairs window of the High Street house and a tool shed in the rear. It consisted solely of a taught string between the two cans. One acted as transmitter and another as a receiver. We talked back and forth over this and could hear quite well. Ethan was very analytical about things and soon became interested in electricity. He obtained some dry cell batteries with which he operated all sorts of electrical motors and magnets that he made himself. My mother recognized his special interest and abilities and gave over to him a wide bay window sill in the new house on Marion St. where he could experiment. None of us could disturb his things there.

It paid off for her. When he was sixteen years old, in 1918, he made a water system for her kitchen so that she had hot and cold running water! None of the other houses in the neighborhood had this at that time. Later he became an engineer and developed a successful company in Chicago. When I was growing up, he was my closest big brother and he taught me many things. When I had a question I could always take it to Ethan for a serious, good answer.

When we finally moved into the new house on Marion Street it was a happy time. We children were intrigued with the amount of space in its six rooms upstairs and four down and with natural gas for lighting and cooking! This was a great help for Mother and there was good gaslight for reading in the evening.

Events of 1914

In November 1914 the Panama Canal connecting the Atlantic and Pacific Ocean for ocean-going vessels was completed by the United States. This had been an ill-fated project started by the French nearly thirty-five years earlier, plagued by complications of design and by the scourge of Yellow Fever. The United States had bought out the French interests after the Spanish-American War in 1898 realizing the value of the canal for national defense. Following this, the Yellow Fever Commission led by Dr. Walter Reed showed that the disease was caused by a virus. The Aedes Aegypti mosquito was next established as the vector of this virus. Col. W. C. Gorgas was then able to rid the Panama Canal zone of Aedes Aegypti mosquitoes and the threat of the dread disease. This allowed the engineering problems of the huge project to be completed. The canal had to cut through mountains where landslides made the job tremendously difficult with the equipment available. Actually, Central America is the extension of the Continental Divide, our Rocky Mountains, connecting to the Andes in South America, and the canal had to be dug through that mountain range. In earlier days a French leader had said that if God had wanted a canal across Central America, he would have put one there. The successful completion of the Panama Canal, a tremendous accomplishment for the United States, was overshadowed by the outbreak of World War I in 1914.

Events of 1915

The steamship *Lusitania* was sunk off the coast of Ireland by a German submarine with the loss of 1198 lives, 114 of which were American. Dr. Joseph Goldberger of the U.S. Public Health Service discovered that pellagra was a vitamin deficiency.

The first transcontinental telephone call was made by the same men who made the original telephone conversation in 1876. Alexander Graham Bell in New York spoke to Dr. Thomas Watson in San Francisco, saying "Mr. Watson come here. I want you." In 1876 they had been in the next room (Carruth, 434–35). The first warships passed through the Panama Canal; the *Ohio, Missouri* and the *Wisconsin*. And the one millionth automobile rolled off of the assembly line at the Ford assembly plant in Detroit (Carruth, 437). The U.S. Coast Guard was established by Congress. The U.S. vessel *William C. Frye,* carrying wheat for Britain, was torpedoed and sunk by a German submarine in the Atlantic Ocean. Haiti became a protectorate of the United States (Wenborn, 207–9).

Events of 1916

General Pershing with federal troops entered Mexico in pursuit of Mexican bandit Francisco Villa. Financial aid was given to farmers (World Almanac, 521). U.S. Marines landed in Santo Domingo to quell a disorder and stayed eight years (Wenborn, 209). A bomb exploded in San Francisco during a parade killing ten people. The United States bought the Virgin Islands from Denmark. A military government was established in the Dominican Republic (World Almanac, 521). The National Park Service was established by Congress. The first birth control clinic was opened by Margaret Sanger, Fania Mindell and Ethel Burne in Brooklyn, New York (Wenborn, 213).

One evening after dinner in our big house on Marion Street there was some unusual activity. Mother was upstairs not feeling well. I, my sister Sylvia, six years older, and Ethan, eight years older, did not know what to make of it. Soon Dr. Stepfield came and rushed up to father and mother's front bedroom. A short while later, Father came down with a smile on his face and said, "You have a new baby sister." This was sister Miriam, a complete surprise to us, welcomed into the family April 10, 1916.

September of that year was the beginning of my formal education, the first grade. The school was less than a mile away and within easy walking distance. Ethan took me on my first day and I was not too anxious to go. Not knowing what I was getting into, I put up some resistance. I dragged my feet in fear of the unknown. He got me there and I soon found out it was not bad at all, in fact it was interesting. My teacher for my first two years was Miss Treuyer, who was a kind person and an excellent teacher who made us pay attention and taught us all a lot of new things. There was no kindergarten at that time.

Scarlet Fever

In about the middle of the term I developed Scarlet Fever followed by Nephritis and was ill at home for nearly six weeks. My urine turned black and I did not pass any for a while. With the aid of Dr. Stepfield, father's good friend, I pulled through. Miss Treuyer coached me in the material I had missed during my illness and with her help I was able to make up my back work. This gained her much gratitude and respect, particularly from my mother and older sisters, and taught me to be thankful when others help when you are in trouble. At the end of the year, with my makeup work, I was promoted to second grade.

Events of 1917
WW I (April 6, 1917–November 11, 1918)

Germany declared unrestricted submarine warfare January 31. The United States declared war on Germany April 6, 1917 (Wenborn, 213). Conscription Law passed May 18. U.S. troops arrived in Europe June 26 (World Almanac, 521). The Lakeside Hospital Unit of World War I from Cleveland, Ohio had arrived one month earlier and joined the British Expeditionary Forces in Rouen, France. December 7, 1917 the United States declared war on Austria-Hungary. The first engagement of U.S. forces was November 3, 1917 (Wenborn, 215).

It was during my first year in school that our country was drawn into the war in Europe. This was a serious thing even for children as older family members left home to serve their country. Young men were volunteering for military duty. The Conscription Law was passed near the end of the school year. My two older brothers, Ernest and Connie, both entered the service. I remember Father's farewell to Ernest the night he left. Father, being a Mennonite, preferred that he would not go to war but told him he respected his decision to go and did not wish to interfere with his plans. His tolerance was appreciated. Later, when I wanted to play football in high school, his attitude was similar. Close friends of my older sisters, Louisa, Esther and Ruth also entered the service. This gave a very special meaning to the war for all of us. Most of the young men were sent to Camp Sherman in southern Ohio or to Camp Taylor, I think in Tennessee, for their military training. Our troops began going overseas in June of 1917 and Esther's friend, Harry (Dick) Galehouse, was one of the early ones to go. (When I left for overseas duty January 10, 1942, he insisted on carrying my suitcase from the car to the 55th Street Pennsylvania Station, Cleveland, for me. He had been through a war and knew what it was.)

During the winter of 1917–18, the influenza epidemic broke out and the son of one of our neighbors, Vincent Dannemiller, died of pneumonia at camp. There were many deaths in the training camps. Everyone was worried.

In the fall I entered second grade. Miss Sweisberger, daughter of the Methodist minister, was the third grade teacher, and she was a close friend of my brother Ernest, which placed another emphasis on the war.

A military tank was brought to town to stir up patriotism and to sell Liberty Bonds. It was taken down in the woods behind the Catholic Church to a steep hillside to show the townspeople how capable and maneuverable it was. It came right up the hill over an old dead stump. After that demonstration, different people, including the Catholic Priest, Father Fastnacht and then Reverend Sweisberger, Methodist Minister, stood up on this tank and spoke to the people telling them to buy Liberty Bonds at the Post Office to support the war effort.

My two older brothers were in training camp and my oldest sister Louisa was working at the Goodrich Rubber Company in Akron making gas masks.

In November 1918 the Armistice in France occurred, the real one on November 11. There had been a false one about a week earlier. I remember being with my father getting gasoline for his International truck at Huffman's Hardware, when whistles started to blow and Church bells ring. There was a din across the countryside as this type of celebration and the setting off of fireworks spread to all the surrounding towns. Everyone was excited and happy that the war was over. Young people gathered and marched around town that evening and I remember tagging along. One of the songs chanted went as follows: "Kaiser Bill went up the hill to take a peak at France. Kaiser Bill came down that hill with bullets in his pants." Some of the older boys fired rifles and shotguns into the air. It was a real celebration!

The best part was during the next weeks and months when the young men began coming home. The Soldiers' Monument on the public square was erected the next year listing those who lost their lives and those who served. The flag pole was also erected.

Father's Automobiles

The First Truck, 1915

A memorable thing in my early boyhood was when Father became the proud owner of an automobile about 1914–15. This was a truck to haul apples to market in Akron. The orchard just south of Doylestown was a distance of fourteen or fifteen miles from the city. This trip took several hours with a horse and wagon and the truck could make it in less than half that time. This was probably the first truck in our town. It resembled a wagon with high wheels and small hard rubber tires. It was a righthand drive with a two cylinder air-cooled engine amidship, under the seat, which chugged along lively at a frisky fifteen miles per hour, faster than a horse could trot. It had headlights in case you did not get home before dark. On the first model, these were kerosene lights and later either carbide or presbide. The truck had two speeds forward and one in reverse controlled by a lever on the right of the seat that the driver pulled upward to engage the clutch. Power was transmitted from the engine to the wheels by means of chains. Each rear wheel had a cogwheel on its inner side on which the drive chains ran. I well remember this because as the cogwheels became worn, the chains would frequently come off. It was my job then to get out and start these chains back on the cogwheels from the bottom and then call to Dad who would start slowly forward and the chain would then pull back into its proper place and we were ready to go again.

This vehicle, an I.H.C. (International Harvester Company), was made in Akron. The factory was on High Street just down the street from the Quaker Oats Company. Later the company moved to Chicago.

Although this machine still had much resemblance to a farm wagon, it worked and pulled a good load and was a true embryo of the trucks of today. The truck body in the back had removable longitudinal seats for hauling passengers on special occasions, an interesting option, although the ride more closely resembled that of a farm wagon from which it was not far descended. Gasoline was purchased by the five gallon can at Huffman's Hardware, where it was poured into the under-seat tank with a funnel. Mr. Huffman was progressive; he saw the "writing on the wall" and realized that these things were for real. Later, Nate Zimmermann put in a gasoline pump right on Main Street and pumped the gasoline directly into your tank for fifteen cents a gallon. He was later

24

followed in this business by Cline, Whitman and Lepley. A later vehicle was called the REO Speed Wagon. We owned several of those.

Nate Zimmermann was an interesting old fellow with his store on Main Street. In addition to his first gasoline pump, Nate also sold jewelry and repaired watches, but you had to be careful if you took a watch to him for repairs. He was a little temperamental at times and if he did not feel good that day, he might throw it on the floor and put his foot on it!

Hiram Dague ran the grocery store at the foot of Marion Street where we shopped. When Father paid the grocery bill at the end of the month Mr. Dague would give me a bag of candy. He was a kind man and this put him tops in my estimation. He even let me pick out the kind I wanted. Chocolate Indian Heads were especially good. I'd look at them in the case thinking when I grew up I'd get a lot of them.

There were a lot of fine people in that town. Another one was Bill Jenior, the blacksmith in the alley behind our home on Marion Street. The barns for the horses and buggies were approached through alleys at the back of the properties. These were narrow unpaved streets running parallel to the streets, but in the rear. Bill Jenior had his shop there behind his house where he shoed horses, put new metal tires on wagon wheels, fixed nearly anything for you and painted it red when he finished. He probably had only one can of paint. It looked real nice but when you saw something painted red, you knew that Bill Jenior had probably repaired it. He prided himself in not charging high prices. He would fix tools and small things for fifteen or twenty cents. It was intriguing to watch him and he sometimes let me turn the crank of the blower for his forge which would heat the horseshoes and metal tires red and even white hot before he hammered them into shape. One day he was chiseling off the end of a metal wagon tire. The piece flew off and hit me on my right leg. I looked down at my leg and saw something protruding which was round and smooth (a lobule of fat). It frightened me and I ran home telling mother, "My intestine is coming out of my leg!" She put a bandage on it for me. It soon healed but I still have the scar, which is my reminder of good old Bill Jenior and his blacksmith shop. He was a great person in my estimation.

When Dad Bought His First Passenger Car

When Dad bought his first passenger car is also a memorable time from my early boyhood. This car was a Metz. It had soft seats and was more comfortable and faster than a buggy or the truck he already owned, when it operated the way it should. It had a very interesting drive mechanism which connected the engine to the rear wheels to make them turn. It was not a gear or fluid drive mechanism such as used today, and it was not chain-drive like the IHC truck. Instead, the engine turned a flat disc. Against this flat spinning disc, a friction wheel connected to the rear wheels was made to engage when the car was put "in gear." The driver controlled the location of the friction wheel on the disc with a lever. The position of the friction wheel on the disc determined the speed of travel, faster the farther from the center of the disc. It also controlled the direction of travel depending on which side from the center of the disc the friction wheel was positioned. (It could be made to go backwards as fast as forward, although no one cared to do that.)

I think Mr. Metz must have developed his car to run on flat terrain. Although the arrangement gave good control of speed and enough power on the level road, it was not good on hills. We soon found this out, about the first Sunday we had the car. There was a steep hill up to a railroad crossing on the way to the Reformed Mennonite Church in the country, six or seven miles south of town. Father didn't judge his speed well enough on this hill in the new vehicle and it stalled. When he tried to get started again, the friction wheel slipped and Father could not get the car to go up the hill. At this point he uncharacteristically used some profanity. That was too much for Mother. She said he could not go to church after talking like that! We backed down the hill and went home without attending church that day. The next time Father kept up his speed and we went over the hill with flying colors, and to church on time.

I remember having a number of those old friction wheels from the Metz to play with as toys. These had flat spots on them from slippage on hills such as we had encountered on the way to church. The flat spots gave a loud thumping sound as you sped along and that lead to replacement with new smooth ones. I was given the old parts for toys.

The Post–World War Period

When World War I ended in November 1918 there was a general feeling of euphoria, which persisted for several years. The conflict was wishfully described by some as "The war to end wars." The aggressive Kaiser had been stopped. This idealistic attitude, although doubted by many, was popular as people busied themselves leaving the service, going back to work and taking part in the many new developments of the era.

Pres. Woodrow Wilson proposed fourteen points for peace, attended the World Peace Conference in Paris and received the Nobel Peace Prize in 1919, but the United States Senate took an isolationist stance and did not approve of our involvement in Europe.

Events of 1918

On July 1 there were one million troops in Europe. May 28—First success with French Forces versus Germans at Cantigny. June 17—Second battle of Marne halts German advance (Wenborn, 521). Influenza epidemic 548,000 deaths (World Almanac, 521). July 18—Marne Offensive launched by U.S. forces September 18—U.S. forces take St. Mihiel with 15,000 prisoners. September 26–November 11—Battle of Meuse-Argonne. 1.2 million U. S. and 135,000 French cut German supply lines. November 11, 1918—German Armistice (Wenborn, 217).

Events of 1919

January 18—Peace Conference, Paris. February 14—President Wilson presents League of Nations Covenant at Paris Peace Conference. March 15—American Legion formed in Paris. June 5—Nineteenth Amendment to Constitution, Woman Suffrage, passed by Congress. June 28—Versailles Treaty signed. July 1—Daily air mail service between New York and Chicago. July 4—Jack Dempsey becomes World Heavyweight Champion. September 15—President Wilson suffers stroke in Colorado while advancing the League of Nations. October 28—Eighteenth Amendment, Volstead Act, passed banning the sale of intoxicating liquors, those containing one-half percent or more alcohol by volume. (Repealed 1933.) November 19—Treaty of Versailles not ratified by U.S. Senate (Wenborn, 1991, 217).

Mother's Final Illness

Mother was operated at the Barberton Hospital for a malignant tumor of her right breast in 1918 by Dr. Roscoe Stepfield and the prognosis was not good. This was a great shock to all members of the family. My older brothers and sisters knew more than I of the consequences, but the feeling of apprehension was apparent to us all.

In this year, 1919, my older sister Ruth married Eldon G. Cleckner in July and sister Esther married Harry W. Galehouse in December. Harry had been overseas in Germany in the infantry during the active fighting and had remained there with the Army of Occupation. He was an excellent marksman, won honors and was known as "The best shot in his battalion."

Mother appreciated two of her daughters being married and the ceremonies took place in the front room of the big house on Marion Street. In April of 1920, Louisa married Joseph Banks Rhine in the same room.

Mother at the time of Louisa's wedding was not feeling well and it was apparent that the breast tumor was recurring. Family resources were pooled and she was taken by train for consultation to Johns Hopkins Hospital in Baltimore, Maryland from Akron in 1919 to see if any further treatment was available for her. The news was bad. She had lung metastases and at that time no further treatment was possible. She returned home to await the inevitable. Her right arm became tremendously swollen. Father made a wooden frame on which it could be elevated to various heights with weights for counterbalance. She could then move about in bed or to a chair more readily. This helped to make her more comfortable. She gradually became short of breath and was finally confined to her bed, which was brought downstairs to the same front room in which the weddings had taken place. Here she was cared for by my older sisters and by Louise Smith, an excellent practical nurse in the community. Marie Dannemiller, R.N., who had taken nurses training at Lakeside Hospital in Cleveland and who later married Dr. Leonard Raycraft, was a great help to mother also. Marie had been a Doylestown young lady who lived on adjacent Howard Street and was a staunch family friend. She was the sister of Vincent Dannemiller who died of Spanish influenza at the Sherman army camp the year before.

Progressively Mother lost strength. The whole family rallied around her. Her adult daughters spent much time with her being on vacation and taking time from their teaching duties during the summer of 1920. She had bad spells followed by periods of improvement. On two occasions in her final weeks of life, thinking that the end was at hand, she called to see us all. On the first one of these occasions I remember Father coming to my bedroom in the middle of the night saying that he thought Mother was about to die and that she wanted to see me. In horror, I quickly donned some clothes and rushed down to the front room. The others were all there except Miriam, who was age four. Mother was sitting up in bed gasping for breath with her swollen right arm elevated on the frame that Father had made. She wanted me to come close to her and she put her left hand on my head and patted it. I don't think she said anything. With her labored breathing, she did not have to. She loved each of the nine of us and we all knew it. She had done everything for each of us that was within her power to do. She had worked very hard for us. She and Father had given us an appreciation and a clear outlook on life that would help throughout our own lives. We deeply returned her love. The nurse gave her some medication and her breathing became better and she dozed off to sleep, temporarily relieved. That crisis passed but the next and final similar episodes were more severe and the end came on August 20, 1920. I was in the room when she died and appreciated being allowed to be there. It was terrible for all of us. We witnessed it together and it bound us more closely together.

Funeral

The funeral was a few days later, held at home in the same front room. Mother's casket was open. She wore her sweet Mennonite garments with the small white bonnet and appeared to be at rest after her suffering. When it became time to close the casket I stood beside her at the head of the casket not wishing to leave. Miss Smith, the nurse, told me several times to get my cap to get ready to go. I ignored her at first. When finally I compiled and returned to the room, the casket was closed. She was doing what had to be done but I held it against her for a long while. Burial was in the family plot next to her infant daughter Bernice who had died of whooping cough in 1906 when was two weeks old. The family plot is on the south side of what is now called St. Michael's Cemetery. The cemetery is located on 95 Wayne County Road, five or six miles south of Doylestown. A brick Lutheran Church stands across

29

the road from the cemetery, and the small White Reformed Mennonite Church is visible at the adjacent cross road just south of it.

Mother's death tightened the bonds of the Weckesser family. Father and the four youngest of the children (Ethan 18, Sylvia 16, myself 10, and Miriam 4) were made to feel that we were welcome at the homes of each of our three older sisters. Father, Miriam and I stayed at the home on Marion Street with Ruth and her new husband Turp (Eldon George Cleckner). Soon needing a home for their own family, they bought the house, but we were still welcome there as guests.

From here I continued in the Doylestown school and entered the fifth grade in September shortly after Mother's death. Brother Ernest married Sadie Liken that fall. Sadie was a secretary at the Miller Rubber Company in Akron where Ernest worked in the Service and Adjustment Department. When people had trouble with their tires, they came to Ernie, who listened and made decisions on replacement or compensation to keep the customers happy. He was good at that. In the early days tires were not as strong or good as they are now, and troubles were frequent. Ernie's services were in great demand. The new couple took an apartment at Stadelman and Exchange Streets in Akron and later bought their own house in West Akron.

Esther and her new husband, Harry (Dick) Galehouse, took up housekeeping just down the road from the new fruit orchard that Father had acquired south of Doylestown. They also made us feel welcome there at all times. I lived with them part of the time and at other times with Ruth and Turp in Doylestown. My two older sisters, Esther and Ruth, worked that out in a congenial way among themselves. I marvel how well they did it. When I was living with Esther and Dick in the country I walked to the same Doylestown school in town so that there was no need to change schools. It was all so congenial that I felt as though I was a member of both families. I think they felt the same way. Later, in college at Duke University, the relationship with Louie and Banks in Durham, North Carolina was the same. It was an unusually close relationship with all members of the family that I think was brought on first by family hardship and then by Mother's early death.

Louisa (Louie) and Banks were taking advanced work at universities about the country; Chicago, Illinois, Yonkers, New York, and Morgantown, West Virginia before settling in Durham. Sylvia graduated from Doylestown High School in 1922 and, the fall that followed, went to the University of Chicago. She lived with Louie and Banks part of that time and worked for members of the faculty for room and board at other times. When Louie and Banks went to Morgantown in 1924, she transferred there to the University of West Virginia where she received a Bachelor of Arts degree in 1927. Louie and Banks were in the Botany Department there at that time.

Sister Miriam also began living with Louie and Banks while they were in Morgantown, attending grade school there. She stayed with them during their subsequent moves until she completed High School in Durham, North Carolina.

Louie and Banks Rhine were especially wonderful people in our family. They not only offered physical help to us younger ones, but also helped us with our visions of the future and the planning of our lives. They opened the door to advanced education in our minds by emphasizing and demonstrating its value as Mother had done. They had each demonstrated that it was possible to earn one's tuition by working while taking classes.

The Rhines were not only wonderful to members of the Weckesser family but also to other university students, many times supplying emergency help when needed. They were loved by many. Weekends at the Rhine household involved all sorts of hiking activities and excellent Sunday dinners prepared by Louie, who was an excellent cook in addition to all her other activities, interests and achievements.

I first used a microscope under the tutelage of Banks in his laboratory at the University of West Virginia. He took time to show me how to use it. It was very impressive for a freshman in high school. I looked at a drop of rain water and felt like Leeuwenhoek himself when I saw the ''animalcules'' in it!

Other Events of 1920
Warren Gamaliel Harding 1921–23, d. 8/2/23;
John Calvin Coolidge, 1923–28

1920 was the three hundredth anniversary of the Pilgrim landing at Plymouth, Massachusetts. Woodrow Wilson was completing his eighth year as president. He had become an invalid, incapacitated by a stroke, but continued in office. He had been a very active president during World War I and through the post–war reconstruction period, and much legislation was passed. However, the Senate was isolationist and had not ratified

31

the League of Nations for which he had worked vigorously but in vain. It was also the year that the sale of intoxicating beverages was made illegal (Prohibition). It was the year that the 19th Amendment to the Constitution of the United States became effective. The wording was, "The right of citizens of the United States to vote shall not be denied or abridged by the United States or any state on account of sex."

Aviation was developing. The first commercial airline was established between Key West, Florida and Havana, Cuba. Installment buying was gaining popularity for consumer items. Instead of waiting until you had the cash in hand to make a purchase, buy the item "on time", with a down payment, and have the use of it while you paid for it by installments! It was the antecedent of today's credit cards, thought by many people to be evil! Maybe it is. The conservative dictum was, "Wait until you have the cash in hand." We may have to come back to that idea. The first public radio station, KDKA Pittsburgh, began broadcasting in November. Sigmund Freud published *A General Introduction to Psychoanalysis* which attracted much attention to the unconscious mind. Warren G. Harding was elected president in November with Calvin Coolidge as vice president. Babe Ruth hit 54 home runs (Gordon and Gordon, 6–14).

Completion of Grade School Education

The next four years of my life were devoted to the balance of my grade school education at Doylestown. My teachers, Miss Shafter, Miss Schafer and Mr. Sellers, were interesting and good. I enjoyed the learning experience. I lived part of the time with sister Ruth and part of the time with sister Esther as already related. In 1922, Father leased the "Black Diamond Farm" adjacent to the apple orchard but over the hill on the next road east. The properties adjoined each other at the top of the hill. On the property were buildings, including a house and barn, which gave Father an independent place to live. But there was no wife or mother to make it a home. We did the best we could. Ruth and Esther were a great help but by this time they were having families of their own. Father, Ethan and I lived there with Connie and Sylvia at different times but it was quite austere. Cooking was a chore that none of us mastered. Sylvia naturally had the most talent and when she was there we ate well. She even made lemon pies with lots of lemon, which were delicious. But, she was not there for very long periods. Most of the time it was Ethan, Dad and I and occasionally Connie. The Black Diamond Farm was planted with all sorts of produce crops that were marketed at the early morning Farmer's Market in Akron. The crops were corn, tomatoes, onions, lettuce, and melons, in addition to the apples and peaches in orchards on the other side of the hill. The trip to the 4:00 A.M. market in Akron was in a class by itself. The wholesale buyers for hotels and restaurants came at that time to get the best produce. If they liked what you had, they might buy all of it. Preparation the day and evening before required a lot of work. The REO truck was packed the night before, usually in the evening so it was possible to get five or six hours sleep before taking off by three in the morning. Older brother Connie made this trip a lot, but there were times when I filled in getting the produce there, leaving it there with Father and returning to Doylestown in time for school. Father gave up driving when his sons were old enough to take over. I never knew just why that was. He drove over the IHC trucks and the Metz passenger car but did not drive later on.

Father was an expert on building greenhouses to get an early start on the season. We had one at the farm that was heated by wood fire since that fuel was readily available. Do I remember cutting wood for the greenhouse on the cold winter days? Yes, indeed I do. It was Ethan and I with a cross-cut saw. This was long before the days of the chain saw. It was really hard work but we did it. As the season progressed it was necessary to fire the greenhouse furnace every two hours at night. This chore we shared but I remember it as a dreadful task. It seemed that no sooner would you get back to sleep than the alarm rang for the next firing. Even though it became almost second nature, it was a task not relished.

Ethan faithfully stayed with the family working for Father until he was twenty-one years old. He then set out for himself to earn sufficient money to attend the Ohio State University Engineering School. It was a tough road but he made it and graduated with a Mechanical Engineering degree in 1928. He joined Miller and James, an engineering partnership, in Cleveland, with offices at East 9th Street and Prospect Avenue. The position lasted about a year and a half and then gave out due to the Great Depression. There was no money and no work. He obtained a job with a dredging company on the East Coast for a period of time until that too gave out. There was then a period of unemployment, during which he worked with Harry Galehouse in Doylestown building bridges on Wayne County roads. About 1932 he went to Chicago where he attempted to design and manufacture toys. He started the Weckesser Company, which soon shifted to plastics. He recognized the value of plastic clips to hold house wiring in place. They were nonconductors and were used widely by electricians. His company made barrels of them. He could make them cheaper than the metal type that had been in vogue. His company became very successful with these and other nonconductive items. It employed nearly one hundred people as he expanded into all types of circuit boards. His ability to make new designs to meet the new demands of the developing market was excellent and the business thrived until his health failed in 1971.

Father and I were pretty much alone on the farm after Ethan left and Father was away much of the time selling apples in Akron and other places, not getting home until late at night. Sylvia was away at college. I walked back and forth the two miles to school each day after feeding the animals in the morning and again after school. The Old Black Diamond could get kind of scary at night and I was always glad to see Father's lantern flickering between his legs as he walked down the hill from the orchard, sometimes having walked from Barberton. I could then relax for a good night's rest. Dad and I slept together in the downstairs bedroom at that time.

On weekends we were usually invited to Sunday dinner at either the Cleckners or the Galehouses. Brother Ethan's advice was, "Don't stay too long, always leave while you are still having a good time." It seemed like good idea to me too, not to wear out our welcome, which was always very warm. I don't remember volunteering to wash the dishes after dinner, which would have been appropriate, but young minds are not apt to think of that. In this routine, my years in grade school were completed.

Events of 1921–24

Current events of the day other than the war had not yet made a great impression on me up to this time. Gradually I was becoming aware of them. Father was impressed in 1921 by *The Outline Of History,* a book by H. G. Wells, and we spent much time reading and talking about that. Vitamins E and D were both discovered that year.

Albert Wallace Hull, an American physicist, developed a radio tube, a diode, that produced ultra high frequency radio waves of high intensity. He did this by using an external magnet to produce a magnetic field in the vacuum tube and called his device a *Magnetron* (Asimov, 482). This device and variations of it would lead to the development of many new uses for microwaves later, including the development of radar during World War II. Radar allowed detection of aircraft through darkness, clouds and mist and was very helpful to us and our Allies in that conflict. In May 1942, in Melbourne, Australia my unit, the Fourth General Hospital and I cared for the crew of a B-17 bomber that made a fiery crash landing at Essendon airport while demonstrating radar to Australian officers. The bombardier in the nose of the plane did not escape but we were able to save the other members of the crew and the two Australian officers who were very severely burned.

In 1922, the Teapot Dome Land Lease Scandal attracted much attention (Carruth, 460). Public lands in Wyoming had been leased to private interests for personal gain. The opening of the 1350 B.C. Tomb of King Tutankhamen in Luxor, Egypt in 1922 attracted tremendous attention. No one seemed to wonder why the tomb had been opened. King "Tut" became the widespread subject of conversation.

Of much more importance in that year, the first United States aircraft carrier, the *USS Langley,* was built from a converted cargo ship. This was the forerunner of the aircraft carriers that would turn the tide of battle in World War II in the South Pacific. The battle of the Coral Sea, the first week of May 1942, prevented an invasion of Port Morsby and of the Australian mainland. This was possible because of two things. We had very fortunately cracked the enemy's code and no carriers were lost at Pearl Harbor. They were not in port. The *USS Enterprise* was due to return from delivering planes to Wake Island on December 6. It was held up by high seas, a fortuitous miracle for us, contributing greatly to turning the tide of battle at Midway in June! In the battle of the Coral Sea, the planes from the carriers *Lexington* and *Yorktown* met the enemy and prevented landings at Port Morsby and probably the Darwin area. The *Lexington* had to be abandoned after the battle due to internal fires but the *Yorktown* made it back to Pearl Harbor for quick repairs, then on to the battle of Midway Island three weeks later where it also played a decisive role.

In 1921 insulin was discovered and produced by Banting and Best in Toronto, which would become a boon to many diabetic patients in America and the world. As the Teapot Dome Scandal unfolded, President Harding is quoted as saying, ''It's not my enemies, it's my friends that make me walk the floor at night.'' He was referring to his Secretary of the Interior, Albert B. Fall, who had leased public oil lands in Wyoming to private interests. President Harding died suddenly in San Francisco August 2, 1923 while returning from a trip to Alaska. The country went into deep mourning as his Funeral Train crossed the country on its way back to Washington. People waited for hours at railroad crossings all across the country to get just a glance at the car carrying the body of their dead president. Father and I waited at the Baltimore and Ohio crossing south of Doylestown until midnight but the train did not arrive. He went back later and saw it at 2:00 A.M. as it sped by. The Ku Klux Klan became active that year. U.S. Steel agreed to a reduction in length of the work day for employees from twelve to eight hours.

High School, 1924–28

In 1924 I entered Doylestown High School when I was fourteen years old. The size of my class was larger than my grade school class due to additional students from the township schools and from the Doylestown Parochial School. This meant a lot of new friends in addition to many new experiences in my classes. In General Science, Mr. Garver produced water from potassium permanganate and another dry chemical which I did not know could be done (as already related). To learn that glass was made out of the silicon of sand was equally interesting.

We obtained our first farm tractor, a Fordson, which facilitated plowing, discing and harrowing in the preparation of ground for planting. I enjoyed operating it and my older sisters worried that it was dangerous for me to do so alone. There was word of tractors turning over on the operator. I was careful and fortunately no accident occurred.

Events of 1925

Calvin Coolidge, known as Silent Cal, was president. He, like his predecessor Harding, believed that the government should not interfere and let the country get back to normal after the war. In Russia, Lenin died and Stalin rose to power. The Secretary of the Interior Albert Fall along with the Secretary of the Navy and the Attorney General resigned due to the Teapot Dome scandal. Leopold and Loeb were sentenced to prison for life for the thrill murder of a young boy, Bobbie Franks (Daniel, 42). In February Woodrow Wilson died at his home in Washington. On March 18 the worst tornado in history struck thirty-five towns in Illinois, Indiana, Tennessee, Kentucky and Missouri. Eight hundred people were killed, three thousand injured and 15,000 made homeless. There were 2.5 million radios in homes across the country. Four years earlier there had only been 5,000. Singles tennis champions were William T. Tilden II for the men and Helen N. Wills for the women. A new Ford car, black of course, and without a self-starter could be bought for two hundred and nine dollars (Carruth, 467).

In 1925 Calvin Coolidge was inaugurated for a second term. A young man named Floyd Collins was trapped in a coal mine and aroused intense national feelings during fifteen days of rescue attempts, which eventually failed. In May the trial of John N. Scopes in Dayton, Tennessee attracted world-wide interest. He was charged with violation of a law of that state forbidding the teaching of the theory of evolution. Clarence Darrow was the defense attorney and William Jennings Bryan the prosecutor. Scopes was found guilty and fined one hundred dollars. The decision was later reversed by the Tennessee Supreme Court. The Scopes Monkey Trial attracted more attention than any other legal proceeding in United States history (Carruth, 470).

The court-martial of Col. William (Billy) Mitchell deservedly attracted extreme attention. He was an aviator who foresaw the potential of aerial bombing and predicted its aerial superiority over the battleship. This brought him in conflict with the naval high command who was of the opinion that their dreadnoughts were superior. Colonel Mitchell was found guilty of making statements to the prejudice of good order and military discipline. Maj. Gen. Douglas MacArthur, one of his judges, voted not guilty but the majority convicted him. He resigned from the army and continued to write and lecture about his ideas. He died in 1936 before his complete vindication, which came belatedly during World War II (Encyclopedia Britannica 15:618). A treaty to outlaw the use of poisonous gas was signed. The National Broadcasting Company (NBC) was formed. Parathyroid hormone was isolated and Vitamin A deficiency was shown to produce night blindness. In Durham, North Carolina, Trinity College changed its name to Duke University with the bequest of over six million dollars from a forty-million dollar American Charity Fund established by James B. Duke, tobacco tycoon. This was an example of Paul's Law. ''There is good in all things including the bad.'' I did not know it then, but in a few years I would be a student at Duke University. Florida land was booming, although some of it was under water. In September the army dirigible, *Shenandoah,* was wrecked in a windstorm in southeastern Ohio with the loss of fourteen lives. This was a demonstration of the vulnerability of lighter aircraft in bad weather. An antitoxin for Scarlet Fever was developed in 1925 (Carruth, 470).

Events of 1926

In 1926 the first successful treatment of pernicious anemia was reported by Drs. Minot and Murphy in Boston. They fed their patients a liver diet with marked improvement. This, it was found, supplied a missing factor, which was later identified as vitamin B12 and folic acid. It was a very worthwhile contribution that provided treatment for a previously fatal disease and lead to a much greater understanding of anemia in general. Henry Ford shortened the work day of his employees to eight hours and the week to five working days. In a few years I would be working at a Ford assembly plant in Cleveland earning money for college tuition. Admiral Byrd flew over the North Pole. There was a severe hurricane in Florida and the Gulf states in which 372 people lost their lives and 6,000 were injured. 18,000 were left homeless. The first airmail service was established between New York and Boston. Gertrude Ederle swam the English channel and Gene Tunney won the heavyweight boxing title from Jack Dempsey. Clara Bow's popularity as a movie star increased and Hirohito became emperor of Japan.

Football Team of '26

I was a junior in high school and became a member of the newly formed football team. Father was not in favor of such foolishness but did not tell me I could not do it. I appreciated his attitude very much. It was an introduction to team sport, working together with others. It demonstrated the value of cooperation and the satisfaction of accomplishment due to that effort. It made me feel as though I was doing something more than just looking out for myself. I felt like I was doing something for the team and for the school. Team spirit was something new and good for me as I was growing up.

The father of one of my friends, Earl Coffman, did not want him to play but we needed Earl on the team. He told his father that he was water boy but his father came to a game and saw him playing. Earl said later that his father did not say anything to him on the way home, he just kept quiet. Earl had played well and he thought that his father was probably proud of him. Actually the team did quite well that season and lost only one game in its division.

Father liked to visit other members of the Reformed Mennonite Church in central and eastern Pennsylvania in the summer and I would drive for him on the trip. In the summer of 1926, primarily in order to make that trip, Father bought a used Ford touring car at a nearby farm sale. It had red wire wheels held on by three bolts at the hub. These wheels looked nice and were supposed to be real easy to change in case of tire trouble. We soon found that they came off much too easily. The three bolts at the hubs would loosen and the wheels would come off while driving! On the trip to Pennsylvania a few weeks later one came off on Route 30 on the top of the Allegheny mountain. We had a terrible time finding the wheel among the bushes and trees but finally did, got it back on and proceeded on our journey without serious damage. This led to frequent tightening of the hub bolts—whenever we stopped! That trip to Lancaster and Philadelphia proceeded without further trouble. But later, even with the bolts tightened, a wheel occasionally came off. This is hard to believe but on one occasion I saw a wheel to the left of the car before the left rear of the car sagged down. It was running on three wheels for a short distance until I could get it stopped. You have probably heard of all the things that a model T could do, well this is another one. Another time, with my friends, we lost one at night on the way to North Canton and were very lucky to find it. You may wonder about the three bolts. They stayed with the wheel under the hub cap in each instance and were not lost. Fortunately, in those days, traffic was not as heavy as it is today and our driving speed was about thirty-five miles an hour. I've never been fond of wire wheels since, probably because of those early experiences.

Events of 1927

The first highlight of 1927 was Charles Lindbergh's nonstop flight from New York to Paris on May 20–21. He flew 3,600 miles in thirty-three and one-half hours. He was welcomed by 100,000 people in Paris and the country here went wild. He had done it alone and became an instant National Hero. His success was in every newspaper and on every radio program. Songs were written about his flight such as "Lucky Lindy Up in the Sky" and phonograph records made. It was like filling a vacuum. It attracted attention to aviation and gave the country something good and clean and upbeat to talk about. I remember where I was, upstairs at 136 Marion Street, when the news came.

On August 2 Pres. Calvin Coolidge announced that he would not run for reelection. Times were good and people were happy. He surely would have been reelected if he had. He chose not to run saying that when his son Calvin Jr. had died of septicemia in 1924 from a blister on his toe from playing tennis, "The power and the glory of the presidency went with him." The country had prospered under "Silent Cal." He went into retirement and died in 1933. In retrospect his retirement demonstrated excellent judgment. He quit when he was ahead, which is difficult. His successor took the brunt of the looming inflationary problems that were developing.

The death of a sixteen-year-old son of a United States president in 1924 from an infected blister on his toe exemplified the great danger of infection that still existed for healthy young people in 1924. This infection was due to the same organism, streptococcus, which had made childbirth dangerous for women for ages past. That danger had been greatly diminished by the recognition and use of asepsis. Another organism, the pneumococcus, was also still killing thousands of young healthy people with pneumonia each year. Gonorrhea and syphilis were rampant.

During WWII, the advent of Penicillin followed by other antibiotics eradicated or tremendously diminished the danger from most micro-organism. The problem now is that many organisms are becoming resistant to antibiotics. But most infections, with the exception of the AIDS virus, are no longer the serious threat to life that they once were.

Al Jolson was featured in the first talking moving picture, *Mammy* (now known as *The Jazz Singer*) in which the soundtrack was on the film itself. It was a stunning success. Talking pictures were a reality. The Holland Tunnel under the Hudson River was opened in New York. The fifteen millionth Model T Ford motor car was produced and the factories were closed down for the change over to Model A, which would feature drastic changes, including a gear shift instead of three-foot pedals on the floor. Babe Ruth hit a record sixty home runs in 1927 (Carruth, 476–79).

Events of 1928

Graduation, Doylestown High School

1927–28 was my senior year in high school and it was a pleasant time. I was elected class president. During that year, I lived with sister Ruth and her family in Doylestown. Extracurricular activities attracted more of my attention. The football team under Coach Stanley C. Neal continued to do well. My position was changed from left tackle to left end. We finished the season winning four of our six games. I played basketball that winter and the team also had a fairly good season. Our class play, directed by Miss Althouse, was a success. It was a comedy entitled, *A*

Turn to the Right about a convict from Sing Sing prison, played by yours truly, who had an embarrassing time when some of his old buddies from prison paid him a visit in his home town after he had made the turn. My grades suffered but not greatly. My responsibilities as president were not fully realized and hence not fully carried out in one respect. I felt bad about it when it was brought to my attention. We, the senior class, had borrowed a davenport from the Catholic school for setting the stage for the play at the high school auditorium and had not returned it. I did not learn of this fact until some months later when I was at Duke University in Durham, North Carolina. It was handled by correspondence but was still a regretful embarrassment to me. It taught me to learn all of the responsibilities involved in any position accepted.

During the summer of 1928 I helped Father at the orchard. My older brother Ethan had helped him until his twenty-first birthday before going off on his own. I was torn by my responsibility to my father who I admired very much and my own development. My feeling for Dad was very acute, especially in view of Mother's death.

With all due respect to him, I finally decided, with the backing of my brothers and sisters, to go on to college that fall. I had meager savings that would pay my tuition, having painted Ernie and Sadie's house in Akron and worked for my brother-in-law Dick Galehouse, sister Esther's husband, putting in a pipe line in Wayne County. Louie and Banks had gone to Duke University the year before and they offered to have me live with them. They were having another university student live with them also, Anthony C. Westerhoff, and he and I would share the same room. He was a droll sort of fellow with a dry sense of humor who said 'just call me 'Sparky'.'' (At that time AC Spark plugs were being widely advertised.) This seemed a little out of character and we wound up with ''A.C.'' instead.

The Rhines were in Ohio that August visiting the Rhine family in Greenwich and Weckesser family in Doylestown. A.C. came to Doylestown the third week in August and the four of us drove to Durham in the Rhine family sedan. This was prior to the birth of the Rhine children. It was a very pleasant trip appreciated and enjoyed by all. On arrival at the newly rented upstairs apartment at 113 Watts Street, Durham, just adjacent to the East Duke campus, Louie fixed a front room for A.C. and me. I was to help Louie about the house and pay what I could toward board. How they could be so nice was beyond me.

42

I immediately busied myself getting some jobs for income. At Banks's suggestion I advertised in the campus paper to start morning fires for other faculty members in the vicinity and obtained several. For a nominal fee, I went at an agreed hour each morning and kindled a fire in the furnace of the house to take off the chill. This was before thermostats and automatic gas heat.

Events 1928
Herbert Clark Hoover, 1928–32

Herbert Hoover became the thirty-first president when Coolidge decided not to run. This was lucky for Coolidge, with the 1929 stock crash and a severe economic depression soon to occur. The Kellogg-Briand Peace Pact was signed in Paris by fifteen nations in an effort to outlaw war, an admirable effort to settle international controversy by arbitration. It was the twenty-fifth anniversary of the Wright brothers' first air flight at Kitty Hawk, North Carolina. The first scheduled television broadcasts took place from station WGG in Schenectady, New York and the first color motion pictures were shown (Carruth, 479–83).

Turkey declared Islam no longer its state religion. British women were given the right to vote. Dr. Papanicalou presented an early cellular test for carcinoma of the cervix of the uterus. Dr. Alexander Fleming noted that certain molds destroyed bacteria on a Petri dish, which would eventually lead to the development of Penicillin about fourteen years later. Vitamin C was isolated and the Asheim-Zondex test for pregnancy was developed (Gordon and Gordon, 78–80).

Duke University

Transmission of Acquired Knowledge

Through my brother-in-law, Dr. J. Banks Rhine, I was exposed, for the first time, to scientific investigation. It was intriguing. Dr. Rhine and Dr. William McDougal, head of the psychology department at Duke, were engaged in testing the hypothesis that acquired learning could be transmitted to successive generations of rats. The experimental animals were a pure strain of white rats that had been bred for a high number of successive generations, each generation being taught to escape from a maze, a puzzle, without receiving a shock.

The maze consisted of a water tank in a darkened room with two exit ramps, one illuminated and the other dark. The test rats were placed in the water of the tank and had to find their way out. If they took the dark metal ramp they received a mild shock which was strong enough to make them squeal. If they took the illuminated metal ramp, they were not shocked and received food by continuing up to another level.

I helped with these rats (Group 2) and with other new generations whose ancestors had not been trained (Group 1). The two groups were compared. There seemed to be a difference. The rats whose ancestors were untrained (Group 1) were more impulsive, immediately rushing over both ramps and squealing when they were shocked on the dark ramp. Gradually they learned to take the lighted exit.

Group 2 rats, whose ancestors had learned to exit the lighted ramp, behaved differently than Group 1 and their scores were better. The Group 2 animals tended to be more deliberate before attempting to exit. They would swim over to one ramp, consider it, then to the other several times before making a decision. They took more time but their scores were better. The statistical difference between the scores of the two groups may not have been significant—I do not recall that—but their behavior in the maze was different. Critics said that Dr. McDougal's training had made the rats more timid. I had to get busy with other things. At the end of my association, the question was still of much interest but not settled.

I had decided on a profession, probably medicine, for my career, as previously noted. My dentist in Barberton, Dr. H. M. Peters, had opened my eyes to a profession. He said, "Learn to do something that everyone else cannot do." This made sense to me and I first considered being a dentist. My Uncle Ray, Father's younger brother, was a dentist in Sandusky. After a time and in further discussions, Dr. Peters told me, and I remember how his eyes sparkled when he said it, that he had yearned to be a doctor of medicine. *Well, that's OK,* I thought to myself, *I can be either one.* They are both down the same track as far as courses are concerned. The final decision was not necessary immediately. Dr. Vern Sharp in Akron, my brother Connie's friend whom I had known in Doylestown, was another confidant who also encouraged me to go into medicine. Later he had much influence in my going into surgery. Were there doctors in my family background? I would soon be asked that question. Even when I entered medical school I answered "No," ignorant of the fact that my Long and Herr ancestry was full of them. Mother was gone. I did not find this out until I studied her ancestry many years later.

College Classes, Duke University

Classes began in a week or so and I found myself quite busy. The size of the assignments was greater than anything that I had been accustomed to. English, History, Mathematics and Chemistry. The English assignments were tremendous, my mind did not and does not manipulate mathematical symbols well and I was not at all prepared for chemistry. I had not taken it in high school. It was completely new to me and I had difficulty understanding the professor's rapid speech and German accent. The change from high school was rather shocking. Putting all of those factors together, I had problems and had to buckle down right from the start. Fortunately I realized it and was able to meet the new challenges.

Hotel Malbourne, Durham, N.C.

In addition to problems, adjusting to the greater assignments, new chemistry, and rapid speech and foreign accent of professors, I had to earn some money to stay afloat. A classmate worked as a night clerk at a hotel in downtown Durham. Taking this as a lead, I applied at the Malbourne Hotel on Main Street. It was the largest hotel in town although the Washington Duke Hotel was under construction. I got a job as Assistant Clerk on the afternoon shift from three until eleven P.M. It was difficult because I had an afternoon laboratory that ran until three o'clock. Included was a seventy-five cent allowance for my evening meal which sounded like an adequate amount since at that time a "blue plate special" (yesterday's food) in many restaurants cost fifty cents. To my surprise, I soon found out that I hadn't allowed for hotel pricing of food. I gained no weight on my diet. The afternoon laboratory was a more serious problem. I worked over the experiments ahead of time and wrote up as much of the report as I could and was able to get by with this technique, but I do not recommend it to anyone.

Graham, the afternoon room clerk who I assisted, was good to me and introduced me to many of the ways of the world. I became acquainted with the clients, especially those who were permanent residents in the hotel. One of them gave me a good suit of clothes, which I accepted with thanks. It fit me and I wore it for several years. One day at the desk a man was showing some card tricks and then after he had people interested, asked for a dollar bill saying he could make it disappear. I innocently produced one of mine. He folded it in a clever way, and sure enough it disappeared among his cards. Then he showed us more tricks and walked away. I then realized that he still had my dollar bill, ran after him and fortunately got it back. It was my introduction to intended deceit—not the last.

Another incident occurred in front of the elevator just across from the front desk where I was stationed. It is worthy of some comment. Otho, the head waiter and luggage handler, was usually stationed beside the front desk or in the area when not busy and we knew him well. One day he was carrying a large dinner tray over his shoulder on his way to a guest room upstairs. Most unusual for him because he was very adept at his duties, for some reason in this instance the tray slipped and the food and breaking dishes clattered all over the floor. He cleaned up and mopped the floor in "nothing flat." Just a short time later, Mrs. Mangum appeared from the kitchen and looked around. Not seeing anything unusual, she said, "Otho did you break some dishes?" Otho answered, "No ma'am, I didn't break no dishes." She looked around again, suspiciously, and then went back into the kitchen. After this was over, Graham said to Otho, "Why did you lie like that to Mrs. Mangum?" He replied, "Mr. Graham, I didn't know how much those dishes cost." I've often thought of that rationalization and wonder how often it occurs. This loss was probably a day's wages to this man. What about greater losses or questions that might endanger a life or a family? A mother in relationship to her child? The question may even be asked about lost causes that once were previously propounded by all about you. An old saying states that all is fair in love and war. I'm sure it is true in the latter but I leave judgment of the former to others. Honesty is still the best course, although special circumstances may make it haunting. Withheld comment can sometimes be practiced.

I passed that semester and soon after that my hotel job gave out. Business was not good. I was laid off. It was probably for the better since I was then allowed more time for my studies. I then worked in the athletic department at the university, taking care of tennis courts. This I could do after class and in the evenings. It was much better. By this time chemistry had become very interesting.

Events of 1929

Herbert Hoover was inaugurated as the thirty-first president of the United States. The Empire State Building in New York City was begun and would be completed two years later. Lt. Commander Richard E. Bird made the first flight over the South Pole. Albert Fall was convicted of fraud, sentenced to one year in federal prison and fined one hundred dollars for his part in the Teapot Dome Scandal. All else was eclipsed by the Stock Market Crash beginning on "Black Thursday," October 24th. Billions of dollars were lost overnight signaling the beginning of the Great Depression (Carruth, 482–85). Charles Lindbergh married Anne Morrow. Babe Ruth hit his 500th home run for the New York Yankees (Gordon and Gordon, 87–96).

The spring of 1929 came early in Durham after a very mild winter. This was a change from the usual cold snowy winter of northern Ohio. I finished out the second semester with grades that were not outstanding but respectable considering the circumstances. I still had the feeling that I had "let down" Father at home by not staying and helping him. I told him this by letter. He had never put pressure on me but I felt that way. I told him I would like to work part time for him and part time for myself during the coming summer to try and raise more money for tuition.

Return to Ohio

Louie and Banks drove me out to the edge of Durham and left me along the main road north. This was before hitchhiking received a bad name. I had Duke stickers on my suitcase and it was quite evident that I was a student. This method was quite common for students at that time. I came up through Washington, D.C. and Pennsylvania stopping with friends in Chambersburg, Pennsylvania and made it home in three and a half days. My reaction coming up the Doylestown hill from Barberton was very vivid after having been away for a year and after hitchhiking back from Durham, North Carolina. I was returning to a village at the top of a green hill. I had come through many villages, but this one had been the center of my universe prior to a year ago. I could now put it into perspective with the other places I had been and the experiences that I had had. I was greeted warmly by my family, who were glad to see me. It had been an interesting year and I was glad to be back. Father was very glad to see me, as were Ruth and Esther. They all welcomed me. I think I realized then that people are more important than places or things.

Real Silk Hosiery

That summer, in addition to helping Father and painting brother Ernie's house in Akron, I took up the house-to-house sale of "Real Silk Hosiery." This was a new venture. Banks and Louie had been successful selling "Club Aluminum" and this was my try at sales. This was pretty good. I could make ten or twelve dollars a day if I worked hard. I also had heard of a new vacuum cleaner by the name of Airway Sanitary System, which had interesting new features, including a hollow handle that could be used to as a cleaning tool. I made a trip to the home office in Toledo at the end of the summer and was assigned to the Durham and Raleigh area thinking that I could sell them down there. When I went back I had actually not yet received all of my summer earnings. I did not have enough money to pay my tuition and decided to work a year.

House Painting

I painted brother Ernie's house in West Akron in the summer of 1929 in about two weeks. All went well with no accidents.

48

Vacuum Cleaners

I also tried selling vacuum cleaners before returning to North Carolina for a few weeks with little success. When I got back to Durham, I teamed up with a Mr. Mayo, a married graduate student who had a car to get around in. We traveled together but worked independently. We traveled all over but sold only a few. The machine sold for seventy-five dollars and people were hesitant about investing that amount of money. Some of them did not know what it was. I remember trying to explain what I was selling to a negro lady at the door. She had a very quizzical look on her face but finally she said, "Oh, you mean one of those old sucking things?" I said, "Yes, I guess I do." There was no sale there. Mr. Mayo did better than I. Then the stock market crashed in October and business went to nothing.

Stock Market Crash

The prices of stock on the Stock Market had become quite elevated in value. On "Black Thursday," October 24, 1929 stock prices began falling sharply and, on October 29th, became extreme. The Dow-Jones Average, which had peaked at 381 in 1929, fell progressively to 41 in 1932 and unemployment reached 25 percent.

Second Return to Ohio (November 1929)

I decided to return to Ohio in November, 1929 hoping that jobs would be more available in Cleveland. At that time my brother Ethan and Dwight Galehouse were rooming together in Cleveland where Ethan had a job with Miller and James, Engineers on E. 9th St. Dwight worked at the Standard Tool Company. I roomed with them by sleeping on a cot. I tried to sell Airways in Lakewood but sales were dismal.

Cleveland Higbee Company

By this time the Christmas season was at hand and I was able to get a job at The Higbee Company then on Euclid Avenue near E. 14th St. I jokingly told friends that I was a director in The Higbee Company (Elevator Director). That job lasted several weeks until they needed people in the package-wrapping department and I was sent there where I learned how to tie packages tightly using a bowline knot, something that I have used ever since. This lasted through the holiday season. One day while wrapping packages the word circulated that Ford Motor Company was going to start hiring on a certain day. Ford at that time was paying more than the usual wage. My ears perked up. I learned all I could about that possibility.

The Ford Motor Company Assembly Plant—A Friendly Voice

Creation of Automobiles

The Ford Motor Co. Assembly plant in Cleveland was at E. 116th St. and Euclid Ave. It might have just been a rumor but I decided I'd check it out. On the day in question I was there before daylight. E. 116th St. was already full of men, hundreds of them. There was a door into the building on the west side of the street and every few minutes someone would open it and call out for a certain number of men wanted for a particular job. Suddenly there was a call for typists. Somehow I was able to get up and into that door and waited. I had taken typing in high school thinking that sometime it might come in handy. Then word came that the two positions were taken and I was supposed to go back outside. But one of the men told me to wait and I used this as an excuse to stay inside amidst the hustle bustle, standing tightly against the wall to avoid being pushed back out.

I heard the same friendly voice that told me to wait, say, "Take that young fellow, he looks good and strong." Someone had failed their physical examination. I had a job at the unloading dock, unloading Ford engines. I felt sorry for the man who failed his physical but could not dwell on that. It was heavy work but I could do it.

The Assembly Line

The job involved taking the engines on two-wheeled dollies from freight cars at the dock into the assembly building where they were put into the chassis of the cars on the assembly line. The men at the assembly line had an overhead crane to lift the engines into position and fix them there as the chassis moved slowly down the line where the next operation occurred. I think the line ran at about twenty cars an hour; it might have been faster. There was no time to spare and the objective was to keep it moving. This was the method of assembly that Henry Ford had developed. It was quite interesting to see all the operations involved down the line until finally, at the end, a driver got in, stepped on the starter, the engine started and he drove it to the parking area.

Occasionally, there was difficulty starting the new engine but not often. When it did occur something had to be done quickly in order not to hold up the line. The people in this area were expert in solving those problems and only rarely was it necessary to stop the line. Shortage of parts somewhere was a more frequent problem. It was remarkable to realize that out of the multitude of parts along the assembly line that a complete automobile was assembled and that the internal combustion engine would start for the first time when a spark ignited gasoline vapor, according to the laws of nature. It was impressive to me at that time to see this happen. All this coordinated human effort created an automobile.

Later, with humble respect, I would realize that it was nearly nothing in comparison to the sequence of events that occur during the development of a human fetus. The fetus spontaneously starts breathing when the umbilical cord is divided at the time of birth. This is an even more amazing thing than the first explosions of a new engine, yet they are both due to physical laws, one much more complex than the other.

On the automobile assembly line hundreds of humans had to use their brains to fit the parts together and choose the final outside colors. The building where it occurred was large and parts were shipped from many different parts of the country. I think the engines at that time came from Michigan.

The development of a human embryo occurs without outside help according to coded instructions within the forty-six chromosomes of *each nucleated cell* of our body. Each cell carries all of our unique characteristics. This code is in each of the trillions of nucleated cells of our body (red blood cells excepted). It constitutes one of the greatest and most complete manuals ever written. It is all done with the variation of sequence of four substances: adenine, thymine, cytosine and guanine, in the DNA of the nuclei of our cells. Mind boggling! In human development, our protein molecules line up due to natural law, forces we do not understand, under directions carried in the makeup of our chromosomes to put our tissues together without outside help. This all happens in a very small space to make the most intricate structure on earth. The procedure is thousands or millions of times more complex than the automobile assembly line that I admired as a college student.

Yes, I admired the assembly line but we had to work fast and hard. It was a fast pace for every one involved. It was noted how often a worker went to the bathroom and how long he stayed there. There was no smoking. Henry Ford had good judgment about more than just automobiles and he was not foolishly paying the highest wages of the time. He was wisely and justly sharing the profits of his manufacturing with his workers. In Durham, the usual wage was twenty-five cents an hour. Here, I started at sixty-seven and a half cents an hour which automatically went to seventy-five cents an hour in thirty days. This was great for me, but let me tell you my next piece of good luck.

The Cunningham Sanitarium, 1928–34 Therapy and Rest under Pressure, Student Evening Telephone Operator, Grounds Keeper, Chauffeur

1930–34 ECW

When I returned to my room one evening, my roommate, Dwight Gale-house had a message for me. "Call Mr. Hoffman at Kenmore 3400." I had answered a help-wanted ad in the *Plain Dealer,* about a week earlier, which asked for a student to work evenings. Actually I had nearly forgotten about it until I received the message.

Mr. Hoffman turned out to be the manager of the Cunningham Sanitarium at 18485 Lake Shore Boulevard. I had an interview and obtained the evening job, which was to attend the switchboard at the front desk and take care of calls and patient requests from six to eleven each evening, seven days a week. It paid twenty-five dollars a month, included a place to live on the unfinished third floor of the hotel portion of the new building and provided board. How could I be so lucky? It was perfect. I could continue my job at Ford and start back to college in the fall.

1920 Ford Sedan

I needed transportation and bought a 1920 (ten-year-old) Ford Model T sedan with one door for thirty-five dollars. It had been a stylish model with a flower vase inside the single door, but its glory had faded. Old cars for transportation had become a specialty of mine and I was quite adept at making them go. I had learned that from my brother-in-law, Dick Galehouse in Doylestown and from Dad's trucks and the tractors at the apple orchard.

Move to Cunningham Sanitarium

I moved my things to the unfinished third floor of the sanitarium hotel building. The walls for the rooms had not been inserted. It was all open. I had a new bed by a front window, a functioning bath at the end of the hall, a dresser and a small desk with adequate heat and lighting. Several patients also lived there who were working for their treatment. I ate in the employee's dining room where the food was good, prepared under the guidance of Ms. Elizabeth Perry, dietitian. All the people were fine and treated me nicely. I detected a few jealousies as reported later among a few employees which gradually became less. I could drive to the Ford plant and return in time for my evening duties. With food and lodging provided, I banked my Ford checks every two weeks in the nearby branch of the Union Trust Company.

My job in the evening was interesting and I enjoyed meeting the patients and made a lot of very nice friends. Edward Hoffman, who hired me, was supportive. He had diabetes. As time went on I was accepted even by Dr. Orval J. Cunningham, the director of the Sanitarium, who called me Alden. There had been another student before me who had not worked out. When they left in the evening, Dr. Cunningham would sometime say, "Alden, you're in charge." I handled the switchboard and took care of patient requests that came by telephone.

The Switchboard

The office switchboard at that time was not automatic, as they are now. It was the center through which all calls passed and the operator was very aware of what was going on. It was the front desk. The operator gave assistance as necessary or called the proper people that needed to be notified for things that were happening. The switchboard itself was actually a bank of sockets. One for each telephone in the buildings and several outside lines. When someone picked up the receiver of their phone, it caused a light to appear below the socket for that telephone on the switchboard and set off a buzzer that attracted the attention of the operator who, after six P.M., was me. To answer the call, the operator plugged a wire connector into that socket and gave a greeting. The caller then expressed their wishes and the operator carried them out. If they wanted someone in another room, you completed the circuit there by placing another wire connector into that socket and rang the bell, with a little black lever, a time or two until the other party answered. All calls went through the switchboard. If the caller wanted an outside line—there were several of those—you gave a connection there. If the caller needed help or attention, you made arrangements for that. The switchboard covered all the rooms in the hotel as well as all the thirty-six rooms and other telephones in the sphere, the engine room, and everywhere else. The compressors in the engine room ran constantly when the sphere was under pressure changing the air and maintaining the thirty pounds gauge pressure there, which made a total of three atmospheres pressure instead of the normal one atmosphere outside. This increased pressure caused the tissue fluids of the body to have more oxygen (and other gases of the air) dissolved in them for use by the cells of the body. Normally in our bodies, oxygen is constantly being carried to our tissues by the hemoglobin of our blood, but by increasing the oxygen tension (the amount of oxygen) directly in the fluid around the cells of the body by the higher pressure, each cell has more oxygen to utilize. Oxygen had to some extent been administered by means of tent, or face mask, which increased the amount of oxygen in the air breathed, but the method was not widely used in 1918. The use of compressed air to get more oxygen to the tissues of the body by keeping patients under three atmospheres of pressure days at a time was Dr. Cunningham's contribution. This was in medical lingo, Oxygen Therapy by Means of Compressed Air.

A huge steel ball on the north side of Lakeshore Boulevard, near E. 185th St., was a familiar and interesting site in the late 1920s and early 1930s. It was a pioneering effort to deliver additional oxygen to patients who had impairment of oxygen exchange in their lungs and other conditions for which the indications were less clear. Oxygen, the substance that supplies energy to each cell of our body every minute of our life, is of utmost importance to us; without it we cannot live. The steel ball, "The Sphere," was erected with great expectations, enjoyed success, then much unnecessary controversy, and finally suffered sad destruction in spite of its many capabilities. Why did this happen? Were the claims of the operator overextended? Was the censor intransigent in his demands?

The huge sphere, sixty-four feet in diameter, five stories high, weighing nearly 900 tons, with 350 porthole windows, was not a strange design meant to attract attention, but a working compression chamber for the treatment of patients. The atmospheric pressure within the ball, or Sphere, was increased to three atmospheres—three times normal, approximately forty-five pounds per square inch. The patients lived under this increased atmospheric pressure for various periods. In the 1930s it was one week in and one week out. The patients who lived nearby went home during their "week out" and those from a distance lived in the comfortable attached three-story brick hotel. Patients came from far and wide, even from the Philippine Islands and other parts of the world.

How did this beautiful silver sphere with its thick steel wall come about? What was it for and what led to its early demise?

The story starts twelve years earlier, in 1918, during the severe influenza-pneumonia outbreak of World War I. This was before the age of antibiotics and pneumonia antiserum. Dr. Cunningham was taking care of large numbers of patients with pneumonia, seeing many of them die a blue cyanotic death due to lack of oxygen exchange through their consolidated lungs. They were dying of anoxia (insufficient oxygen). A method of getting more oxygen into their systems was required.

Let us first consider this thirty-eight-year-old doctor, an internist and anesthetist at the University of Kansas.

Orval James Cunningham, M.D., 1880–1937

This interesting pioneer, responsible for the huge sphere, Dr. Orval James Cunningham demonstrated that compressed air is an effective method of oxygen administration. He was also the first person to show that large numbers of patients can live safely and comfortably a week at a time under three atmospheres of pressure.

Dr. Cunningham was of Scotch, English and French descent. The Cunningham Clan of Ayrshire, Scotland is represented by a beautiful red Tartan (Gimble, 61). He was born January 30, 1880, at Odell, Nebraska about sixty-five miles south of Lincoln, the eldest son of James Dorian and Mary Isabell (Crooper) Cunningham. He had two sisters and one younger brother, John, who became a very successful inventor by devising a mechanism that became widely used to prevent fire in oil storage tanks. He died an untimely death during the influenza outbreak of 1918. This death of his brother brought the problem into his own family and was an additional stimulus to him.

Dr. Cunningham's father operated a farm implement store, Cunningham and Cropper, which supplied farm machinery to the farmers of the surrounding plains area. When Dr. C. was about ten years old the family and business was moved to Keytesville, Missouri, about ninety miles northeast of Kansas City where he attended local schools. He continued his education at the University of Oklahoma and University of Nebraska

58

(1899–1900), University of Chicago (1900–1902), and then Rush Medical College, where he obtained an M.D. degree in 1904. He then became licensed to practice medicine and opened an office in Kansas City and practiced internal medicine and what later became known as anesthesiology. He was associate professor of physiology at the University of Kansas City 1905–1909 and later associate professor of medicine at Kansas City University. His mother died in 1905 of placenta previa when he was just starting practice. His father died of uremic poisoning seven years later while Dr. Cunningham was practicing medicine on the staff at the University of Kansas.

Who's Who in American Medicine of 1925 additionally lists the following for Dr. Orval James Cunningham:

Associate Professor of Medicine Kansas State University 1915 to date. Devised several types of apparatus for Administration of nitrous oxide, oxygen and ether, 1908–17; experimental work with compressed air for therapy since 1918; Member Jackson Co. Medical Society; National Anesthesia Research Society; Missouri State Med. Assn.; A.M.A.; Author several articles in Med. Journals; Member Phi Beta Pi, Christian Clubs, City and Meadow Lake Country Club; Res. 3424 Gillham Rd., K.C., Mo.; Office 3310 Harrison St., K.C., Mo.

June 7, 1914, he married a lovely lady, Grace Margaret Quinlan of Chicago, and they had two fine children, a son, Orval Jr. and a daughter, Dorothy. Orval Jr. married Louise Coppage of Cleveland, daughter of Dr. Everete Peter Coppage, Sr. They have a son Robert Young Cunningham who is now married and operating a successful employment agency in New York City. Dorothy was married in California to Leslie Duryea with whom she had four sons. Sadly, she passed away prematurely in 1985. Orval Jr. died in 1996.

Dr. C. was a very private person. He did not enter into conversation freely with strangers and yet was a brilliant conversationalist when his interest was aroused. Patients often remarked on that. He was also very modest, not flaunting his ideas or accomplishments and also very kind and generous. There were a number of patients who Dr. C. allowed to work in payment for their treatment. Several of them lived on the unfinished 3rd floor of the hotel where I stayed. His son Orval Jr. tells of a situation that also bears this out. Dr. C. and his family lived on the same property behind the sanitarium at the edge of Lake Erie. Milk was delivered to a box at the back door by the milkman. Mrs. Grace Cunningham began to notice a bottle of milk missing each morning from the milk box. She checked with the milkman who assured her that he had left the proper order. This was at the depth of the depression, 1932–33. She brought it to Dr. C.'s attention with the idea of watching for the thief. His reply was, "These are hard times, Grace; many are out of work. Order an extra quart." She did so and there was still one bottle missing each day but the family had enough milk. Several weeks later the daily deficit ceased to occur. When Grace told Dr. C., his reply was, "The poor fellow probably found a job." Grace then cancelled the extra milk order.

Oxygen Therapy by Means of Compressed Air

As stated before, many people were dying of anoxia (insufficient oxygen) in 1918. Dr. Cunningham's adult brother died of this disease. A method of getting more oxygen into these people's systems was critically needed. This is the stimulus to which Dr. Cunningham responded, as the loss of his brother inspired him greatly.

The author vividly recalls, when he was eight years old, the 1918 epidemic of Spanish influenza and pneumonia in the military training camps. Two of his older brothers were at Camp Sherman, Ohio where deaths were occurring in great numbers. The concern of our mother, father and entire family was very great especially with the death of one of our neighbor's sons, Vincent Dannemiller, a very healthy young soldier in training who we all knew well. I also remember the shocking death of another strong healthy middle-aged neighbor who suddenly became ill and died on the third day of his illness. He lived just a few streets away in my home town. His son, also away at army camp like two of my brothers, became engaged to my older sister Ruth and later became my brother-in-law, Eldon Cleckner.

The cyanotic (blue) death from Lobar pneumonia that caused the patient to gasp for breath was a horrible thing to witness, which made it a dreaded killing disease feared by all in the days before pneumonia antiserum and antibiotics. The fact that it struck healthy, active, young persons as well as old people, leading to death in just days, made it more fearful. This situation continued pretty much unchanged into the days of my internship at the Cincinnati General Hospital the winter of 1936–37 when pneumonia antiserum was first introduced. This stimulus of treating seriously ill and dying pneumonia patients appeared to be primary in leading Dr. Cunningham to develop the use of compressed air for the administration of oxygen. Methods of oxygen administration by adding the gas to the air the patient breathed had not been well developed and there was hesitancy in using it.

Survival of pneumonia patients was said to be better at low altitude, at the seashore, rather than in the mountains where people went to escape malaria and yellow fever, away from swampy areas. This was indicative to Dr. C. who, with his training and experience, thought of gases in relationship to their partial pressures. On a trip to the Grand Canyon looking into the deep gorge in 1918, it is said that Dr. C. conceived the idea of mechanically increasing atmospheric pressure to get more oxygen into the tissues of the body (Trimble, 53). In his work with anesthetic gases, he was well aware of the composition of air and of Henry's Law. When the pressure of a gas over a liquid is increased, as with air containing oxygen and nitrogen, more of both gases enter into solution in proportion to their pressure. He probably used both lines of reasoning—they reinforced each other—in deciding he could provide oxygen therapy in this manner. The theory seemed good but it needed proof. It is interesting and remarkable how the brain can synthesize fragments and bits of information and knowledge, which are striking it constantly, into logical postulates, possibilities, and theories. These postulates and theories, useful as they are, are tentative conclusions, actually questions, which have value in our thinking but need to be proven as facts before they can be relied upon. If not, serious errors can occur. In addition, when peers attack, we can fend them off with factual proof.

Dean Sudler, University of Kansas City

In 1918, Dr. Cunningham presented his idea of pressure treatment to Dr. Sudler, dean of the medical school, University of Kansas, who thought it was a good idea and requested animal experimentation to verify it.

With Dean Sudler's support the first tank was constructed on the grounds of the University of Kansas in suburban Rosedale, Kansas (Trimble, 54). Tank One was a cylindrical tank, eight feet in diameter, twenty-four feet long, made from a used steam boiler. Dr. C. directed its construction using secondhand parts and many of his own funds. It was completed and ready for operation in November, 1918 at the time World War I was ending. It was ready for experiments to begin.

A young cyanotic comatose pneumonia patient was referred to him by a local doctor and Dr. C. could not turn the referring doctor down. The patient was moribund and there was no other treatment. The patient was placed in the newly constructed pressure tank and the compressors started. The pressure was raised an additional ten pounds and held there (Trimble, 55). The young patient's color improved; he regained consciousness and made a remarkable recovery. Word spread and other cases followed. Experiments were delayed. Months went by, then a year. Criticism began to occur among his peers. Experiments were again requested by the Dean.

Science and Medicine

Science was coming into and affecting the practice of medicine and it's quite possible that Dr. Cunningham did not fully realize it. At this stage it seems that Dr. Cunningham misjudged the degree to which the scientific community was requiring a factual approach to the practice of medicine. It was a change that had begun in the mid-nineteenth century and had increased tremendously, even since his medical training at the turn of the century. In the past, false claims by practitioners of many sorts had been made. There had been many abuses and very few corrections. Patients were being victimized by valueless treatments.

In 1920, nearly two years after the first tank began operation, Dr. C. had not begun the experimental procedures necessary for his acceptance at the university. Some of his contemporaries were becoming more critical of him for this and were putting pressure on Dean Sudler. It was a controversial situation. Why did Dr. C. resist doing experiments? It is a difficult question to answer. He procrastinated further. Perhaps he thought the request ridiculous in view of the fact that patients were responding and getting better. Scientific methods and the necessity of using them was not foremost in his mind and he next made a decision that would have grave consequences. There was another factor of which Dr. C. was probably not aware. The American Medical Association was carrying out a campaign, the first one, to stop unscientific practices, an effort considered commendable by most people in view of many forms of treatment in use at that time that were costly to patients, but not of actual value.

Experience is a wonderful thing. In a new situation, however, the person who needs it does not have it until after it is needed! With hindsight, always clear, Dr. Cunningham made a mistake in 1920. He should have written up clinical reports on cases treated at the University of Kansas, especially since he did not have animal experimental proof of its value. This would have given him the advantage of a clinical study, which was one of the things that the AMA was asking for. The first pneumonia case treated or, even better, the first ten pneumonia cases treated could have been submitted for clinical publication, but it would have required making careful records of treatments given and detailed responses of the patients to the treatment. And the reports would have needed to be carried out enough times to show them repeatable. It also could have been done in a similar way for patients with syphilis, even though speaking about the disease was taboo in 1920. In Dr. C.'s report in *Anesthesia and Analgesia,* April 3, 1927, he states that the spirochete of syphilis is anaerobic and killed by the increased oxygen tension in the tissues and tissue fluids. This was a postulation based on the results he was obtaining. He needed to present the evidence to convince others. This could have made an excellent report, showing, as he claimed, that the Wasserman tests became negative. Of the first 175 cases of syphilis patients completing five months of treatment, only two did not remain Wasserman negative, which is what he reported in a talk given to anesthetists at Kansas City in 1926. This was very pertinent before other treatments for the disease had been demonstrated. This would have required record keeping and follow up. Why did he not do that? Perhaps he, himself did not know.

Dr. C. Leaves University of Kansas City

There was something in his nature that made him take another route. Instead of making clinical reports of his cases, or doing animal experimentation as requested, he obtained a loan in 1920 of $70,000 and built his own larger Tank Two in a residential area of the city (3310 Harrison Avenue) away from the university. Leaving the university would not substitute for providing a scientific basis for his new treatment although he probably thought it would. Subsequently it did lead to further problems and in retrospect was not wise. A scientific basis for the treatment needed to be established to make it secure against all onslaughts. We are looking back with hindsight, which is good only for other similar events in the future.

Tank 2, Away from U.

The new tank was larger but demand for hyperbaric treatment grew. With one satisfied patient telling another, they were keeping it filled. He had unsolicited but favorable publicity in a 1921 article by Floyd W. Parsons, a science writer for the *Saturday Evening Post,* which was very complimentary. Dr. C.'s name was not given but the "Tank Treatment in Kansas City" left no doubt about the reference. He became even busier. Flu, pneumonia, asthma, hay fever, heart failure and syphilis patients were treated. Some of the patients also had diabetes according to the General Manager, Edward Hoffman, who himself was a diabetic and had improved with the treatments. Diabetes was added to the growing list of conditions being treated. The patients felt better. Some were even able to stop taking insulin, it was said. If this could have been backed up with specific data, it would have been extremely helpful to Dr. Cunningham. The diabetic patients received low carbohydrate diabetic diets and insulin under medical supervision of Dr. C., postulated that the disease was due to an anaerobic germ, a new idea then. This was a postulate that needed proof. When none was given it lead to criticism even though results with diabetic patients were very good. (Cases could have been written up and published to verify this.) The anaerobic organism postulation as the cause of diabetes was unfortunately without proof. It was used against Dr. Cunningham by his opponents.

In spite of this, the fame of the "Tank Treatments" continued to spread widely. Well-known public figures viewed it favorably. The wife of Mr. J. H. Rand II found that it lowered her blood pressure from 200 to 150 with a one week stay in the tank. She came periodically to the Kansas City Tank for treatment. With demand for the treatment increasing, Dr. C. became busier. Patients were rested and invigorated at the end of their stay under pressure. They felt better and the word continued to spread, The Tank Treatment became a popular subject of conversation, especially in high circles. A third tank, 100-feet long, 10 feet in diameter, housed in its own building, and more elaborately furnished, was built next door to 3310 Harrison Ave., which greatly increased capacity. Business was good, the mortgage was paid off and the Cunninghams bought a new car and moved to the country club area (Trimble, 63).

Mr. Henry Timken, Patient

Among satisfied patients was Mrs. Reynolds, sister of Henry H. Timken, president of the Timken Roller Bearing Company of Canton, Ohio. When her brother became critically ill at his home, through her influence, he was brought by special train to Kansas City to be treated by Dr. Cunningham. According to Trimble, (63), he was in uremic poisoning and sinking fast. Another version of the story claimed that he had pneumonia. He was critically ill, whatever it was, and on the verge of coma. Dr. Cunningham at once placed him in the tank under pressure, and stayed with him. It was one crisis after another with the outcome uncertain for several days until the patient's high fever suddenly broke and he began to improve. The crisis was over and in a few more days he was able to convalesce in the sanitarium outside the tank, where he made a complete recovery (Trimble, 64). Mr. Timken realized that he had had a very close call with death and praised Dr. Cunningham for saving his life. It was not all words. He wanted to do more to show his appreciation. He would build a pressure chamber for Dr. Cunningham large enough to be a hospital! Dr. C. could hardly believe his ears knowing Mr. Timken's wealth. According to legend, Mr. Timken told him he would provide a million dollars to build the "Pressure Hospital"! The appointments would be of the very best, like a first class New York hotel. It would be in pleasant peaceful surroundings in Cleveland, Ohio where his engineers from Canton could more readily carry out construction. They would be equal partners (Trimble, 56). Dr. Cunningham, unable to speak, dumbfounded, shook Mr. Timken's hand. It was unbelievable for him!

American Medical Association (AMA)

The American Medical Association had been formed in 1847 to promote the science and art of medicine and betterment of public health (Encyclopedia Britannica 1:794). It was instrumental in setting standards of education and medical practice. Somehow Dr. C., though he knew this and was a member in good standing in his medical society in Kansas City, for some reason did not fully appreciate the necessity of publishing facts to gain the backing of that organization.

In the summer of 1925 Dr. Cunningham and his family took a trip to Cleveland to look at the new location site and to visit the Timken engineers in Canton. When he returned from that trip, the summer of 1925, at the pinnacle of his success, he had a letter that would change his life.

Request from the American Medical Association

The letter was from Dr. Morris Fishbein of the American Medical Association with questions about the Cunningham treatment. Dr. Fishbein was also a graduate of Rush Medical College in Chicago, class of 1912, eight years Dr. C.'s junior. The AMA had been receiving requests from doctors about the country asking the information concerning "The Tank Treatment" for diabetes. The questions asked Dr. Cunningham were:

1. What claims are made for the Cunningham treatment?
2. Has a report of this treatment been published in a Medical Journal?
3. Has the treatment been put on a commercial basis? Patented?

Dr. Cunningham made a trip to Chicago in answer to this request. When he arrived at the AMA Headquarters, Dr. Fishbein did not want to talk with him. Dr. C. was told that the answers should be in writing. He returned to Kansas City deeply hurt, especially since he was a member in good standing with his local medical society.

New Ideas

Frequently a person with a new idea is inherently distrustful that his idea will be stolen by others before he gets credit for it. He, with historical precedent, worries that his discovery will be taken from him and another will get the credit. In 1918 the demand for scientific verification for new ideas had developed further than Dr. C. realized. It was a new era that required the backing by scientific data of any new method and he did not fully realize this or at least did not realize it soon enough. I think

66

this was particularly hard for him because he worried about the disclosure aspect and that he apparently might lose control if he let others know of his method, when in reality that was necessary to keep publicity favorable. As mentioned previously, Dr. C. was a very private person who did not share his thinking freely with others. When construction was taking place on Lakeshore Boulevard in 1928, the newspapers were not taken into confidence and reporters were not allowed on the grounds. It was and is a very difficult thing to know how to use publicity and keep it favorable. In fact it is a problem of such magnitude today that special attention is given to avoid problems such as Dr. C. encountered.

When Dr. Fishbein would not talk with Dr. Cunningham, he continued with plans for the new Cleveland "Tank Hospital." These were completed about five months later in February 1926. The decision had been made; it would be a giant steel sphere requiring no internal bracing, sixty-four feet in diameter, five stories high with two additional cylindrical tanks sixteen feet in diameter, thirty-five and seventy-feet long respectively, with a ten by twenty foot central air lock at ground level for all three units. There would be 350 ten-inch portholes in the sphere, twenty in the small and forty in the large cylindrical tank to let in light. The sphere would have three mid-diameter floors with twelve rooms each for patients and an elevator centrally surrounded by a staircase. The bottom floor just inside the air lock was the dining room where heated special trays were "locked in" from the hotel kitchen in heated food carts at mealtime. The top floor was a recreation room with a library, billiard and card tables and other games. In the oxygen enriched atmosphere combustion was intense and dangerous. A match, if struck, would flare up intensely. There was no smoking in patient rooms for this reason. The recreation room at the top had a special smoking area equipped with a sprinkler system. All patients were made keenly aware of the necessity of smoking only in this area. The air conditioners kept the temperature at 68 to 70 degrees Fahrenheit and the humidity at 65 to 85 percent. The huge compressors in the engine room pumped 3,100 cubic feet of air per minute.

Reply to the AMA

In February 1926 Dr. C. replied to Dr. Fishbein as follows:

1. Compressed air is a practical efficient way of administering oxygen.

It is of temporary benefit in high blood pressure, acidosis and conditions needing heart rest. Relief has been obtained in anaphylactic conditions of asthma and hay fever. For syphilis all but two of 175 cases became Wasserman negative. He added that many cases of diabetes mellitus, hypertrophic arthritis and pernicious anemia were benefitted.

2. He had written no clinical reports for medical journals.
   (The experience with syphilis, 175 cases with persistent negative Wasserman Tests in all but two cases would have made a very good clinical report for a medical journal.)

3. The treatment was not on a commercial basis. It was not incorporated. There were no patents that would prevent use of compressed air that he knew of. He held a patent on a method of compression and use of compressed air, which affected economy.

Dr. Cunningham's Presentation in 1926
Oxygen Therapy by Means of Compressed Air, by Orval J. Cunningham, M.D.

Read at the Sixth Annual Meeting of Mid-Western Association of Anesthetists in conjunction with the Kansas City Fall Clinical Conference, *Baltimore Hotel, October 12–16, 1926.* Published in *Anesthesia and Analgesia* April 1927, pp. 1–3:

The conventional methods of oxygen administration are listed as face mask, breathing tubes, tents and enclosures in which the content of oxygen in the inhaled air is increased. Face masks give 50 percent rebreathing. The cost of manufactured oxygen is high. Carbon dioxide is necessarily removed with soda lime from the exhaled air of an oxygen tent.

Compressed air furnishes the oxygen of the air to the patient at any desired tension and for any length of time without additional cost of oxygen. Dr. Cunningham has had eight years experience with it. He gives a description of the Kansas city tanks. Thirty pounds gauge pressure, two additional atmospheres of pressure, making a total of three atmospheres is equivalent to the 60 percent oxygen enrichment to inspired air.

Describing the tank treatment, Dr. Cunningham says the treatment varied from ten to thirty pounds of pressure per square inch above atmospheric pressure. The treatments last from three hours to thirty-one days.

Most are three to nine hours or seven days. In the seven-day treatment, the last forty-eight hours are used for uniform step decompression. The air is scrubbed with water and air conditioned to 72 degrees and relative humidity of 65 percent.

1. Is compressed air a means of oxygen therapy?
2. Do we get more oxygen into the tissues with it?
3. Is it of therapeutic value?

Dr. Cunningham thinks the answers to these questions are positive, here is how he answers: "Many tests have shown the physiological effects of high and low altitudes. The mountains and the seashore. *If the tissues did not absorb large amounts of gas under higher atmospheric pressure there would be no disease such as Caisson's Disease!* (*A very true Statement.*) He also quoted an early report by Dr. Paul Bert at the Sorbonne in Paris, France in 1878, which stated that the oxygen content of various tissues under one atmosphere of additional pressure at the end of five hours contains 90 percent more oxygen. Dr. Bert also showed that the oxygen tension of different tissues varied greatly. Nerve, bone and connective tissue have low oxygen tension.

"We use the treatment principally for anaerobic infections or because of good response to treatment. Spirochetes of syphilis are anaerobic and killed by increased oxygen tension. The general condition of the patients improves and the Wassermann tests become negative."

Response to the treatment of diabetes mellitus, hypertrophic arthritis and pernicious anemia has been such as to indicate that the cause of these diseases are also anaerobic infections and many of these patients are apparently cured by compressed air. "Disregarding the possible relapse after long intervals, I believe it is safe to say that many of these cases are cured." (The diabetic patients received diet and insulin treatment as well. Nothing available at that time was omitted.)

"Beneficial effects in asthma and hay fever are observed. Many cases have had no return of their disorders. Encouraging results with carcinoma are observed." The same mechanism is postulated.

He then asked his audience of doctors if compressed air treatment might be a good preparation for surgery. No data given; it was a question to the audience. "Should operations be done under increased pressure to ensure better outcome? How will patients react to their anesthetic gases under increased pressure?" He aimed his questions to his anesthetist audience.

Dr. Cunningham told what he was doing, how he was doing it and postulated why the treatments should be helpful. His statement regarding Caisson's disease is very meaningful. Unfortunately, he did not give any actual data upon which independent judgment could be based for diabetes, pernicious anemia or carcinoma.

Hypoxemia, Professor Nelson
Professor C. F. Nelson, M.D., Chairman, Department of Biochemistry, University of Kansas, Lawrence, Kansas, *Anesthesia and Analgesia*, November–December 1931, pp. 1–6

Read at the Joint meeting of the Southern Association of Anesthetists with the Mid-Western Association of Anesthetists in Conjunction with the Southern Medical Association, Hotel Seelbach, Louisville, Kentucky, November 12–13, 1930:

Dr. Nelson, speaking to anesthetists, told them that one of the greatest advances in modern medicine was the relief of pain. (This true statement should have been well received by his audience!) He expressed the opinion that modern man has become more sensitive to pain. As man becomes more civilized his nervous system becomes more delicately sensitized.

He then gave a detailed discussion of hypoxemia, the condition of abnormally low partial pressure of oxygen in the capillaries of the various tissues of the body and indicated how critical this is to the life of the cells. He said that whatever theory of narcosis is found true, it shall be intimately bound up with oxygen tensions in the capillaries in his opinion. He differentiated three types of hypoxia:

	Hemoglobin	**Circulation**	**Alveolar Oxygen Tension**
Anoxic	N	N	Reduced (e.g. altitude, pneum.)
Anemic	Reduced	N	N (e.g. aplastic anemia)
Stagnant	N	Reduced	N (e.g. shock, hemm.)

Alveolar air has one-third less oxygen than inspired air. Gas poisoning can diminish passage of oxygen from alveoli into hemoglobin. Symptoms of acute hypoxemia are light headedness, dizziness and difficulty concentrating. Symptoms of chronic hypoxemia are tiredness and fatigue resulting in increased depth and rate of respiration on exertion.

70

Treatment of Anoxemia

1. Evans of Buffalo, New York—Administration of oxygen in inspired air. Advocated in 1900 by Smith.
2. *Cunningham of Cleveland—Compressed air.* Original cost of equipment high but once installed *it truly becomes a deluxe method of giving oxygen.*

Research

In 1924, animal experimentation was carried out by Dr. C. F. Nelson, professor of biochemistry at the University of Kansas. The original compression tank constructed at the University of Kansas in 1918 was moved to the Harrison Avenue location. There Professor Nelson and associate Woodard carried out experiments on rabbits to determine the effect of compressed air on animals made anoxic by two methods. This was done to simulate the impairment of oxygen exchange in the lungs, similar to pneumonia.

1. Six rabbits were made short of breath and cyanotic (blue) from pneumothorax (air injected into their pleural cavities). This produced partial lung collapse. These animals were greatly improved under compressed air at 21 pounds pressure.
2. Six rabbits were made short of breath and blue from gum acacia injected into their tracheas, to simulate the blockage of secretions from pneumonia.
   A. Their arterial oxygen saturation dropped 30 to 40 percent.
   B. The arterial saturation was restored to preinjection levels under compressed air.
   C. Three of these animals were then decompressed in the chamber.
   When this was done, their arterial oxygen saturation again dropped to the pre-compression levels.

This work was published in the *Journal of Pathology and Bacteriology, 381 [1925]: 507–513.* The beneficial effect of compressed air in these animals was similar to the beneficial effect seen in the clinical cases of pneumonia that Dr. C. had treated. (A reprint of this work was sent to Dr. Fishbein at the American Medical Association.)

Dr. Nelson's experimental work with rabbits indicated that compressed air is helpful to animals with diminished pulmonary function. This supported his success with human cases of pneumonia. It is unfortunate that his pneumonia successes were not individually recorded in detail and reported in a medical publication, and the same for the cases with syphilis.

Changes in Spinal Fluid Oxygen and Nitrogen Content of Dogs under Pressure

During the summer of 1933, my last complete summer at the sanitarium, James H. (Jim Rand) Rand III and I carried out an interesting experiment on dogs to determine the changes in the oxygen and nitrogen content of their spinal fluid under an additional thirty pounds of gauge pressure. This was the additional pressure being used for the treatment of the patients, a week at a time, in the Sphere. This experiment with dogs was to gain some objective data concerning nitrogen and oxygen content of their cerebrospinal fluid under normal atmospheric pressure and when under thirty pounds of gauged pressure. Our paper was accepted and published in *The American Journal of Physiology* in January 1934. Unfortunately, it came too late to help Dr. Cunningham with his problems with the medical society.

Although James H. Rand and I came from very different family backgrounds, we became good friends. The fact that we had both lost our mothers at an early age may have contributed to that congeniality. Jim and his family were close friends of Dr. and Mrs. Cunningham and he periodically came to the sanitarium. He had been in medical school at the University of Virginia and had a theory on the cause of cancer that excited his professors. When it did not work out, he had left school and came to the sanitarium. The published data of our study was as follows:

72

Relation of Oxygen and Nitrogen Content of Cerebrospinal Fluid to Increased Barometric Pressure (30 lbs. Gauge) by Cunningham, Rand, and Weckesser
American Journal of Physiology *107, no. 1, January 1934:164–167*

Sixteen dogs were used. They were housed in the cylindrical tank 35 feet long and 16 feet in diameter, the front cylindrical tank shown next to the Sphere in aerial view of Sanitarium on p. 163. Samples of cerebrospinal fluid were withdrawn by cisternal puncture with local anesthesia when the animals were under normal atmospheric pressure and examined with Van Slyke apparatus to determine the content of oxygen and nitrogen.

The pressure in the tank was then raised to 30 pounds gauge pressure and kept at that level. All animals were under pressure at least 10 hours before new samples of fluid were drawn. The temperature was maintained at 72 degrees F. and the humidity at 65 percent using the same compressors as the large sphere. Duplicate analyses were made of all specimens throughout.

Results in volume percent, averages for the 16 animals:

	Atmospheric Pressure		Atmospheric Pressure plus 30 Lbs.	
	Oxygen	Nitrogen	Oxygen	Nitrogen
16 Dogs	0.20%	0.91%	0.44%	2.69%
	(0.18–0.27%)		(0.35–0.55%)	

The nitrogen increased 196.7 percent nearly according to Henry's Law. The oxygen content increased 120.0 percent. Could this lesser increase in oxygen content be due to its constant utilization by cells?

This study gives actual data showing the increase in both oxygen and nitrogen content of spinal fluid in dogs under one atmosphere and under three atmospheres of pressure.

Letters to Dr. George Crile Sr., 1929

These letters are of particular interest in retrospect. On May 15, 1929 a terrible disaster occurred in Cleveland. It was described by William Ganson Rose as one of the city's greatest tragedies. This occurred at the

Cleveland Clinic at East 93rd Street and Euclid Avenue when a fire broke out in the basement of the building, probably due to a short circuit in an extension cord. Noxious gases were released probably from stored X-ray film as it unknowingly burned. The fumes permeated the building, where many patients and medical personnel were housed. The fire created an unexpected serious lethal situation in which 124 people died. Many others received very serious damage to the lining of their lungs and alveoli and had difficulty breathing. Dr. John Phillips, one of the founders of the clinic, died in that disaster. Dr. Henry John, a diabetic specialist, was injured by the gases, reported dead in the headline of the evening paper, but survived. He and I were very good friends in later years and he showed me a copy of the newspaper reporting his death. When inhaled the noxious gases seriously damaged the delicate lining cells of the alveoli of the lung and those patients had respiratory distress and needed pulmonary support. An urgent request for oxygen tents was circulated. The letters were in response to this call. The first is a letter from Dean Marvin Sudler, dean of the medical school at Lawrence, Kansas, enclosing a letter from Professor Nelson, chairman of biochemistry which is self-explanatory.

This is a touching appeal to Dr. Crile, from Dean Sudler and Prof. C. F. Nelson, chief of biochemistry at the University of Kansas, to get in touch with Dr. Cunningham for use of the Sphere with its compressed air to relieve the hypoxia of the victims.

I do not think anything ever came of it, but the benefit could have been great if the victims of *endothelial alveolar* injury had been placed under increased atmospheric pressure to get more oxygen into their tissue fluids.

Physical Aspects of the Cunningham Sanitarium

Mr. Timken himself picked the beautiful thirteen-acre former estate of banker Henry Payne McIntosh as the location of the new sanitarium. It was a rectangle of land between the Lake Erie Shore and Lakeshore Boulevard eight miles east of downtown Cleveland. The mansion located on the lake shore provided a beautiful home for Dr. and Mrs. Cunningham and their two children, Orval Jr. and Dorothy. The sanitarium was along the front of the property just back from Lakeshore Boulevard with very nice landscaping, many trees and separate well-kept lawns. There was no smoking while the pressure was on except in one area of the recreation room, which was equipped with water sprinklers. In front of the engine room building was a brick hallway leading to the locking chamber or lock. This room was necessary to gain access to and from each of the tanks when they were under pressure. The lock, into which the hallway ended, served the two smaller cylindrical tanks on each side of it and also the large sphere. All were made out of thick steel to withstand the high pressures. The three tanks supplied increased atmospheric pressure while people lived in them.

The Treatment Cycle of the Sanitarium

The pressure treatments given in the Sphere were intermittent. The patients went home between treatments or, if they were from long distances, they lived in the attached hotel building that housed the front office where I worked evenings. The length of time that patients remained under pressure varied, but when I arrived at the sanitarium in January, 1930 the treatment cycle was six days in, a day to change over and six days out.

The patient's rooms, with radios and telephones, were nicely decorated and had light from portholes. The upper floor was a recreation room with reading material, a billiard table and card tables. The ground floor was a dining room where the trays were ''locked in'' and ''locked out'' for each of the three daily meals.

During the years 1930 to mid-1934, patients entered the sphere on Sunday afternoon. The doors were sealed and pressurization began. Over a period of three or more hours the pressure was raised to thirty pounds gauge (three atmospheres total). The patients were instructed by two nurses, who also lived in the Sphere, to equalize the pressure on their ear drums by chewing gum, swallowing or increasing pressure in their mouth and pharynx by blowing and holding their noses while the pressure was being increased. The new patients were kept under observation and helped by the nurses as necessary during their first experiences. They soon became experts at equalizing their ear pressure and frequently developed special techniques of their own. The increased pressure in the Sphere was maintained for four days. During this time the patients were free to move about and noted no unusual symptoms. They could read or carry out any projects that they brought with them. It was a good rest in an isolated, comfortable atmosphere. The heart patients, as well as all others, said they felt invigorated on leaving the Sphere.

Events of 1930–31

The U.S. Senate confirmed the London Naval Treaty with Britain and Japan. A protective tariff, the Smoot-Hawley Act, was signed by President Hoover. Duty was raised on 890 articles that favored farmers. There were four and a half million unemployed people. Dr. Karl Landsteiner was given the Nobel Prize for the discovery of human blood groups. Boulder (Hoover) Dam was begun at Las Vegas, Nevada to be completed in 1936. The Bank of United States with 400 branches closed in New York City (Carruth, 484–89).

A rise in the stock market was only temporary. There was a severe drought in western U.S. leading to "dust bowl" conditions. Crops failed and the dry land literally blew away causing severe hardship for farmers. France began construction of the Maginot Line. The Democratic party won control of Congress for the first time since 1916. Emergency public works provided 116 million dollars. A public poll showed a majority of people opposed to continued prohibition of the sale of alcoholic beverages.

Models of molecular structure of common molecules were made and demonstrated for teaching purposes (Gordon and Gordon, 100–107).

Events of 1931

In 1931, the Massachusetts Senate made the first resolution for the repeal of Prohibition. Unemployment was near 16 percent of the working population. Two of three auto workers in Detroit were unemployed. Striking coal miners battled guards in Harlan, Kentucky—four were killed. Hunger marchers to the White House were turned away. There was a Japanese invasion of Manchuria. Chiang Kai-shek's nationalists in China clashed with Mao Tse-tung's Communists (Gordon and Gordon, 109).

Adelbert College Matriculation

I matriculated as a sophomore at Adelbert College of Western Reserve University in the third week of August. My evening work fit nicely with my college schedule. After things quieted down there was usually time for study. The instructors were excellent and the classes were interesting. I was very glad to get back to my studies.

Professor Montcastle was an inspiring teacher of physics, regarding the ultimate nature of things. For a while I seriously considered making physics my career. Then came Professor Cleveland in chemistry and Professor Lankelma in biochemistry. Professor Montcastle's lectures were lucid and the experiments intriguing. It was wonderful to be able to understand more about the physical laws of nature and how they reacted one with the other. The professor himself was an inspiring enthusiastic person and I felt a bond to him and his ideas. It was exciting. I considered making the study of physics my main line of interest for some time. I've often thought about that and think it would have been very rewarding. The possible understanding of the ultimate nature of things was intriguing. I had also taken biology in my previous courses and liked it. In the consideration between medicine and physics, which I weighed carefully, my main mission in life, I thought, was to help others. All of these things were considered. Mother's early loss of life and the death of an infant older sister from whooping cough were often spoken of in the family and Father's experiences in his early life on the farm, losing brothers and sisters from diphtheria when he was a boy. Later when applying for medical school another factor arose, the question of preceding doctors in my family. I answered "NO" to the question on the application form not realizing then that the Herrs and Longs on my mother's side of the family were full of them. She was gone and could not correct me. All these factors combined led to my decision, which has never been regretted.

The school year went quickly. I traveled by bus to Euclid Avenue and then by streetcar to University Circle, and vice versa after class, to save gasoline and expense. Being able to read in transit was an additional help with my studies.

Care of the Sanitarium Grounds

When the school year ended in June, Ed. Hoffman asked me to take care of the outside grounds by watering, mowing and trimming. This was with the help of two patients who also lived on the third floor, where I stayed. Similar to the tractors at home, the tractor and mower for the large lawns were down my alley, and I found the patients quite cooperative.

In addition to the grass mowing, which was practically continuous, the sprinkling was also a large task. With a water intake from Lake Erie that had to be put into place in the spring and taken out in the fall, it was no small task. The first season we did not get the intake out soon enough in the fall. Cold weather set in, which made it a terrible task. That only happened once. The sprinkling was not automatic. There were multiple water outlets and large circular sprinklers that were self-propelled, but had to be changed and hoses dragged around to keep the grass green. There were flowerbeds to tend and shrubs to trim. Experience in Father's greenhouses came in handy with that.

It was a busy place in other ways too. There were trains to meet and people to be taken to the station and other places. There were three sedans for that purpose, a Cadillac, a Franklin (air cooled) and a Chevy, which meant a great deal of chauffeuring.

A Matthews Cruiser

About the second summer, Dr. C. surprised everyone with the purchase of a thirty-eight-foot Matthews Cruiser, which was docked at the Cleveland Yacht Club in Rocky River. This caused interest and excitement. It was a very nice cruiser with a small galley midship that converted into bunks at night, and a comfortable compartment for two in the bow with a head. The stern was open with multiple cushioned seats. Most meals were taken ashore.

The doctor was very proud of his cruiser and used it to entertain patients and friends on trips to many places among the islands of Lake Erie. Favorite spots were Pelee Island and Put-in-Bay with an overnight stay in the latter harbor and a leisurely trip back to Rocky River next day. I frequently was first mate and cabin boy on those trips and Dr. Cunningham frequently gave me one of his cigars, a special treat, to smoke while we were in port.

The switchboard was usually tended by one of the nurses when I was away. They were responsible for Sunday coverage of the switchboard and some bargaining occurred when one or the other wanted time off. The ladies tried to tell me that I did not mind working Sundays and therefore should give them time off but I did not buy it unless there was a reasonable exchange. It worked out fine.

78

The summers of 1931 and 1932 passed rapidly with these many duties. In the summer of 1932 Grandfather Emanuel Long died in Williamsville, New York, my mother's home, just outside of Buffalo. I did not attend his funeral. It is something that I am not proud of. I admired him greatly. In addition to my work, I was getting ready for medical school, but that was not an adequate excuse.

School of Medicine of Western Reserve University (Now Case WRU)

I entered the School of Medicine of Western Reserve University in August of 1932 with the Depression at its lowest ebb. Thankfully, I had money for tuition from my savings account. I was a senior in absentia at Adelbert during my first medical year and received a B.A. degree from Adelbert College, the undergraduate school of Reserve, in June 1933. Things were so busy that I did not go to the graduation exercises and had my diploma mailed to me. My main interest was obtaining my medical degree and all efforts were to that end.

"Through the Air Lock"

In order to get into the sphere when it was pressurized required a special technique or sequence of events, going "through the air lock." We went down the connection hall from the hotel. We started with pressure in the Sphere and none in the lock. The doors to the lock could be opened inward in a normal or usual way because the one atmosphere of pressure was the same on both sides of the door. We opened the door into the lock and entered taking whatever else we wished along with us. The steel-walled room ten by twenty feet could accommodate six or eight people. The food tray carts, for example could be taken in with us, only usually those were trapped in by themselves to the nurses on the inside. We closed the heavy steel outside door behind us (they opened inward to seal tighter as the pressure increased) and threw its steel bolts. After closing all valves to the outside we opened the valve of a pipe leading from the interior of the Sphere. With all the exit valves from the lock closed, the pressure rather rapidly rises in the comparatively small lock. We could feel the pressure on our eardrums. It was like coming down to land in an airplane. Swallowing or blowing with our mouth and nose closed caused the pressure on our eardrums to equalize through our Eustachian tubes. We also soon noticed that it was getting quite warm. The increase in pressure of the air about us led to an increase in temperature of the air about us—a law of nature, Boyle's law. Pressure and temperature are directly related to each other. Soon the noise from the air rushing into the lock from the pressurized Sphere decreased and then ceased.

80

This indicated that the pressure on both sides of Sphere door had equalized. We now could unbolt that door, push it open, inward and walk into the pressurized Sphere. The pressure on each square inch of our body was forty-five pounds per square inch instead of the usual fifteen pounds. We actually were not aware of this increased pressure and could move about freely. If we wanted to go back out without decompressing slowly, we could only stay a short time, fifteen or twenty minutes. The shorter the time, the better.

Bends

Normally, if one is under increased atmospheric pressure longer, more than a few minutes, rapid decompression may lead to the *bends* or Caisson Disease, which are other names for decompression sickness. The name was derived from the fact that divers working under increased pressure in caissons bent over in extreme pain if they came out of high compression rapidly. This condition is caused by the fact that our tissues and body fluids absorb more gases than normal from the high atmospheric pressure if we stay in it more than five to fifteen minutes. If we suddenly leave the high atmospheric pressure after a long stay and decompress rapidly, this large amount of nitrogen and oxygen in our tissues comes out of solution rapidly foaming and forming bubbles in our blood and tissue fluids, tissues similar to the carbon dioxide escaping from the liquid of an uncapped carbonated beverage.

Scuba diving, which involves the diver being under increased atmospheric pressure, has become very popular. The problems of decompression are present in that sport.

"The Physiology of Decompression Illness", by Moon, Vann, and Bennett, in the August 1995 issue of *Scientific American*, gives a very good review of these problems and points out additional difficulties in a patient with a patent Foramen Ovale, which offers additional risk by allowing venous blood containing gas bubbles to get into the systemic circulation. Normally, excess gases are diffused out in the pulmonary circulation and do not get into the systemic circulation. Air in the systemic circulation can cause air embolism, which is not well tolerated and can be fatal. Therefore persons with a circulatory abnormality that allows crossover into the systemic circulation from the pulmonary circulation are at a much greater risk from bends than those with a normal right and left heart circulation. It is unwise for persons with abnormalities of their pulmonary circulation to deep sea scuba dive or work in Caissons. At least this is true unless they do so with very slow decompression and return to normal atmospheric pressure gradually. It's quite possible to have circulatory abnormalities without being aware of them, which makes this an important and sobering consideration.

Short Stay or Slow Step Decompression

The safe thing is not to stay under high pressure more than a few minutes if we are going to decompress rapidly. If we have been under high pressure more than fifteen or twenty minutes, it is safest to decompress slowly, allowing our blood stream to carry the excess nitrogen and oxygen to our lungs where it can escape instead of forming bubbles. Prevention is by far the safest. The best treatment when it occurs is recompression as soon as possible followed by gradual step decompression over a period of time. The patients in the Sphere went through step decompression of about five pounds every twelve hours during the last forty-eight hours of their treatment.

To leave the pressurized Sphere after a short stay, the process of entering was reversed. When both lock and tank are equally pressurized, we enter the lock and close the steel door of the Sphere behind us, throw the bolts, and close the air valve that we opened coming in. We next open another air valve to the outside of the lock, which lets the pressure within the lock equalize with normal atmosphere pressure outside. We hear the air rushing out of the lock. Now the air in the lock becomes very cold, the opposite of coming in, and fog appears and gets quite heavy. This process of releasing gas under high pressure is the same one that is used in refrigerators, only here it is just incidental and serves no useful purpose. Finally the noise of the air rushing out gets less and ceases, meaning that the pressure in the lock has equalized once again with the outside atmospheric pressure. We can now open the exit door from the lock to the outside and return to the hotel.

Caught in the Lock

It was possible, of course, for someone to make mistakes with the valves, leaving one open when it should be closed or vice versa. Occasionally this happened with someone caught in the lock. When this occurred, it was possible to make the necessary corrections with emergency valves on the outside. The engineer ordinarily took care of that. A few months after I arrived someone was caught in the lock one evening and the engineer was busy. Understanding the situation, I left the switchboard, corrected it on the outside with the emergency valves and went back to my station. The engineer, when he was free, was surprised and, not being an admirer of mine, said, "The kid did that?" He held a grudge against me for a while, but it gradually lessened.

Requirements for Hyperbaric Treatment

1. Special equipment:
   Compression chamber.
   Adequate mechanical equipment.
   Compressors, air conditioning.
2. Special experienced personnel.
3. Cost efficiency. Sharing of facilities probably necessary.

Final Days

Next, Dr. Cunningham's relations with his benefactor, Mr. Timken cooled (Trimble, 76). Business at the sanitarium slowed down greatly in 1934. This was probably secondary to his difficulty with the American Medical Association. It was scoring him for claiming, without proof, that diabetes was due to an undiscovered anaerobic organism. He was giving all necessary treatment for diabetes that was available at that time, including diet and insulin, but had not made a report of his results in a scientific journal as requested. He was also being criticized for his attempts to treat malignancy, which were actually turning out negative.

In 1934 business dropped off sharply. The causes for this, although not entirely clear were probably mainly related to Dr. C.'s difficulties with organized medicine. He had been a member of the Medical Society in Kansas City, but the Cleveland Academy of Medicine had rejected his application for membership. His work had become included among those methods of treatment without scientific backing, a tremendous blow to his pride and self esteem. This hurt him greatly. Next, probably for this same reason, his warm relationship with Mr. Timken, his great benefactor, became cool.

At school, Dr. Wiggers, my professor of physiology, for whom I had great regard, expressed doubt about the compression treatment in that hemoglobin was 97 percent saturated with oxygen under our normal one atmosphere of pressure. This was not true for the body and cell fluids, of course. It was controversial. My single and most pressing need was to continue with my medical education. Dr. Cunningham told me he did not want me to be hurt by the controversy. After talking things over with my brother Ernie and Father, I left the sanitarium at the end of my sophomore year at the Western Reserve Medical School in the summer of 1934, ending a four-and-a-half-year stay at the Sanitarium, which had been a tremendous benefit to me. I had met many very fine people.

James H. Rand III

James H. Rand III bought rights to the sanitarium from Mr. Timken and tried reorganization for about a year. His efforts were unsuccessful and the sanitarium closed in 1935. In 1942 the Sphere and the cylindrical tanks were sadly dismantled and sold for scrap for $25,000 to support the war effort of World War II while I was in the South Pacific.

Death of Dr. Cunningham

The controversy about Dr. Cunningham's claim that diabetes, carcinoma and pernicious anemia were due to an anaerobic organism continued to his detriment and I think his health began to fail at about that time. He moved from the sanitarium grounds to another home in Cleveland where he died in 1937 of congestive heart failure, a slow agonizing death according to his son Orval. This occurred when I was interning at the Cincinnati General Hospital.

Some Fine Patients and Other People at the Sanitarium

Aldenese Family. Mrs. Aldenese was the patient. Mr. Aldenese was insular collector of customs for the Philippine Islands. There was a son,

Carlos, a daughter, Paula, and grandmother, who was a sweet elderly lady who gracefully smoked cigars with a pleasant smile and spoke very little English. The family lived in the hotel for several months while Mrs. Aldenese underwent treatment. After returning home, Carlos became a Philippine Scout during World War II. General MacArthur formed a corps of Philippine scouts just before the onset of World War II when he was in charge there. He took great pride in them, which I was about to learn. Many of them were brought to Australia in March, 1942 with MacArthur when he arrived in Melbourne where my hospital had assembled three weeks earlier. The Philippine Scouts were sent to my post to be admitted to the U.S. Army. This offered a difficulty for Captain Weckesser (ECW). The army regulations specified a certain minimum height for each inductee. These were just little fellows, far short of the minimum requirement. ECW was new at the army game and hesitated. He turned one down because of short stature. A curt call came from MacArthur's headquarters in nearby Toorak School. *"Admit those Men!"* My reply was, ''Yes, sir.'' That was all I needed to know! Learning is rapid in situations like that. I looked for Carlos Aldenese but did not find him. He was not among the group brought to Melbourne, Australia.

Mr. Gabaldon. A high ranking official in Philippine Government.

Henry Holcumb. Founder of Conneaut Lake Park in Pennsylvania. (Warned me of bank failures in 1933 in time for me to transfer most of my tuition money safely to Postal Savings, which kept me in medical school.)

George Melbourne. President of the construction company that built the Sphere.

The Shibe Family. Shibe Park and Philadelphia Athletics baseball.

Connie Mack. Visited while the Shibes were there. I chauffeured him and players to the Union Terminal Station when they left town.

The Pruitt Family. Pruitt Department Store, Tulsa, Oklahoma.

Mr. Timken. The benefactor was not a patient during my four-and a-half years at the sanitarium.

Miss Elizabeth Perry. Dietician. A very fine person. She was the dietitian later at City Hospital, Metro General Hospital, Cleveland and later for the Stouffer Corporation.

Mrs. Gladys Wales. Laboratory technician.

Edward Hoffman. General manager of the Sanitarium, from Oshkosh, Wisconsin, Edward continued to be a good friend after the sanitarium closed. In the 1950s, he often visited Katy and me in our Shaker Heights home on his trips to Cleveland. At that time, after World War II, the children were growing up and I was practicing surgery at University Hospitals. He was associated with the Golfing Association in Oshkosh and arranged tournaments and that type of thing. We enjoyed his visits, reminiscing about former days and the people at the Sanitarium until he died in 1962.

And many many more fine people.

Physical Laws of Gases

Dalton's Law: Pressure exerted by a mixture of gases is equal to the sum of the partial pressures of those gases.

Boyle's Law: The pressure of a given quantity of gas, temperature constant, varies inversely with volume.

Henry's Law: The amount of a gas forced into solution in a liquid is proportional to its partial pressure.

Summary and Conclusions

1. The Cunningham Sanitarium was an extremely well-designed, equipped and operated facility.
2. It offered rest and an efficient method of treatment for:
   A. Caisson's Disease (Bends). The surest and best treatment. Prevented preferably by short exposure or slow step decompression from a hyperbaric environment.

B. Oxygen for respiratory insufficiency. Pneumonia, emphysema, etc.
C. Asthma, hay fever. The washed air was quite free of allergens.
D. Rest.
3. The method has since been shown effective for:
A. Carbon Monoxide Poisoning
B. Gas Gangrene
C. Tetanus
4. Destruction of the largest and best compression chamber ever built and operated was a tragedy. In addition to offering an excellent method of oxygen administration, it had many features of an Aesculapian spa. It was a comfortable, pleasant place. The patients were invigorated and rested when they left the Sphere.

An Epicrisis

Dr. Cunningham's use of compressed air for oxygen therapy, in order to force more oxygen into the tissues and tissue fluids of the body, was sound. Animal studies were desirable at the earliest time. Those that were done were supportive. Case studies and reports on example patients were also highly desirable and would have probably prevented much of his difficulty with the medical society. At least he could have benefitted himself greatly by making published clinical reports of successes and failures, particularly for pneumonia, syphilis, hay fever and allergic conditions. Dr. Cunningham's treatment of diabetes was carried out according to the methods of that day, including proper diet and insulin in addition to increased atmospheric pressure. There were no omissions in treatment. Studies and reports of his results with that disease would have shown a high score in my opinion even though his theory of causation had not been proven. There was no significant benefit for malignancy. Arthritis was indeterminate.

Now approval by the Food and Drug Administration or other regulatory body would be required to operate the Sphere. That was not true in Dr. Cunningham's day.

Postulates and theories, useful as they are, should be converted to proven facts as soon as possible for security. However, a postulate, if a true one, has its true quality even before it is proven fact, but it takes the factual proof to make sure of that. It is not known why Dr. Cunningham did not comply with the requests for clinical case reports and waited so long to produce experimental evidence. It was probably something deep in his nature that he himself did not understand.

Dr. Fishbein could have and should have talked with the man he severely censored when a meeting was requested. That man with brilliant inventive ability was not fully cognizant of the new necessity for scientific proof. To our detriment, he was sadly caught in the "jaws" of scientific requirement and intransigence.

To Cleveland Clinic

I was able to get a night position at the Cleveland Clinic for the summer of 1934 after leaving the sanitarium. I lived with a friend in a boarding house on nearby East 81st Street. I took care of the switchboard at the clinic and made out the operating schedules for the next morning cases. I frequently watched Dr. Crile Sr. and Dr. Lower operate on their cases that I had scheduled the night before. Both men were very nice to me.

National Bank Holiday

A lucky thing happened one night at the front desk that was very fortunate for me in 1933. One of the patients, Mr. Henry Holcomb who had developed Conneaut Lake Park in Pennsylvania, said to me, "Elden, where do you have your savings?" "Union Trust Bank," was my reply. He shook his head and said, "Union Trust is van Sweringen, van Sweringen is railroads and railroads are no good now." On this admonition I withdraw all but two hundred dollars and placed it in Postal Savings, a branch of the Post Office that was then available. A few weeks later the Union Trust Bank closed with the "Bank Holiday" (March 1933) called by newly inaugurated President Franklin D. Roosevelt. I was able to stay in school with my Postal Savings funds. The Bank Holiday, actually the causes of the Bank Holiday, were terrible for everyone. Business practically came to a halt. It was not possible to cash checks and money was very scarce. Practically none was circulating. The day before the Bank Holiday I went to the local Union Trust branch to withdraw some cash. My teller, with whom I had become acquainted, with tears in his eyes, told me none was available. The bank closed its doors next day. In the midst of this crisis, a day or so later, I received a letter from my sister Sylvia, from Texas, with a ten-dollar bill enclosed! I was touched by this, a demonstration of real family loyalty in time of need. We had been through a lot and knew each other's problems.

Several years later I did receive my principle sum of money from the Union Trust Company after the crisis was over, but it was my Postal Savings that had kept me in school.

Actually, closing of the banks throughout the country, 'The Bank Holiday', ordered by President Franklin Delano Roosevelt, as one of his very first acts on taking office in March, 1933, was a very good strong move that prevented further financial collapse. It was the first of many strong steps he took during World War II. Another that I must mention, since I was in an area where it was particularly appreciated—Melbourne, Australia—was the appointment of Gen. Douglas MacArthur as army commander in the South Pacific. Until his arrival from the Philippines three or more weeks after the arrival of our hospital unit, Fourth General Hospital, in the end of February 1942, desperate plans for defence of Australia involved trenches north of Brisbane. MacArthur changed that with the use of air power and "leap frog" invasions of strategic locations of the jungle shore lines along the north coast of New Guinea, Guadalcanal, Dutch East Indies and finally the island of Leyte in the Philippine Islands.

Events of 1932
Franklin Delano Roosevelt,
1932–45 (d. 4/12/45) and
Harry S. Truman, 1945–52

The Great Depression of the 1930s was the worst since the Panic of 1893 (Manchester, 37). The Panic of 1893 had caused my father to lose his properties in Sanborn, New York and on Cayuga Island in the Niagara River and to finally, six years later, return to Ohio in 1899 with his family of four children.

The Depression was considered even worse than that of 1893, and 1932 has been considered its cruelest year. A bonus bill proposed to help World War I's unemployed veterans was defeated in Congress. This led to a Bonus March to Washington, D.C. Many men took their wives and children along. This group was called The Bonus Expeditionary Force (BEF). The men did not have jobs, were not able to feed their families and were asking for help. Auto sales were down 80 percent from 1929 and unemployment reached 24 percent in 1932. The marchers were asking that a bonus due in 1945 be paid to them then, in 1932, to relieve their distress. Many of these marchers, on reaching Washington, took up quarters in old buildings on Pennsylvania Avenue. A larger group located at the edge of the city across the Anacosta River over the Eleventh Street bridge. President Hoover was not sympathetic to their demands. The gates to the White House were chained and an unfortunate event took place. President Hoover called on the Chief of Staff of the Army, Gen. Douglas MacArthur, to forcefully evacuate the group from their Pennsylvania Avenue location. When they refused to leave, the group was forcefully driven back across the Anacosta River. The second officer in charge was Maj. Dwight Eisenhower (Manchester, 1–2).

Japan proclaimed a new state Manchuko in former Manchuria, which it had invaded the previous year. U.S. Secretary of State Henry Simpson made a public statement: "The United States will recognize no territorial acquisitions of aggression." Japan was branded the aggressor in China by the League of Nations (Gordon and Gordon, 118).

Col. Charles Lindbergh's infant son was kidnapped from the Lindbergh home in New Jersey and later found dead. Amelia Earhart made a solo transatlantic flight.

In 1932 there was an increased interest in microwaves that had been used by Italian-born Guglielmo Marconi (1874–1937) for transatlantic wireless transmission in 1901 followed by development of a company that carried out that service. Marconi had shown that microwaves, though traveling in straight lines, were bent and transmitted further around the curvature of the earth than previously known, which made them useful for long-range transmission. These microwaves would later lead to the development of radar during World War II, and subsequently to the post-war transmission of telephone and television signals, in addition to the popular microwave cooking of today.

The Neutron

The greatest event for me in 1932, the worst year of the Depression, was entry into medical school. A greater, by far more valuable thing for the people of the world, however, was the experimental proof of existence of (discovery of) the neutron by Sir James Cavendish at Cambridge, England. This was shown to be a particle of the atomic nucleus of all atoms except hydrogen, which had no electrical charge. It had been postulated by Lord Rutherford in 1920 but never proven. Cavendish made his observations on rays emitted from beryllium when bombarded by alpha particles. These rays were previously thought to be gamma rays. He proved otherwise. It turned out that these uncharged particles, neutrons, when passed through a cyclotron, were excellent for bombarding elements to change their atomic weights and actually *split atoms!* The absence of charge allowed them to enter nuclei without being repelled. Neutrons became the propagating agent of the chain reaction. It was the use of *neutron bombardment of uranium that lead to development of the atomic bomb* in the 1940s and the development of peaceful production of energy.

Atomic Scientists to the United States

Important work leading to splitting of the atom carried out by a number of European physicists, including Szilard in Hungary, Hahn & Strassmann in Germany, Fermi in Italy, Meitner and Frisch could have gotten into the hands of the Axis powers. It is remarkable that the physicists mentioned above all successfully fled to the United States where coordination and proper support of their work provided the outcome that occurred. The opposite could have led to unthinkable disaster for the Allies if Hitler had gained control of the experimental work that was taking place within the borders of his own country. The course of history could have changed dramatically. The policies of our free society and astute leadership by Franklin Roosevelt saved us.

While working at the Ford Motor Company Assembly Plant at East 116th Street and Euclid Avenue during the day and at the Cunningham Sanitarium evenings and during the two years at Adelbert College, I had contemplated where I could, or would be able to, attend medical school. It was difficult to be accepted into medical school in those days. About one in ten candidates made the grade and I was not sure I would be a lucky one by any means. I first applied to Duke University where I had spent my Freshman college year and, after interviews, was accepted there. I went by bus to Pittsburgh to meet a doctor for my final interview. Duke was just opening a Medical School and I could be in the first class. This acceptance gave me courage.

School of Medicine, Western Reserve University

Western Reserve Medical School had been in existence since 1843 and was much in demand. With encouragement from very nice ladies in the Adelbert front office in Adelbert Hall, Helen Doolittle Stewart and Muriel Mays Kline, I decided to also apply at Reserve. They told me I could apply to enter after my third year of college and could be an Adelbert student in absentia to receive my B.A. degree at the end of my first year in medical school. That would be very helpful to me in my financial situation.

At this time the registrar at Reserve Medical School was a large forceful woman with a loud voice by the name of Hunter—Miss Hunter! I think from my observations, and those of classmates, that she took great satisfaction in frightening medical candidates. She had the upper hand and she let you know it.

I had interviews with professors at the Medical School and all seemed to be going well. My grades at Adelbert were good but Miss Hunter needed a transcript of my grades from Duke for my freshman college year. My Duke acceptance was my ''ace in the hole'' and I did not wish to reveal or jeopardize it. I feared I might do so by asking for a transcript of my grades to Reserve. I also hesitated to tell Miss Hunter that I had been accepted at Duke because I thought, with the limited number of spaces for candidates available, that she would say that I should go there since medical school opportunities were so scarce. After a period of time, she called me in saying she had to have those grades. I knew the jig was up. I could delay no longer. I told her why I had not asked for the grade transcript thinking she would probably throw me out of the office. Not so. She was ''nice as pie'' and said, ''Oh, you've been accepted at Duke and want to come here. Well now, I think you should!'' What a relief! I asked for the grade transcript and there was no further problem. I had been very much impressed with the caliber of my instructors at Adelbert and felt that the same would be true at the medical school.

During this time, my older brother Ernie, to whom I was very close, encouraged me to go to Reserve. I consulted Dr. Marion Blankenhorn, professor of medicine at Reserve, originally from Wayne County (same as myself). His father, a fine doctor, practiced in Orrville, Ohio, just across the Chippewa Valley from the Weckesser Apple Orchard. He was known by my family but I had never personally met him. He was a member of the staff at Lakeside Hospital. I contacted him by letter and he wrote back that Western Reserve was "a fine provincial school." I accepted this as a recommendation since the eastern schools were out of the question for me. We became friends later through medical school and my internship at the Cincinnati General Hospital (1936–37) where he had gone as professor of medicine the year before. During my year at Cincinnati, Dr. Blankenhorn had some detractors, who were jealous of his position and his scientific methods. Those people received no sympathy from me. I was a Blankenhorn man all the way and let them know it. He was a very fine person and my friend.

Year One

And so it was, in the third week of August, 1932, I matriculated at Western Reserve University School of Medicine, Cleveland, Ohio. I enrolled with some trepidation having heard from many sources that it was a long, hard course of study. This was amplified by Dean Torald Sollmann in his introductory talk to freshman. He said that what we had heard was going to be true. It was, there was no question about that, and the Dean and the others were correct, but it was well worth it. The dividends have been very great.

The first class was biochemistry (under Victor Carl Myers, Ph.D.) concerning the chemical makeup of living tissues. Myers was not considered an inspiring lecturer by many in the class, referring frequently to his former teachers, Folin and Wu, but his subject matter was great. This started with a one-hour lecture followed by a three-hour laboratory, lasting until noon.

One hour for lunch, then I went to anatomy class. This also began with a one-hour lecture, by T. Wingate Todd, M.B., Ch.B, F.R.C.S. (Fellow of Royal College of Surgeons), Henry Wilson Payne, professor of anatomy. This man, we would soon find out, had a lot "on the ball," but he was tough. He didn't believe in "mollycoddling" anyone. Part of your training was to learn to stand up under pressure and he let you know it. On the first day, in his first lecture, he showed a slide of a beautiful nude woman pointing out the beauty of the curves of her body, with which none of us disagreed, doing it from an artistic standpoint. He also prepared us for the dissecting room, which was to come next. It was a great privilege, he told us, to be allowed to dissect the human body and we were to be reverent while we did so. This was observed. There was no nonsense in the dissecting room. The physical form and relationships of skin, subcutaneous tissue, facial layers, muscles, tendons, blood vessels, nerves, and so on were developed with care and precision. Eight students shared a cadaver, two on each extremity. We were on our own the first day. No one told us what to do. I think this was intentional. After a period of indecision on that first day, during which time our anatomy texts were avidly perused, dissection began cautiously with a skin incision, looking about frequently to see what the others were doing. There was plenty of scouting going on. When one group developed a structure, others went back and did it too. The accomplishments of that first day were not great, but it was a beginning.

On succeeding days the tempo picked up. The lectures and demonstrations were quite informative. At mid-semester, at about seven weeks, we were to have an oral examination in the medical library with eight examiners at eight different locations there. The tales about the approaching examination were terrible. It was like running the gauntlet, we were told. About every ten minutes a bell rang and you went from one examiner to the next on that signal. It had the reputation of being a killer. We all studied hard for it but you didn't know if that would be enough. The day finally came. My first examiner was Dr. Insull, a short, stout, gruff man who did not speak loudly or clearly and often mumbled. Dr. Insull mumbled his first question and I could not make it out. I thought to myself, *I don't even know what he is saying,* but said, "Pardon me, Sir," and he repeated, "What are the malleoli?" What a relief; I could understand him and could answer his questions. He graded tough. If you knew all the answers you were given seventy-six, if you knew most of them, you received seventy-five and if you did poorly you were given seventy-four, which was failing. Dr. T. Wingate Todd, professor of anatomy and head of his department, liked to quiz with X-ray films of different portions of the body. He would give you a baton-like stick pointer to identify what you saw. This was to see how much you were shaking. I was lucky and made it. A number of us did not.

In the second semi-semester, histology, under Dr. Frederick Clayton Waite, Ph. D., was added to our morning classes. Here we became quite familiar with the histological appearance of cells of different organs, drew pictures of them and became able to identify tissues by their microscopic appearance. We continued with anatomy in the afternoons, and had another oral exam on anatomy in the library at the end of the period.

In the third semi-semester, embryology, under Dr. Bradley Patten, took up the mornings. Here we used the microscope and studied the development of the chick embryo, on which he had written a book. This was fantastic to see how the cellular structure developed and made one wonder what directed it. Anatomy continued in the afternoons with the usual oral examination at the end. This made three semi-semesters of anatomy. We really knew it quite well when we finished. Dr. Todd gave class demonstrations of the X-ray appearance of the stomach and intestines under the fluoroscope, which was quite advanced at that time and we "ate it up" and, of course, received some extra irradiation, about which there was little concern then. After all, it was common practice then in good shoe stores to stand under a fluoroscope and be shown how well your new shoes fit before you paid your bill! The fluoroscope in the shoe store was used to clinch the sale!

In the fourth semi-semester, we had organology and began physiology under Dr. Carl Wiggers in the morning. Dr. Wiggers was an outstanding lecturer who made his subject matter extremely interesting. We learned the function of the various organs and even carried out metabolism experiments and measured oxygen consumption under exercise. Dr. Wiggers was particularly interested in cardiac function and the physiology of the vascular system, which he demonstrated with mechanical and hydraulic models. We did experiments on the effect of various ions on cardiac function and many other things. The afternoons were given over to bacteriology under Dr. Emerson Megrail, a wonderful person. Our microscopes showed us the "animalcules" that the Dutchman Leeuwenhoek had first demonstrated in the 1670s but which were not associated with disease until the time of Pasteur, Lister and Virchow, two hundred years later.

Events of 1933

Hitler became German Chancellor assuming dictatorial control. President Franklin Roosevelt escaped an assassination attempt in Florida. Mayor Anton Cermak of Chicago was struck by the gunfire and died. The Governor of Michigan, William A. Comstack, declared an eight-day bank holiday in his state to stabilize the outflow of funds from banks. A week later Governor Albert C. Ritchie of Maryland declared a bank holiday in that state also and others followed. Finally Franklin Delano Roosevelt was inaugurated on March 5 and immediately declared a Federal bank holiday (Manchester, 86).

An Economy Act was passed by Congress that reduced veterans' pay and Federal salaries. The Civilian Conservation Corps (CCC) was created by the Unemployment Relief Act to create employment for young people. The United States left the gold standard for our currency. The Tennessee Valley Authority bill was passed allowing the government to produce electric power. Oil was struck in Saudi Arabia. Japan and Germany withdrew from the League of Nations. Prohibition of the sale of alcoholic beverages in the United States was repealed (Gordon and Gordon, 127). The World's Fair, a big event, was held along the lakefront in Chicago.

Summer 1933

With this, the first year of medical school came to a close and I went back to my summer day job of grounds care at the sanitarium as soon as classes ended. I had worked evenings throughout the school year at the front desk, which gave me room and board. The school year had been rewarding but truly was a tough year and I said to myself at the end of it, "I'll think this over before going back."

In June, I received my B.A. degree from Adelbert but my yard work at the sanitarium was so heavy that I did not go to the graduation ceremony. My diploma was mailed to me. Grandfather Emanuel Long, a person I admired greatly, died in Williamsville, New York and I did not take time off to attend his funeral. Someone should have made me go but I was young and intent on what I was doing.

Year Two

By the time the summer was over I was ready to go back to my studies. With my Postal Savings account, thanks to Mr. Holcomb who had warned me about the Union Trust Bank, I could pay my tuition. This second year of instruction, similar to year one, was considered preclinical, but in the second semester we were introduced to the Departments of Medicine and Surgery. Each of the first two years consisted of thirty-five weeks—one thousand, one hundred and twenty hours of instruction.

The first semi-semester of the second year was given over to neuro-anatomy and physiology in the mornings and physiology, chemical pharmacology and applied anatomy in the afternoons. Physiology continued under Dr. Wiggers as the chief with the aid of Dr. Quigley, Dr. Ray and young assistants. One of the latter caused me some trouble. In a written examination he asked the question, "What is the significance of the intermittent nature of the nervous impulse?" I hadn't learned yet that you should give back what had been given in an instructor's lecture and answered in some detail about sustained muscle contraction which I thought was a very valuable thing. This produced a big red zero on that question. When I saw him about it after the examination he apparently thought I was impertinent and would make no change. At the final oral examination at the end of the year he asked to examine me alone after the others were finished. The quiz subject he then selected was osmosis, which I knew well, and he finally said, "Oh, alright," threw up his hand and passed me. I was limp as a rag when that was over and had to sit down for a while in the hall after leaving the room.

In hygiene, we studied the spread of epidemic disease under Dr. J. Angus Doull. The subject of the spread of smallpox on the Philippine Island of Cebu was intriguing. I last saw Dr. Doull years later in the officers' quarters at our Fourth General Hospital in Melbourne, Australia during World War II. He was on a special mission for the army and stayed with us a few days in 1942. He remembered his former students and we appreciated the time with him. He had Australian friends from previous trips there.

Pathology, under Howard Thomas Karsner, M.D., was added to our schedule in the second semi-semester of the sophomore year. Here was a man of form and principle. He dressed immaculately, smoked cigarettes with a fancy cigarette holder, insisted on proper English and would not tolerate carelessness. We could not use the word bluish without giving the color that it modified. The word was an adjective. It had to be bluish green, bluish red or something of that nature and you had to designate which it was. In group presentations you spoke distinctly without hesitancy. "Ah" and your slides were to be clean. If not, you might get, "Stop! Clean that slide!" The presenter was so impressed that it never happened again. Later, during my surgical residency, I spent three delightful months in his department. I learned to do a proper autopsy, identify diseased and malignant tissue and write an epicrisis at the end that reiterated pertinent features of the case and summed up what you had learned. It was a fine department, with Dr. Harry Goldblatt, Dr. Alan Moritz, Dr. Enrique Edwardo Ecker and others. Dr. Karsner conducted the department with some class, the same way he dressed. At three in the afternoon, the members of the department met in the conference room for tea and brief conversation for about thirty minutes, then went back to work. Karsner's textbook *Pathology* was a classic of its day. He did not care for Boyd's *Pathology*, which I thought was good also.

Pharmacology, under Dean Torald Sollmann (referred to affectionately as Solly among his students but always Dr. Sollmann when spoken to), was very instructive but difficult. At that time most prescriptions were written in Latin and compounded by the pharmacist before the days of the pharmaceutical houses. There was much interest in it because we all wanted to know how to write prescriptions. These were as indicative of the profession as the stethoscope. Dr. Sollmann's pharmacology text was a storehouse of information and all students bought it. I still have mine and think of it with affection.

Clinical Departments

The third semi-semester continued with pathology, pharmacology and applied anatomy and we were finally introduced to the department of medicine. This was after a year and a half of medical school training. This would change with the new curriculum of the 1960s but we knew nothing of that then. We finally felt we were getting somewhere when we were told about real diseases and were appreciative to hear about them.

The last semi-semester of the second year continued with clinical pathology, pharmacology, applied anatomy and finally surgery, believe it or not. The surgery lectures were given in the Lakeside Hospital Amphitheater! These lectures were given by members of the department. Dr. Ernest Bright gave the first one. Not only were we having lectures on surgical diseases but we also had afternoon sessions on surgical technique in which we did operations on dogs. However, this course was not given in the hospital, it was given in the dog laboratory of the medical school. It was a very popular course while it lasted but a few years later it gave way to other types of instruction that were considered more necessary.

Events of 1934

Nine hundred and fifty million dollars was authorized by Congress for emergency relief and work projects for the unemployed. In Germany Adolph Hitler killed off a rival storm trooper, Ernst Roehm with seventy-seven of his followers. This was the start of Hitler's rise to power. Dust storms continued in the midwest states. The Security and Exchange Commission, the National Labor Relations Board, and the Federal Communications Commission were established. In China Mao Tse-tung began his long march into the interior with his Communist followers. A Farm Bankruptcy (Frazier-Lemke) Act relieved farmers from mortgage foreclosure. Japan renounced the United States and British Naval Limitation Treaties. At home, public enemy number 1, gangster John Dillinger, was cornered and shot by G-men outside the Biograph Theater in Chicago, betrayed by ''A Lady in Red.'' Bruno Hauptman was arrested for the kidnapping of Charles Lindberg's son. The wooden cruise ship *Morro Castle* burned off the New Jersey coast with the loss of 130 lives. The wooden sister ship of this vessel, *The Oriente*, quickly converted to a troop carrier after the Pearl Harbor attack would take the Cleveland Lakeside Hospital Unit to Melbourne, Australia in January–February 1942. This was by convoy from the Brooklyn Navy Yard through the Panama Canal with six other vessels. In 1934, a seventeen-jewel Elgin watch could be bought for thirty-five dollars and a full-course dinner for under a dollar (Gordon and Gordon, 136).

Summer of 1934

The second year came to an end with a flourish but I had a problem, or at least I thought I did. I wanted my training and my associations to have no tarnish. I thought I should break my connection with the sanitarium, which had been very good to me. Some of its treatments were based more on theory than fact and were not well accepted by the medical community at large. Dr. Cunningham's claim that diabetes mellitus was due to an anaerobic germ was not proven. Jim Rand and I had shown that oxygen in the spinal fluid of dogs was doubled when the animals were under an additional thirty pounds gauge pressure. This agreed with Professor Nelson's finding that rabbits with impaired pulmonary ventilation were greatly benefitted when placed under twenty-one pounds of gauge pressure. It also supported Dr. Cunningham's success in treating patients with pneumonia, the details of which had never been written up and published in a clinical medical journal. It was inexplicable why this had been omitted as already related. The evidence showed that compressed air was a good method of administering oxygen but Dr. Cunningham was being castigated for claiming diabetes, carcinoma and pernicious anemia were due to an anaerobic organism that had not been proven. I did not see any way that I could contribute further or help in the controversy. It was a tough emotional thing but I finally made up my mind that I should leave.

The Cleveland Clinic

I obtained information that students worked nights at the Cleveland Clinic at East 93rd Street and Euclid Avenue. I applied there and was interviewed by Dr. William E. Lower, one of the founders along with Crile, Bunts and Phillips. He hired me for a night job at the front desk for the summer. This was similar to the one I had had at the sanitarium. I attended the switchboard and typed the operating schedules for the next morning. During this time I went back and lived with my friend Dwight Galehouse, who was employed at the Standard Tool Company and had a room on East 81st Street. I had roomed on East 71st Street with Dwight, my brother Ethan, and Donald Galehouse, all from my home town of Doylestown, when I first came to Cleveland in the fall of 1929. Ethan had left Cleveland and was then located in Chicago where he was starting the Weckesser Company. Times were really tough but he was persisting. Don Galehouse had gone into social service work and was out of the city.

I worked nights from seven in the evening until seven in the morning. My friend Dwight and I were good friends and we got along well. The room was such that I could sleep there during the day. There were Clark Restaurants about the city at that time where good food could be obtained at reasonable prices. The Blue Plate Special, which sometimes may have been yesterday's food, was good and usually cost about fifty cents. On Sunday, however, we would walk to East 55th Street, have a good breakfast there, then walk to East 105th Street, where we had another one. That was an economical way of having Sunday dinner. The streets were safe at that time.

The job at the clinic was fun. I became acquainted with the residents there who were called Fellows. Having made out the schedule the evening before and knowing what cases were to be operated, when possible I went to surgery the next morning and watched Dr. George Crile Sr. operate. He knew I was a student working downstairs and he was very good to me. One morning after completing an operation, he thumped me on the chest and said, "Come on over in the next room for this next one." He frequently scheduled (and I typed) ten or twelve thyroid operations for a morning and doctors came from far and wide to watch him. He had two teams of house officers, or Fellows. These teams opened the wound ahead of his arrival and closed after he left. The second team would have the incision made on the second patient by the time Dr. Crile had finished the first, so that he could go from one room to the next very expeditiously to the approval of his audience.

At that time he operated in the patient's room for two reasons, he said. First, he was of the opinion that there was less chance of serious infection since the organisms in the rooms were less virulent than those in the operating room. Secondly, and perhaps more important, he was operating on hyperthyroid patients before the days of antithyroid drugs when "thyroid storm" was a very real and serious post-operative complication. The patient was given oxygen inhalations in his or her room by a nurse anesthetist in the mornings and the patient's pulse and blood pressure monitored. After receiving these inhalations for several days, if pulse and blood pressure were favorable, the anesthetist proceeded by adding nitrous oxide to the inhalations producing general anesthesia and the operation took place. This became known as "snatching the thyroid" and Dr. Crile carried it out with great success. His incidence of thyroid storm was considered lower.

Care for the Down and Out, Wayfarers Lodge

I needed a place to work that provided board and room for the school year. Students worked at Wayfarers Lodge at 1701 Lakeside Avenue under Dr. Samuel Gerber who later became the county coroner. The Lodge was just what its name implied. Remember, these were hard times. Work was scarce. It offered overnight lodging and meals for the homeless and the down and out. This was part of Pres. Franklin Roosevelt's response to the depressed economy to help the disadvantaged in a time of need.

After an interview with Dr. Gerber, I was given a post at the Lodge with five other students. Brother Ernie was not taken with the place, which was quite a come-down, he thought! He went along with the change but shook his head. We lived in the east end of the building, sleeping on double-deck bunks, and took our meals in a staff dining room at the other end.

Our job in the evenings was to hold sick call at the dispensary in the central part of the building and supervise the men as they entered the dormitory after they had disrobed. This was necessary and actually mandatory to prevent transmission of communicable diseases. Anyone found to have a communicable condition was isolated in a separate area. After the men were bedded down in the evening, it was possible to study. We alternated night call among the five of us. Actually, the experience, although not classy, was good from a clinical standpoint. We became experts in those conditions associated with the homeless and down and out. One day in the dermatology clinic at Lakeside Hospital, our instructor, Dr. Gammel, a very good man, became quite excited about a case that he had in one of the cubicals. He asked us, the students, to look and see if we could diagnose the case. It was quite a come-down for him when we looked at it and said scabies was all we could see, nothing more. We saw that every night and treated it with sulphur ointment at our dispensary!

Life at the Lodge was quite different than that at the sanitarium or the Cleveland Clinic. The food, though not of the same caliber, was adequate. It was nice being with other students who shared similar problems and experiences. They were from Pennsylvania, southern Ohio, California and Maryland. Some were a year ahead and some a year or so behind me in class. It was a pleasant association.

Year Three

The third year encompassed applied anatomy, pharmacology, and hygiene classes but also clinical pathological conferences, which were in regard to sick people and made the student feel that he was involved in the treatment of patients (or at least learning about how to treat them). I remember one case presented at the Pathological Conference that involved a young man who died after eating mushrooms. We saw the interior of his small intestines, which had been destroyed by the toxin of *amanita phalloides,* a very poisonous species of mushroom that looks like the ones served in restaurants. I still think of it whenever I eat mushrooms and hope whoever picked them knew what he was doing. Another impressive case was a lady who cleaned her davenport with carbon tetra chloride cleaner and then foolishly laid down on it and went to sleep. She died of kidney failure, which would now be tided over by dialysis but that did not come until the late 1940s, after World War II.

We had medical and surgical lectures and assignments and took physical diagnosis, during which we examined each other under instruction by members of the medical department. We learned how to properly take a history, examine a patient and use our stethoscopes. We felt we were really progressing. There were excellent lectures at then City Hospital by Drs. Glover, Freedlander, Lazzari, Roy Scott, Karnosh, Toomey and others. At Lakeside it was the same with Drs. Lenhart, Beck, Holloway, Joelson, and Harbin, just to name a few. Elliott Cutler had preceded Dr. Lenhart but left earlier in 1932, the year that we began our medical studies. We rotated through dispensaries at Lakeside, City (now Metro), Charity, St. Luke's and Mount Sinai in most all of the specialties. There was some chance for choice of hospital; the two main ones were Lakeside and City. The thirty-five weeks of the year were soon over. It was interesting and went quickly.

It turned out that the Wayfarers Lodge jobs were largely held by members of one of the medical fraternities. I was not one of their members. Membership was financially out of my reach. They had allowed me in because they were not able to fill a position. They now wanted it back and I finally yielded. One of my friends went back on me. I had obtained a job for him there at the Lodge and in spite of that he sided with those against me. I was idealistic and did not yet appreciate the art of politics, the art of influence. I continued with my ideas of compassion for others and search for facts and truth.

Crile Fellowship

During the summer of 1935, between my junior and senior year of medical school, I applied for and was granted a three-hundred-dollar Crile Fellowship in the bacteriology department under Dr. Emerson Megrail. My subject was "The Lipolytic Action of the Streptococcus." The studies showed that the organism definitely had the ability to split fats. Dr. Megrail and I wrote a paper showing this. I presented this paper at a local medical meeting in the Pathology Amphitheater at Lakeside, but to my knowledge it was never published. I do not think that any of us recognized its significance. It was later shown that this was the quality of the streptococcus organism that made it so dangerous. It could readily enter the cells of the human body due to this ability. We had a significant finding and did not recognize its value.

The old 1920 Ford had finally given out. I bought an old "experienced" Chevy at Mr. Painter's used car lot at Eddy Road and Euclid Avenue, again for thirty-five dollars, but it was a klunker; it was too "tired" for the task. It broke down on my first trip down Carnegie Avenue to City Hospital. It had to be towed back. Mr. Painter game me credit and I took a 1928 Chevy Sedan instead. This one cost seventy dollars. It had a good engine but a leaky roof. That car was a good buy and lasted several years. I was driving it when I met Katy a year and a half later at the Cincinnati General Hospital. The leaky roof persisted in spite of attempted repairs. When it rained hard we had to put up an umbrella. When you are young you can handle things like that.

Events of 1935

The Social Security Law was enacted to provide retirement income for those over sixty-five years of age. This was to be financed by salary deductions during working years. Up to this time there was no legal arrangement to pay workers after retirement. It was quite controversial at the time. Providing for one's latter years was considered to be a problem of the individual. The word retirement was not in wide usage. People worked as long as they could and then hoped that some member of their family would provide care for them if necessary. Pneumonia was a frequent solution, a frequent cause of death among the elderly. Most people did not live beyond their seventies. The overall life expectancy at birth in 1930 was 59.7 years. This was rising rather rapidly. In 1980, fifty years later, it was 73.7 years and in 1990 75.4 years (World Almanac, 956) due to better living conditions, better nourishment and better health care. However, it lengthens the post-working, post-income period of life. Providing income after age sixty-five, desirable as it may be, was thought by many to put an undue burden on government. It has lightened many burdens for the elderly and is a desirable thing. Its cost must be budgeted. In the state of Louisiana, Gov. Huey Long, a near dictator nicknamed Kingfish who had done many good things for the people of his state, was feared by many politicians for his autocratic, dictatorial methods. He was shot in the abdomen by a young Dr. Carl Weiss, and died. Dr. Weiss was riddled with bullets from the governor's body guards and also died (Manchester, 139).

In 1935 Alexander Watson Watt improved mechanisms for producing microwaves and tracked the flight of an airplane with one of his devices (Asimov, 527). This was a great step forward leading to perfecting radar referred to previously.

There has been concern that microwaves are harmful to those that are in close contact to them such as in the operation of microwave ovens in the kitchen. The issue is not completely settled. Care should be taken to follow the directions of the manufacturer. They are not ionizing rays such as X-rays and are apparently safe when directions are followed.

George Gallup conducted his first poll in 1935. People were caught up in a chain-letter writing craze that year. It may be considered the beginning of the electronic age. A great number of things were happening and developing. The electric door opener was first demonstrated that year. An entering person interrupted a beam of light which in turn activated a motor which opened the door—"an automatic doorman." This was just the beginning of automation, which would spread through industry.

Splitting the Atom for Energy

The most significant event, probably, although not appreciated at the time, was the splitting of the uranium-235 atom by the Italian scientist Enrico Fermi. The first chain reaction (Manchester, 141). The tremendous release of energy with this accomplishment was appreciated by only a small group of physicists at that time. Following that discovery in Italy, the knowledge of it somehow did not come under the domination of Mussolini and Hitler. It is most fortuitus for us as described earlier (See atomic scientists on page 91). It was the repressive conditions at that time in Europe for the scientists who came to understand the possibilities that lead them to migrate to the United States and carry on their work here. The tenets of our democracy created the attraction. Actually, much of the knowledge did exist in Germany. The possibility of what could have happened had Hitler gained possession of the bomb ahead of us is chilling. The danger of a present or future enemy remains (Manchester, 142). General Motors introduced knee action on the front wheels of their cars for a softer ride.

Soil Conservation Act was passed in response to soil erosion in the midwest. The National Labor Relations Act provided for collective bargaining, the Works Progress Administration (WPA) was created to provide more jobs and a Rural Electrification Act was passed by Congress. An Employment Relief Act allowed the government to provide jobs and the Federal dole was discontinued.

Federal Deposit Insurance Corporation (FDIC)

An inheritance gift tax was enacted and the Federal Reserve Bank was reorganized. It set up a Federal Deposit Insurance Corporation (FDIC) to insure bank deposits in case of bank failure.

Abroad, the name of Persia was changed to Iran by Shah Reza Pahlavi, Heinrich Himmler began state breeding under Hitler to produce ''perfect Aryans'' and the Saar Valley voted for union with Germany. Italy invaded Ethiopia and the League of Nations imposed sanctions. A Neutrality Act permitted embargo of Foreign Arms Shipments. The Congress of Industrial Organizations (CIO) was formed by John L. Lewis. A tropical hurricane killed 400 people in the Florida Keys and destroyed the road and railroad bridges to Key West. Will Rogers and Wiley Post were killed in an airplane crash in Alaska. There were 161,359 physicians in the U.S. and 1,014,000 hospital beds (Gordon and Gordon, 145).

Year Four

Otis Steel Company

Dr. Donald Glover was one of my instructors at City Hospital. He also took care of the Otis Steel Company in the flats behind City Hospital and used students there also. This was night work again, an eight-hour shift at a dispensary next to the blast furnace of the plant. I spoke to Dr. Glover and he gave me a job there for my senior year. For my sleeping quarters, I was asked if noise bothered me and I answered that I did not think so. Well then I could sleep in the same building as the dispensary in a back room near the blast furnace. One night there made me change my mind! The intensity of the noise from the blast furnace was greater than anything I had anticipated, but worst of all, a switch locomotive went by about ten feet away and would blow its steam whistle just outside my window! The dirt was horrendous. I do not mean dust in the air, I mean dirt. Any exposed surface was covered with it in an hour. A few nights of that and I had to give up. Dr. Glover then found a room for me at the back of an office building in another part of the factory, the Riverside Plant near the rolling mill instead of the blast furnace, which was cleaner and quieter. I could sleep there when I had the opportunity. My duty hours were from 11 P.M. to 7 A.M. at the dispensary every other night. In addition to manning the dispensary I took care of a gate that opened by pressing a lever after proper identification, to let vehicles in and out of the factory yard. The Protective Service police wanted to put a man on that gate and would try to catch me napping. The dispensary was not usually busy but getting rest was the problem. I had to stay awake and practiced sleeping while standing up like a horse. I could dose a little while standing but one night I fell down. It was tough but somehow I made it. After my nights on duty usually there was no extra time to get across town to class. The job paid enough money so that I could afford to buy my meals at restaurants. During this time, I was in close contact with the men on the Protective Service department and in the factory. The profane language that some of these people used was astounding to me. I was then twenty-six years old and had been around quite a bit, but had never heard that sort of foul, repulsive talk.

The fourth year was a great one, the most interesting of all because we were dealing with patients. The school year consisted of forty-eight weeks instead of thirty-five weeks for the previous three years. We began the third week of August. The students were divided into groups and assigned to services at City Hospital, now Metropolitan General Hospital, and Lakeside University Hospital. The members of our group were all good students and we became very close friends during the course of the year. Webb Chamberlain and I are the only survivors of our group of six. The paths of Webb and I have crossed frequently over the years and have run parallel, to a degree, in that we both practiced in Cleveland and remained associated with the university, he in ophthalmology and myself in surgery. We were together in the Fourth General Hospital in the South

108

Pacific during World War II. Harry King practiced in Dayton. I operated upon his mother at one time but physically we became separated and now, for our sixtieth medical school reunion, I have learned that he has died.

Medicine, City (Metro) Hospital

Our first month of rotation in 1935 started in the department of medicine at City Hospital. We took histories on new patients admitted to the wards, examined them and wrote up our findings, which were then checked by the intern on the floor and the senior attending doctor. Dr. Roy Scott was in charge of medicine and we saw him on frequent ward rounds at which time the individual cases were discussed. The student would usually present the history and the visitant would then discuss his line of reasoning, with frequent questions to the student, which led to reaching a diagnosis. The wide variety of cases seen on the wards and the discussions of the attending doctors and frequent lecturers were very instructive and the month went quickly. Dr. Scott was an excellent speaker and teacher, as was Dr. Karnosh in Psychiatry, and we followed them whenever we could.

Surgery City

The second month was on the surgical service, also at City Hospital. We were introduced to the service by Dr. John (Tony) Lazzari. He was a very positive, outgoing person with whom you always knew right where you stood. There was never any doubt. He told us what our duties were and how to do them. We operated in the morning on the tenth floor at seven-thirty and we were supposed to be there twenty minutes ahead of time to help pick instruments for each case. During an operation we would either pass instruments or second assist by holding retractors so that we all could see. You might not like it, but it was important and someone had to do it. We saw a large number of operations and assisted on many operations on the thyroid gland, the stomach, the appendix, and the large intestine. The surgeons in addition to Dr. Lazzari were Dr. Glover, Dr. Freedlander and many others. We were kept quite busy and the time went quickly.

109

Ob/Gynecology

Next came a month on obstetrics at Maternity Hospital at the University. This was under Arthur Holmbrook Bill, A.M., M.D., F.A.C.S. Dr. John Thomas gave the lectures on the subject. At that time Dr. Bill had set up a district service so that deliveries took place at the patient's home under the care of a medical student and a resident obstetrician from Maternity Hospital. The student went to the home first, examined the patient and determined the condition of the patient and the foetus, the frequency of the uterine contractions and the dilation of the cervix. This was phoned back to the hospital. Actually, the obstetrical nurses there, who were very good, took the information and relayed it to the doctors as necessary.

When the patient was having regular contractions and the cervix was dilated, you called the resident who then arrived with an obstetrical nurse to help with the actual delivery. We each had to have credit for twelve deliveries. If the baby was born before the resident arrived it was termed a "precipitate" and you went back on first call for the next case. This required excellent timing involving factors over which you had very little control. The residents usually came quickly when called. If you called them too soon, of course, that was not appreciated. But if you needed them, they were good at coming. We had code words such as Dr. Hypotension and others that we would have a family member call in for us if we were not able to get to the phone. In a breach presentation I had one of the family call for Dr. Breech and the resident and nurse came promptly. Another time it was Dr. Footling for an unmarried mother, which actually was a miscarriage. It was a hands-on, interesting experience about which each student had many tales to tell when it was over.

Blood Transfusions

A method for students to take quick money was to give blood transfusions when the opportunity presented itself. I was on the volunteer list and was called while on the obstetrical district delivery service, which as I have mentioned was a strenuous service. At that time blood transfusions were relatively new and were given by the "Vincent Tube" method. This was then still a variation of the direct method in which the blood was drawn from the donor's arm directly by cutting down on one of his or her arm veins; drawn directly into a vertical sterile waxed Vincent Tube. It was

110

then administered directly into the recipient arm's vein by a similar surgical procedure. Both donor and recipient were in the same operating room. Each lost one arm vein in the process. It was direct whole blood still warm from the donor which had not been anticoagulated. Modifications and the use of sodium citrate greatly simplified the procedure several years later. The donor was paid fifty dollars a unit, which was about a pint of blood.

I was the blood donor for an anemia patient who needed two units. The first unit was taken from my arm and I felt fine. Everything went well. The doctor said my pulse rate had not changed. (I have a slow pulse.) He then asked me if I would like to give the second unit also for the patient instead of using the second donor. It would simplify things for them and I would be paid for two units of blood. I was laying down and felt good so I said yes and the second unit was taken from my arm.

I dressed and started back to the obstetrical unit in McDonald House. There was an outside stairway at that time behind the tennis courts that I had to climb. I got part way up and had to sit on the steps due to weakness and shortness of breath, but then made it back to my quarters. Fortunately I did not need to go on a call that night, but the next day developed a terrible cold. It was a striking demonstration of the effects of acute blood loss in a young healthy person. I also gave a blood transfusion in Cincinnati before I married Katy.

Gynecology

Next was gynecology at Lakeside under Drs. Weir, Faulkner, Folger, Mowrey, Reycraft and others. Here we worked in the dispensary and on the wards. Much of McDonald House, the obstetrical hospital, was closed because of the Depression. It was an economy measure. McDonald House surgery was being done in the tenth-floor Lakeside operating rooms. Panhysterectomy was the new, more radical operation of that day. Dr. Weir advocated this to prevent the occurrence of carcinoma in cervical remnants left in place by the previously performed popular super cervical hysterectomy. Dr. Keith Folger, one of the younger men at that time did the operation of panhysterectomy particularly well and I remember passing instruments for him. It was a great loss when he died of a brain tumor at an early age.

111

Surgery, U.H.

Next, in December 1935, we went to the department of surgery at Lakeside Hospital under Dr. Carl H. Lenhart. Dr. Lenhart had taken over the department from Dr. Elliott Cutler when the latter went back to Harvard in 1932. He was a fine teacher, a sound practical man with no frills. He had previously worked with Dr. David Marine on the function of the thyroid gland in the laboratory at Western Reserve University and together they had established the fact that the Great Lakes Region was a goiter belt because our pure fresh water from the Great Lakes lacked the element iodine. As a result of their work, the addition of iodine to the diet was carried out and iodized salt was adopted.

Next in line on the staff came Dr. Claude S. Beck, a large strong-willed man with independent original ideas and the courage to carry them out. He was a graduate of Hopkins who had come to Cleveland from Harvard as a resident with Cutler in 1924 when Dr. George Crile Sr. left Lakeside Hospital at the mandatory retirement age to start the Cleveland Clinic. Dr. Beck had operated at Harvard with Cutler on the first operation for mitral stenosis a year earlier. He was carrying out extensive research in the laboratory on heart valves and the pericardium. He had also worked in Boston with Harvey Cushing, a Clevelander who became known as the "Father of Brain Surgery." In 1935, Dr. Claude Beck was also the neurosurgeon at Lakeside Hospital, in addition to his interest in the heart and blood vessels.

As students, we watched Dr. Beck operate. He was a very meticulous operator and a good teacher, who taught gentleness at operation in the handling of tissues. Dr. John Holloway was highly respected. He was especially interested in diseases of the spleen. He was particularly good in diagnosis of conditions within the abdomen before all modern methods of diagnosis were available. He taught us how to diagnose pathological conditions in the abdomen. Dr. Frank Gibson did beautiful abdominal surgery. Dr. James Joelson taught us diseases of the genito urinary tract and made that specialty very interesting and appealing. We were avidly watching each experience trying to decide which to go into. We talked among ourselves, trying to decide where the new developments would be in the next thirty years. Maxwell Harbin taught orthopedics and did a good job of it. Herniation of the intervertebral disc had just been recognized as a specific cause of lower back and leg pain, which he was

112

pursuing with much interest. This was a specific type of "Lumbago" which could be treated surgically with much success.

It seemed to us that specialization was the way to go with all the new knowledge accumulating. Surgery, with its direct approach to illness, appealed to me. The work of Lenhart, Beck, Holloway, Joelson and Harbin was all attractive. It was a very pleasant two-month experience.

Dr. Lenhart's Party

After the two-month service on surgery, the six students on the rotation were invited to Dr. Lenhart's home for dinner. This was a real treat. The members of the staff were there and we all mingled together for cocktails in his recreation room where he played the piano and the group sang. This was followed by a very nice dinner upstairs. Mrs. Lenhart was very gracious. It was a generous and much appreciated event.

Stool Clinic

Next came pediatrics under Dr. Henry Gerstenberger. Our first four weeks were under Dr. Toomey on the clinic service at City Hospital where we learned a lot about infectious diseases. We also spent time at one of the city clinics downtown. Following this we were on the service at the Babies' and Children's Hospital in the university group. Here Dr. Gerstenberger taught the illnesses of children. He had just developed Synthetic Milk Adapted (SMA), which was cow's milk adapted to equal human milk for feeding formulae. This was very popular and widely used. He considered it superior to another one called Similac. Dr. Gerstenberger taught that much could be learned from the examination of infant stools.

At "stool clinic" he demonstrated fresh stools in diapers as we stood in a circle around him while he demonstrated and described the characteristics of the various specimens to us holding them close under our noses so that each of us got a good smell. It seemed that was important to our professor but we students were skeptical.

Medicine, U.H.

We wound up the year and our formal medical school training with two months in Lakeside Medicine. We took histories on the new patients being admitted to the ward, made examinations and wrote up our findings, following which we presented the cases to the resident as well as our written material for his approval. I discovered a gall stone in the stool of one of the patients that I admitted with abdominal pain. The pain had gone away and it was thought that I probably discovered the cause. Dr. Wearn, professor of medicine, complimented me for my discovery. Stool clinic may have helped me after all!

Dr. Blankenhorn had gone to Cincinnati to be director of the service and professor of medicine there. Dr. Hayman made frequent instructive ward rounds in which each ward case was discussed. Other visitants included were, Beams, Christie, Leas, Egeberg and a number of bright younger men, all of whom made the service very worthwhile. It was a good experience at the end of medical school.

Events of 1936

Dust storms continued in the Midwest, while floods in northeastern states made many homeless. Democrats renominated FDR to run against Republican Alf Landon for president. The reelection of FDR was a landslide, 523 to 8 electoral votes. The Panama Treaty ended the U.S. Protectorate there. Bruno Hauptmann was executed for the kidnapping and death of Charles Lindbergh's son. Civil War in Spain began. Francisco Franco and Emilio Mola led the army against the Republic. Germany and Italy backed Franco. The United States declared a non-intervention policy for Spain. There was a new kind of strike, a "sit-down strike," on the assembly line at the General Motors Fischer Body Plant in Cleveland. Instead of the men not coming to work, they sat down on the job in order to get their demands. This rapidly spread to Flint, Michigan and across the country idling sixty plants. John L. Lewis backed the strikers. On the third week General Motors gave in. This led to the formation of the Congress of Industrial Organizations (CIO) (Manchester, 188).

King George V of Britain died and was succeeded to the throne by Edward, Prince of Wales. Hitler repudiated the Locarno Treaty and German troops reentered the Rhineland. Mussolini's troops were of course triumphant in Ethiopia. Stalin began a bloody government purge. Japan and Germany announced an Anti-Comintern Pact and a Rome-Berlin Axis was proclaimed. Edward VIII abdicated the throne of Britain for

114

love of Wallis Warfield Simpson. Unemployment was 16.9 percent. Rudyard Kipling died (Gordon and Gordon, 154).

Choosing Internship

I had pretty much decided that my interests were in surgery. Where should I take training? It seemed good that I go to a different location at least for a while. Going east was beyond my grasp financially I thought. Applications were made to the University of Wisconsin, the University of Cincinnati and to the University of Buffalo. Dr. Mont Reid at Cincinnati General Hospital had a good service at that time patterned after the Johns Hopkins program in Baltimore. When this came through, it was accepted. Claude Beck spoke highly of Hopkins and Dr. Blankenhorn had gone to Cincinnati as Chief of Medicine the year before.

Graduation School of Medicine, Western Reserve University

My medical school classes were over and it was a great feeling of satisfaction. I put my hands in my pockets and felt that I had accomplished something. When I was elected a member of Alpha Omega Alpha (AΩA) it was more than I hoped for.

Graduation exercises were held in the Allen Memorial Library Auditorium. Father was a Reformed Mennonite whose religion prevented him from attending many public functions. He was very proud to have a son graduating from medical school and attended. Dr. Howard T. Karsner, professor of pathology, made an excellent address on the high calling of the medical profession pointing out how it differed from business by putting the welfare of the patient first above monetary considerations.

After the conclusion, when we came out to the sidewalk on Adelbert Road in front of the building, Father said, ''That was great,'' in a very pleased tone. Looking back at my sisters he also said, ''Did any of the rest of you graduate?'' He realized that he had missed something. This was embarrassing for me because they had, and he, because of his religion, had not attended. We all forgave him though because it was a remark made on the spur of the moment.

Father knew that Louisa and Sylvia both had Ph.D. degrees and that his sons, Ethan and Constant (Connie), had both graduated from Ohio

State University, Ethan in engineering and Constant in journalism. My oldest brother Ernest (Ernie) went directly into business after World War I and advanced in the sales department of Miller Rubber Company in Akron. When people asked him what school he was from, he would say, ''W.A.O.'' Usually there was a short silence and then the party would ask, ''W.A.O., where is that?'' to which he replied, ''Weckesser's Apple Orchard.''

Father was a person of many interests who would have made a fine professor of horticulture if education had been available to him as it was to me forty years later. He had done very much in his life with very limited resources and had given us very much in our upbringing, although money had always been scarce.

Internship Cincinnati General Hospital

My internship at the Cincinnati General Hospital started July 1, 1936. I packed all my worldly goods into my old Chevy sedan with the leaky roof and headed south on Route 42, the CCC Highway. When driving through Delaware, Ohio, I passed my brother Connie and his family coming north. This was something unexpected. We each saw each other at about the same time and pulled over for a very pleasant chat. They were heading back to Wayne County after visiting friends.

My plan was to arrive at the hospital two days early so that I could observe a bit before my assignment started. The weather was exceedingly hot and Cincinnati, along the Ohio River valley, was even hotter. I found the hospital, parked my old car and reported to Dr. Harry Langdon, the superintendent of the hospital, then waited by the switchboard near the front entrance for a house officer to show me to my room. In a short time I was greeted by someone who I would know for many years, Dr. Joseph Kahn. There is only one like him. His training path took him to Cleveland the next year where I returned for mine. We were together in the South Pacific during World War II with the Fourth General Lakeside Hospital Unit and remained in Cleveland after the war.

Joe, whom I had never seen before my arrival at the Cincinnati General Hospital, greeted me with, "What the —— did you come to this —— place for?" It was quite a greeting for a young medic just out of the oven from medical school, so to speak, ready to help humanity. You soon learned that Joe's outlook on life was a little different than usual and you had to discount some of the things he said. He had a droll sense of humor. My experiences at the Cincinnati General were of the highest caliber and I almost stayed there when my year was over.

Joe Kahn showed me to an upper-floor room, which I shared with another intern, Dr. Harry Jerow, who later went to Michigan in GYN.

Surgery

I expected to observe. Well, they had something better than that for me. An intern had left early. Within an hour I was in charge of Surgical Ward B3 with thirty patients under my care and eight new ones just being admitted. The train was leaving the station, so to speak: Grab the door rail and climb on board if you want to go along; you'll do more than

117

observe! I climbed on board and that is the way my internship began at the Cincinnati General Hospital in 1936.

The nurses on the floor were a tremendous help. One said we had to do dressings and introduced me to the dressing cart that had all the sterile things on board. Together we changed all the dressings on post-operative patients. Then history and physical examinations on all the new patients had to be done and medication rounds made on everyone to be sure each person was receiving the proper medicine. I worked late that first night stopping only for dinner and then getting back to the ward. The resident for that floor was knowledgeable and helpful, but also busy. I made notes on questions to ask when we made rounds together.

We, the interns, worked every night for the first ten days we were there. Then we had a meeting and arranged a sign-out schedule for each other so that we could get some much needed rest.

The patients were recovering from all sorts of abdominal operations, stomach and bowel resections (partial removals). Gastric operations had gastric suction by means of Wangensteen suction. This gave gentle gastric suction through a naso-gastric tube in the stomach. The suction was provided by having water flow from an inverted gallon jug elevated on an intravenous stand to a second jug on the floor. The naso-gastric tube was connected to a glass tube that extended upward through the stopper of the inverted gallon jug nearly to its bottom where a vacuum was created. This caused gastric contents to be drawn out from the stomach during early post-operative stages. The amount of fluid removed had to be measured and a similar volume of sterile fluid replaced containing the proper electrolytes. The intravenous administration of fluids was new and being used freely. It was much more effective than hypodermoclysis, putting the fluid under the skin of the chest wall or thigh, which was also used part of the time. The intravenous route was more effective and was gaining favor rapidly.

There were also severe injury cases from farm, railroad and some traffic accidents. The latter were becoming more frequent. Infections were of many kinds. This was before antibiotics when certain organisms produced lethal infection.

Postoperative pneumonia was very common after an operation and was a frequent cause of death. Preventive measures consisted of frequent turning of the patient and inhalations by face mask of oxygen–carbon dioxide–oxygen mixtures to make the patient breathe deeply. This was to keep the lungs expanded and avoid *atelectasis,* lung consolidation due to a mucous plug in a bronchus. Early ambulation was talked about and being considered. It had not become established treatment.

Infections before Antibiotics

I had a young lady seriously infected on my floor who attracted much attention. She had developed an ulcer of the lower abdominal wall, which did not respond to treatment and which continued to enlarge. At the edges of this ulcer was a necrotic (dead) black margin that would recur after being trimmed away. Cultures showed streptococcus. In spite of our efforts, this ulcer continued to enlarge and spread. Chief of the department of surgery, Dr. Mont Reid, and Dr. Max Zinninger became involved and finally, with intensive Dakin's irrigations and repeated trimming of the wound edges, we were able to bring it under control. About that time Dr. Frank Meleny described a similar case. The streptococci under the dark margins of the wound used very little oxygen and were able to burrow under the normal tissue. Later, when penicillin came onto the scene, this organism was found to be sensitive to it and the serious problem that it produced was over. Until that time the situation was a dangerous one. President Coolidge's son had died in the fall of 1924 of a streptococcus infection secondary to a blister from his tennis shoe. He was sixteen years old at the time of his death, which occurred during his father's presidential campaign, a sad national event, which stirred everyone and demonstrated our inability to deal with serious infection at that pre-antibiotic period. This was the same type of infection that had been such a scourge in obstetrics for women following childbirth, especially before the time of Dr. Simmelweiss. In 1994 there has been an occurrence of streptococci that do not respond to penicillin, which created new problems.

Pavex

Dr. Louis Herman, who had taken part of his surgical training in Cleveland under Dr. Cutler, was active in the department. He was particularly interested in peripheral vascular diseases of the blood vessels of the extremities, particularly the lower extremities that are the farthest from the heart. Vascular replacement had not yet come upon the scene. He and

Claude Beck in Cleveland were good friends and I think both of them were dreaming of it. There was no heparin to inhibit thrombosis. Repair of acute injury had been done but was infrequent. In this interim, in 1936, Louis G. Herman was using his head. He had an entire ward set aside for Passive Vascular Exercise (PAVEX) treatments. He had invented a rigid boot into which the foot and leg were inserted. It was sealed at the thigh and pressure applied into the boot pressed on the tissues of the leg intermittently to stimulate vascular circulation. It was sort of a vascular massage, which gave some improvement. Later when heparin was developed the doors were opened to vascular replacement and he was one of the early ones to adopt it.

It is interesting to compare the work of Claude Beck before the advent of heparin and vascular replacement with that of Lou Herman. Both were working in that vacuum and both made contributions. Claude Beck brought new blood supply to the heart by bringing the *omentum,* a very vascular tissue, up from the peritoneal cavity and wrapping it about the abraded heart surface so that adhesions occurred. He was able to show that crossover circulation did occur between the adherent omentum and the myocardium. His work was later superceded by direct vascular repair and replacement when that became available.

Lobar Pneumonia

Following two active interesting months on the surgical service, I went on the medical service and found things very interesting here also, but in a different way. In these pre-antibiotic days lobar pneumonia due to pneumococcus) was a serious killer that developed suddenly in healthy people and sometimes led to death on the third day. The name was due to the fact that portions of the lung, usually a lobe at a time, would consolidate preventing oxygen exchange. This could rather rapidly extend to other lobes so that suddenly, with a very high fever, rapid heart rate and respirations, the patient became blue and could die suddenly. This was true even for young healthy people, which made it particularly dangerous. Death from pneumonia was widely feared. Typing of the pneumococcus organism had been carried out since 1913–16.

Immune serum had just been developed in 1936 for each of the different types of pneumococcus. This new serum was just being brought to Cincinnati, by a Reserve graduate from the class of 1931, Dr. James

Ruegsegger. It required injection of organisms, from the patient's sputum into the peritoneal cavity of mice for a period of incubation, to determine which type of organism was involved. In the early winter of 1936–37, a pneumonia epidemic occurred filling several wards with patients. It was an all-night job to get these injections carried out so that the proper sera could be administered to the patients as early as possible. The serum was effective and it was very gratifying to observe this in the patients. I had one of these pneumonia wards during that epidemic and was greatly impressed by the benefit of the serum.

Katy: Paul's Law

About this time I developed a severe sore throat, myself, with a temperature of 104 degrees. My resident, Dr. Eugene Stead, carried my suitcase himself and put me in the hospital as a patient, which lasted four or five days. I was honored by his personal attention.

According to Paul's Law (the apostle Paul), "There is good in all things, even the bad." I had heard Father refer to it in my early life but it was impressed upon me by one of my patients, Dr. Perry Gresham, former president of Bethany College, years later when I was in practice. Being laid up with a strep throat was the bad thing, but while there, I met my wife-to-be, a beautiful young lady named Kathryn Alice Tuttle, senior nursing student.

In addition to sore throat, I unexpectedly developed extreme nausea and vomiting which I had never had before. This miserable unexpected condition was soon credited to codeine by my good doctors.

Katy's sympathetic tender care during that unpleasant episode and many times since have made a deep impression on me and my daughters. We have agreed that it's actually fun to get sick when she takes care of you. I was soon out and back on duty in January 1937 on the busy pneumonia ward with memories of this young lady.

The Ohio Valley Flood of 1937

Dire events occur when the waters of the earth get out of balance. A serious example of this occurred in the Ohio River Valley during the winter of 1937, soon after the pneumonia epidemic. Heavy rains had occurred during the month of December, which saturated the earth and filled the tributaries of the Ohio River. These rains did not let up. A low-pressure system developed over the Ohio River Valley, which was locked between two high-pressure systems, drawing in warm, moist tropical air, which then fell as rain. Four inches of it fell in Cincinnati on the night of New Year's Day, and the deluge continued. On January 8 the Ohio River was at flood stage from Paducah, Kentucky, to Cairo, Illinois, where it emptied into the Mississippi. By January 18 the waters reached flood stage (fifty-two feet) at Cincinnati, and they continued to rise, reaching a crest of eighty feet on Black Sunday, January 26 (*Audubon,* 89 [May 1987]: 28–37). This far exceeded the flood of 1913 and the previous record flood level of water of sixty-four feet in 1884. Imagine a wall of water twenty-eight feet high flowing through the city! The City Water Filtration Plant, the power plant, and Lunken Airport were all underwater. At Crosley Field the upper stands rimmed what appeared to be a lake.

During the flood all but emergency services came to a halt with the lack of power and water and difficulty of personnel getting in. Those of us there remained on duty. Emergency surgery was carried out by catching our "scrub water" in buckets, boiling it, and using it over. This lasted for a number of days.

Only Hot Shave in Town

Fellow intern Elmer Maurer met the emergency with ingenuity. He continued to give haircuts in his room in the intern's quarters, topped off with a hot shave with hot water from his steam radiator air vent—*The only hot shave in town.*

Courtship

Cincinnati is a city of seven hills as you probably know. The Cincinnati General was and is on the high ground of one of those hills, but Katy had a two-month assignment at Branch Hospital in a tuberculosis unit, on another hill with swollen, flooded Mill Creek between. This was a problem. The roads were closed due to the high water. Not deterred by water to the running boards, through alleys and back streets I finally made it to Branch Hospital and we had dinner together at a remote little cafe to our mutual enjoyment. This was repeated on several occasions until the flood waters receded. It was against the rules of the Nursing School for a nurse to be married while in training. I had no income, just room and board at the hospital. Brother Ernie faithfully sent me ten dollars a month for incidental expenses. I gave a blood transfusion for fifty dollars and we were quietly married on March 17 without fanfare. Each of us then returned to our posts of duty.

Additional Services

Other services for me beside medicine and surgery were psychiatry, obstetrics and Holmes Hospital. Psychiatry was interesting trying to delve into the problems of the mind but the paucity of treatment methods was too limited, I thought. This was before the advent of good tranquilizers when phenobarbital and paraldehyde were the main sedatives. The obstetrical service, under resident Stan Garber, gave a good exposure to many of the complications of pregnancy and to methods of handling them. Medicine under Blankenhorn, McGuire, Rich, Schiff, Heyn and residents Eugene Stead and Morton Hamburger was a very good experience. Visiting Professor Soma Weis from New York made a great impression on all of us. Among other things he showed us how to perform femoral puncture for venous access when peripheral veins were not accessible, a very useful procedure. This was new then. It could have been his own technique.

I wound up on surgery as I had begun the previous July. Louis Herman was doing new things with peripheral vascular disease, Mont Reid with more central vascular problems, Max Zinninger with the biliary system and John Caldwell with fractures. Among the residents, Paul Hoxworth was doing very useful things in perfecting macro methods of blood typing. Jean Stevenson, Harry Fry, Ed McGrath and Dan Early were excellent instructors and Vinton Siler was doing much work on fractures and injuries of the hand. It had been an excellent internship experience and had given me a broad exposure to the problems of both medicine and surgery.

I worked late on my last day on the surgical service trying to clear things up and not leave them in the condition that I had found them upon my arrival. Late that evening a patient was admitted with vaginal bleeding

123

from a miscarriage. In carrying out the procedure used at that time there was a question that the instrument I was using penetrated the uterus. This was heart breaking for me on my very last case. I reported it that night to my resident, Dr. Paul Hoxworth. On examination we could find no untoward physical signs. She was placed on nothing by mouth and observed. Dr. Hoxworth watched her closely and reported to me later that she recovered without incident. A load off my mind.

Further Surgical Training

As the year drew to a close it was necessary to finalize plans for further surgical training. The training period at Cincinnati was a long one of five years patterned after the Halsted School at Baltimore. I was offered a post starting with a year at Holmes Hospital, which added a year to it. This was a compliment as competition was great. The offer was considered seriously. In the meanwhile I had been in touch with Dr. Lenhart in Cleveland and he offered me a second year appointment directly in the program at University Hospitals, which was a year less. Both programs were good ones. After much soul searching we decided that I should return to Cleveland at the end of the school year after Katy graduated from nursing school.

Events of 1937

Amelia Earhart Putnam and her co-pilot Fred Noonan disappeared over the South Pacific near Howland Island on July 2. No trace was found. Wild speculation later questioned whether she may have sighed Japanese fortifications in the Marianas and been forced down (Manchester, 150). President Roosevelt's request for six more justices on the Supreme court was defeated. Auto and steel unions won big contracts (World Almanac, 445). British Minister Neville Chamberlain appealed to Hitler for cooperation in keeping peace. The dirigible *Hindenburg* burned at Lakehurst, New Jersey with the loss of thirty-eight lives in a fire due to use of hydrogen gas. The stock market declined sharply (Gordon and Gordon, 163).

University Hospitals, Cleveland

This second year of hospital training would pay me twenty-five dollars a month, plus room and board. The first year had paid only room and board. Katy would do nursing to help with the budget. I drove back northeast on the CCC highway to Cleveland retracing my route down the previous year, checking in at Robb House, the residence hall at University Hospitals of Cleveland. Katy followed me to Cleveland as soon as her commitments were completed. We first lived on Euclid Avenue just east of East 109th Street in a one-room basement apartment with a formidable large steel grating in front of the ground floor window which we thought made the place secure. One day one of us did not have a key and the janitor easily lifted the grating aside so that entrance could be made through the window! We were happy there but soon moved to a larger apartment, College Row, on Cornell Road, which was a little nicer and nearer to the hospital and provided an additional living room. Sister Miriam visited us there on her way to the University of Colorado in 1938, where she would soon meet Randy Whaley, her husband-to-be.

Surgically, my return to Cleveland was like coming back home. I already knew the people there and was immediately immersed in the surgical problems of the day, which were many, complicated and interesting. Dr. Frank Gibson, Theron Jackson and Tod Sloan were very active with private patients in Hanna House. The clinics were busy and the conferences good. I was soon on the staff service where responsibilities were even greater and where I was in contact with Drs. Holloway, Beck and Lenhart, all of whom were busy surgeons and good teachers.

Events of 1938

A Naval and Army Expansion Act was asked for by President Roosevelt and passed by Congress. The country was predominantly isolationist but events abroad were ominous and Congress, with the president's leadership, was taking note. A national minimum wage was enacted. Radio personality Orson Welles caused a nationwide scare October 30 by broadcasting a dramatization of "War of the Worlds" without adequate announcement that it was a dramatization (World Almanac, 445). The public had never previously heard a dramatization of this type and believed an invasion of the country was actually occurring in New Jersey and "proceeding south on Route One" as described. It was so very real that a resident at Lakeside Hospital called his parents at their home one hundred and fifty miles from Cleveland and warned them of the attack. When the true nature of the broadcast was learned, he was given the nick-name "Buck", for Buck Rogers, a wild character of the day. Orson Welles made a name for himself but the event scared so many people that adequate announcement of the true nature of such broadcasts was made mandatory thereafter.

Winston Churchill protested Neville Chamberlain's policy of appeasement. Germany invaded Austria. Hitler visited Mussolini in Rome. FDR urged arbitration of the Czech Crisis. The Japanese advanced and captured Canton in the war against China. Mussolini proclaimed Libya part of Italy. Hungary annexed Slovakia from Czechoslovakia. The fascists were running wild. Anthony Eden warned America of "Fascist Peril" on New York radio. Mud slides in southern California killed 144 people. Howard Hughes set a round-the-world flying record of 3 days, 19 hours and 8 minutes. "Wrong Way" Corrigan, supposedly heading for California, flew non-stop to Dublin, Ireland (Gordon and Gordon, 172). Italian born Enrico Fermi received the Nobel Prize in physics for his production of radioactive isotopes by neutron bombardment. This was a significant step on the road to nuclear fission and the release of huge amounts of energy.

Events of 1939

President Roosevelt asked for $535 million for defense. Germany invaded Czechoslovakia. The United States recalled its Ambassador to Germany. Franco took Madrid. Loyalists surrendered and the United States recognized the Franco government. Hitler and Mussolini signed a ten-year pact. King George VI visited the United States. A big fuss was made of his being served hot dogs on the White House lawn. Germany and the USSR signed a non-aggression pact.

Cornell Road

Katy found a one-room apartment across the street on Cornell Road that she liked. It was small but a little nicer than the one we were living in.

Friends lived there. There was back-door access across Abington to the hospital. We moved there and slept on a Murphy bed, which pulled down from the wall and which was put back out of sight in the daytime. We were poor but happy. I made twenty-five dollars and Katy seventy dollars a month. We tried to go on a budget but Katy said after a month that we didn't have enough money to be on a budget! She could not make it balance. I think no one could have. In spite of that, even here, in her little tiny kitchenette, after duty, she began to demonstrate her culinary abilities, which have been a delight all of our married lives.

Vacation with Pay, 1939

At the end of a year back in Cleveland, senior interns received a month's vacation with pay, believe it or not. We went fishing in Canada for two weeks, which was a very welcome change after a busy year on the surgical wards. On September first as Assistant Resident in Surgery, my responsibilities were greater and I was assigned independent operating on the staff service and also assisted Dr. Holloway and Dr. Lenhart with their private patients. The year went quickly. In August of 1939, we took a vacation trip starting east to visit brother Ernie and his wife Sadie then living in Summit, New Jersey. Necessary arrangements were made to have the hospital mail our checks there so that we could travel further. By this time we had traded the leaky-roof car for a more recent model, but still another "experienced" brown Chevy Roadster with six cylinders.

Our trip took longer in those days, before interstate highways. I remember phoning sister-in-law Sadie in Summit, New Jersey about eight in the evening from Scranton, Pennsylvania, saying that we had dinner and had used our last money to fill the car with gasoline, and would she please leave a door open for us? We arrived about two in the morning! Believe it or not, our checks arrived also a few days later, and we had a nice trip to the seashore to Deal Beach, New Jersey. This was the place where Grandfather Weckesser was ship-wrecked on his arrival in America. We had difficulty locating the spot but were able to locate the general area. Our information that had been handed down was that the shipwreck occurred at Sandy Hook, New Jersey. Actually it was about fifteen miles further south at Deal Beach.

On a later visit it was very touching to actually find the place on the beach and to look out over the Atlantic Ocean across the shallow waters where the *New Era* was wrecked on a sand bar during a storm November 13, 1854. Grandfather, a healthy strong eighteen-year-old at that time, clung to a mast all night before rescue came the next day. The memorial marker for the grave of the 240 passengers who lost their lives in that disaster is in the cemetery of Old First Methodist Church near the intersection of Locust and Cedar Avenues, West Long Beach, New Jersey about five miles inland from the Atlantic Ocean.

We arrived back at our little one-room apartment on Cornell Road with its folding Murphy bed in the wall the evening of August 31. The main window of our apartment opened onto a courtyard. It was customary among the tenants, many of whom were young doctors and nurses from the hospital, to open our windows for ventilation at night.

Hitler Invades Poland—Start of World War II

We were awakened about daylight by the blaring of radios in the adjacent apartments. On tuning in, we learned that Hitler had invaded Poland and was advancing rapidly across the country, something that had seemed inevitable for the previous year. Now it had happened. On September 1, 1939, German armies had invaded Poland and Britain and France would declare war on Germany. World War II had begun.

The German battleship *Graf Spee* was scuttled in Montevideo to prevent it falling into allied hands. USSR invaded Finland. Golden Gate International Exposition began in San Francisco and the New York World's Fair opened in New York. Pan-American Airlines opened the first transatlantic flight to Lisbon, Portugal. Edward R. Marrow made nightly broadcasts on the rapidly changing world events each night (Gordon and Gordon, 181). Enrico Fermi arrived in the United States.

Isolationism

The general feeling in the United States in September 1939 was that we should not get involved again as we had in World War I. This was augmented by the opinion of Col. Charles A. Lindbergh, who had visited Germany on two occasions at the invitation of Hitler and spoke openly against our involvement there. Pres. Franklin Roosevelt thought differently. The world had changed, become smaller with modern means of communication and transportation and our welfare depended on the stability of Britain and France and the rest of the free world. Hitler's plan was to take the free world piecemeal. Roosevelt disagreed openly with Lindbergh and the latter resigned his commission in the U.S. Air Force. There was never any disloyalty. These were honest differences of opinion. In fact, Lindbergh gave civilian assistance to our air force later during the war. He flew missions from our air base at Finschaffen, New Guinea in 1944, when the Fourth General Hospital was there.

On December 7, 1941, the country was stunned by the audacity of Japan to attack us at Pearl Harbor without warning while negotiations were still in progress in Washington. It was also stunned by the fact that an enemy could take us completely by surprise and produce such havoc. How did our field commanders allow this devastating attack to succeed? The nation was in shock. Where was reconnaissance? People wondered what was coming next? Isolationism disappeared at once. President Roosevelt addressed Congress the following morning, describing the attack as *"A date that will live in infamy"* and Congress declared a state of war December 8, 1941. I listened to the radio broadcast in my office at 10515 Carnegie Avenue as the President spoke realizing the grave consequences of the situation for all of us.

Surgery Residency, 1939–40

In 1939–40 surgical specialties at University Hospitals, Cleveland were in the early process of formation to meet the demand for many developing new special techniques. It was perfectly natural that this should happen as knowledge increased in all areas. The indications for surgical procedures greatly increased with insight into the cause of shock and the role of body fluid replacement in preventing and treating it. This understanding, new medications, special anesthesia, better trained personnel, including nurses and special therapists, and many other developments brought new surgical procedures safely within the realm of possibility.

The approach to vascular repair and anastomosis in humans as demonstrated by Carrel in dogs in 1903, was on the verge of happening, and did so in World War II, 1941–45. The problem of lung ventilation giving oxygen and carbon dioxide exchange with the chest open was being approached. These things, leading to the expansion of surgery and the formation of specialties were happening within the department of general surgery at Lakeside Hospital, the general hospital unit of University Hospitals, Cleveland.

Genito-urinary surgery was under James Joelson and orthopedics under Maxwell Harbin. Both of these men were in the general surgery department under the direction of the professor of surgery, Carl Lenhart. Pediatric surgery, plastic surgery and hand surgery were still an undifferentiated part of general surgery. Chest surgery was on the verge of development, awaiting only the perfection of endotracheal anesthesia to maintain ventilation of the lungs with the chest open. Obstetrics and gynecology, ophthalmology and nose, ear and throat, however, were already separate departments.

Infections were a scourge in the pre-antibiotic days, which interfered with results in the operative field and plagued the surgeon in the post-operative period with *atelectasis* and pneumonia, even with the strict *asepsis* of that day. Things were happening in these areas also. A red dye called Prontosil was introduced in 1939 that turned the body tissues bright red when given intravenously. The first sulfonamides followed in the same year. Both were recognized as an effective aid to the surgeon and sometimes life-saving for the patient. Penicillin, known to be inhibitory to bacterial growth by Fleming since 1929, was further developed in America during World War II and became available in small amounts by the end of the war in 1945. This substance and other antibiotics that

130

followed selectively interfered with the metabolism of the invading organisms with little or no damaging effects to the body's tissue cells. This gave the surgeon even wider latitude to invade areas of the human body that needed structural repair and artificial replacement. It cleared the way for vascular and joint prostheses. In prior times the danger of infection prohibited large foreign bodies being left in the wound.

The prevention and treatment of shock by proper fluid replacement was just developing in 1939. The need for it was recognized and the intravenous administration of fluids was rapidly replacing hypodermoclysis (injection under the skin). The replacement of blood loss by blood transfusion followed the recognition of blood types by Landsteiner, who was given a Nobel Prize in 1930 for his work. The HIV virus fortunately had not entered the scene and did not complicate things at that time. George Crile Sr. had transfused human blood in 1906 and the technique for the procedure had been gradually developed in many centers. This procedure would become more and more used as the magnitude of surgical procedures increased.

In 1939 Gas Oxygen and Ether (GOE) was most widely and capably administered by nurse anesthetists for most abdominal operations under the able direction of Mrs. Gertrude Fife. The gas in this mixture was nitrous oxide. With the increased scope of surgery requiring anesthesia for special situations and longer periods of time, anesthesiology would later became a specialty in its own right with its own department. Spinal, local infiltration and nerve block anesthetics, when chosen in 1939, were performed by the operating surgeon.

Post-operative complications (atelectasis and pneumonia in particular) required a lot of attention. Prophylactic oxygen–carbon dioxide inhalations were administered and efforts made to keep patients moving. Early ambulation had not yet arrived in full force, but we were thinking of it. The concept of extended rest after surgery was still strong not recognizing the adverse effects on muscles and joints when extended beyond the usual nocturnal amount. Post-operative pneumonia was a very serious complication that took a high toll before antibiotics were available.

Operative Procedures 1939–40

The procedures being carried out in 1939–40 are outlined as follows:

1. Congenital anomalies:

   Hypertrophic pyloric stenosis.
   Imperforate anus.
   Congenital cysts including branchial cleft cysts.
   Omphalomesenteric fistulae and cysts.
   Renal developmental cysts and tumors.

2. Infections:

   Skin and appendages.
   Pilonidal cyst.
   Appendicitis.
   Diverticulitis of sigmoid colon.
   Cholecystitis and lithiasis.

3. Trauma:

   Stab wounds in predominance of all parts of the body, including penetrating wounds of peritoneal cavity and chest. Endotracheal anesthesia was being developed but was not perfected.
   Some gun shot wounds.
   Fractures treated by closed reduction mainly with x-rays before and after.

4. Thyroid:

   Goitre.
   Hyperthyroidism.

5. Biliary systems:

   Cholecystitis.
   Cholelithiasis.

6. Tumors and malignancies:

   Skin and appendages, carcinoma, and melanoma.
   Breast, early radical surgery for malignancy.

Neck, radical resection for malignancy.

Small and large bowel, resection and reanastamosis.

Two stage resection for colon carcinoma mostly.

Combined abdomino-perineal resection for carcinoma of rectum.

7. Gastro-intestinal tract:

Appendicitis, diverticulitis.

Resection esophageal diverticulae.

Obstruction of small and large bowel. Resection and reanastamosis as indicated.

Ulcerative colitis.

Partial resection of stomach for ulcer not responding to diet.

Resection of carcinoma of stomach.

The above list includes most of the procedures that were being carried out on the general surgical service in 1939–40 when I was resident. This was a wide experience at that time provided by assisting Doctors Lenhart, Holloway and Beck with their cases and carrying out the procedures independently myself on staff cases. Dr. Claude Beck assisted me for my first partial gastrectomy, after which I did many more for peptic ulcer and for malignancy. Vascular surgery was confined to repair of injuries. Vessel replacement awaited complete control of infection post–World War II.

Events of 1940

With Britain and France now at war with Hitler, British Prime Minister Neville Chamberlain, who had vainly tried to appease Hitler at Munich in 1938, was replaced by Winston Churchill. This gave a strong stand against the aggressive Hitler. The Nazi armies invaded Denmark and Norway and installed a puppet government in Norway under Quisling. President Roosevelt vainly appealed to Mussolini to help with peace efforts. Hitler's armies next invaded the Low Countries (Holland, Belgium and Luxembourg) with the same Blitzkrieg tactics used against Poland in September 1939, with the same success. The port city of Rotterdam was literally destroyed by the bombing with tremendous loss of civilian life. Italy declared war on France and Britain. President Roosevelt described this in a fireside chat as "Stabbing of its neighbors in the back" and pledges "Material aid to the opponents of force." Japan, Italy and Germany signed an Axis pact. Germany began daily aerial bombing attacks on Britain for the next stage of conquest. The Royal Air Force fought back with its Spitfire fighters. Hitler's armies entered Paris unopposed in June 1940 (Gordon and Gordon, 194). With the fall of France, Allied troops evacuated through Dunkirk in small boats to regroup in the homeland. Churchill sent dispatches to the prime ministers of Canada, Australia, New Zealand and South Africa: "I do not regard the situation as having passed beyond our strength" (Churchill, 194). Britain succeeded driving back Italians in North Africa.

With the urgency of these times, President Roosevelt was renominated for an unprecedented third term and defeated the Republican candidate Wendell Willkie. United States supplied fifty destroyers to Britain under the Lend-Lease Act. Militant Konoye became Japanese premier and Tojo became war minister of Japan (Gordon and Gordon, 196).

At home, the first "peace-time" draft began requiring all men between the ages of twenty and thirty-six to register and a tax increase was voted in. FDR asked for $1.8 billion for defense. The American Federation of Labor and the Congress of Industrial Organizations pledged war aid. The population of the country was 131,669,275. Unemployment dropped dramatically.

Private Practice

My training was such that at the end of my residency I felt very competent to go into practice for myself, which I did at 10515 Carnegie Avenue. I sublet office space from Dr. Wallace Duncan there and assisted him with patients in his office during my first year in practice. Because his practice was orthopedics, I made a change in July of 1941 to the office of Dr. Ralph Elliott, where I had more space to myself for the practice of my specialty, general surgery. The possibility of war was on everyone's mind. With Hitler's advances it seemed inevitable. Dean Sollmann at the medical school had been asked by the U.S. Surgeon General to form a new Lakeside unit similar to that of the World War I unit, which went to France. I, as well as many other young people, signed up to serve in it.

Events of 1941

In 1929 Sir Alexander Fleming described his observation that the growth of certain molds inhibited the growth of organisms on the agar plates in his laboratory. This mold was called *penicillin notatum.* Pasteur in 1877 had observed that the growth of one microbe could prevent the growth of another. Moldy bread was an old-fashioned remedy for certain illnesses. Only a few bread molds are effective (Encyclopedia Britannica, 464). In 1939 a team of Oxford doctors headed by Sir Howard Florey, purified penicillin. In 1941 he brought his methods of production to the States for further development. This would lead to the availability of some of the substance for general use in the armed services in 1945 and a little later in civilian practice.

An office of productive management was created to coordinate defense production between government and the private sector. President Roosevelt declared a state of "Limited National Emergency," froze Axis funds in the United States and closed consulates. An embargo of oil and scrap metal to Japan was set up. Germany invaded Yugoslavia, Greece and, later, Russia. President Roosevelt and Churchill met in the north Atlantic and declared an eight-point charter for a post-war world. Selective service was extended to thirty months. A United States destroyer sank near Iceland with the loss of 100 lives. German armies reached the outskirts of Leningrad.

President Roosevelt appealed to Emperor Hirohito for peace. Japanese Premier Konoye claimed Japan wanted peace but militant Tojo became Japanese premier (Gordon and Gordon, 203).

Pearl Harbor Attack, December 7, 1941

The Pearl Harbor attack by Japan came as a complete surprise to all Americans. I was practicing general surgery from the Carnegie Medical Building when it suddenly came at 7:55 A.M. Sunday, December 7th, 1941 (1:00 P.M. Cleveland time). I had been in practice eighteen months, trying to get established, and we had a three-month-old daughter, Jane, at home. I was driving home from Lakeside Hospital, after patient rounds, to our apartment at 2320 Murray Hill Road, when the announcement came over the car radio. At first I thought the attack was in the Philippines where it was more expected, but then realized the almost unbelievable truth of it. The broadcast was from Hawaii! It was a direct broadcast and the attack was still in progress. Explosions of bombs could be heard in the background. The stark reality of war for the United States had actually arrived after two years of expectation. The audacity of Japan to make a sneak surprise attack against us at Pearl Harbor was almost unbelievable.

When I arrived home, Katy was equally surprised as we listened to our radio there for all the news possible about what was happening. Our daughter Jane, two and a half months old, was in her crib. When the success of the attack was revealed with seven battleships sunk or seriously damaged, in addition to innumerable smaller craft, the destruction of nearly 300 planes and the loss of 2,409 lives, great uncertainty existed as to the limits of the disaster. Was a West Coast invasion attempt possible? President Roosevelt addressed a joint session of Congress next morning, which was broadcast live on radio. The nation listened. I listened in my office at 105th and Carnegie. War was declared on Japan by Congress after Roosevelt's address on that day, December 8, 1941. The president made an historic reassuring statement to the people of the country on radio: "The worst thing we have to fear is fear itself." He was strong and reassuring.

The declaration of war meant mobilization of the Lakeside Unit we all knew. That word came by telephone and by telegram Christmas Eve from the surgeon general to our commanding officer, William McCally. Germany and Italy declared war on the United States. The draft was extended requiring all men eighteen to sixty-five years of age to register. The war news was terrible. Hong Kong, Wake Island and Guam fell to the Japanese and two British battleships, the *Repulse* and the *Prince of Wales,* were sunk off the Malayan coast. The enemy was "running wild."

Events of 1942

Manila fell January 2. MacArthur retreated to Bataan peninsula with his remaining forces and then to the island fortress of Corregidor in the harbor. From here he is called by President Roosevelt to take command of the U.S. Army Armed Forces in the southwest Pacific. The U.S. Navy remained under the command of Admiral Chester Nimitz.

General and Mrs. MacArthur and his young son were secretly taken from Corregidor on March 17 by PT boat and safely transported to Melbourne, Australia, where he arrived by air on March 21, 1942. This was nearly four weeks after the arrival of the Fourth General in Melbourne. I was on detached duty at Port Melbourne on the day he arrived. He left General Wainwright in command at Corregidor with the words, "I shall return," which he did in 1944. His critics, looking to find fault, probably justifiably, criticized his use of the first person singular since that accomplishment was to cost the lives of many. On April 9, Bataan fell to the enemy.

Death March

April 10. American and Filipino prisoners were forced to march eighty-five miles in six days with little or no food. This caused the death of 5,200 (Carruth, 534).

April 18. Air raid on Tokyo! The most heartening thing of the war up to that point. Gen. Jimmy Doolittle. The Japanese landed on the north coast of New Guinea and attempted to cross the Owen-Stanley Mountain Range of Papua, New Guinea in an effort to take Port Moresby on the south coast of the island.

May 4–6. The Battle of the Coral Sea (as described below).

May 6. General Wainwright surrendered Corregidor and the Philippines to the Japanese.

June 4–7. Battle of Midway Island, a decisive victory for the United States.

August 7. U.S. Marines landed in Soloman Islands. Fierce fighting.

August 21. Japanese reinforcements at Guadalcanal repulsed (Carruth, 536).

Sept. 15. U.S. carrier, *Wasp*, lost at Guadalcanal.

Oct. 23. Japanese attack U.S. Marines at Henderson Field. Three days of heavy fighting. Marines hold field.

Nov. 28. Coconut Grove Nightclub disaster in Boston, where 487 lives were lost in the fire.

When Australian and our newly arrived American forces and the adversities of the jungle warfare were able to stand off the land attack on Port Moresby, through the jungle, over the Owen-Stanley mountain range, the Japanese navy next tried to take Port Moresby by coming south around the east tip of New Guinea.

The Battle of the Coral Sea, from May 4–6, prevented enemy landings at Port Moresby and on the north coast of Australia. It was the first sea battle in history in which no shots were exchanged between enemy ships. All action was carried out by planes launched from carriers, which were never in sight of each other.

Other key personnel also escaped to Melbourne to join newly arrived officers from the States and set up MacArthur's headquarters at Toorak School. Children had all been evacuated to the country.

Also coming with MacArthur were a few platoons of native Filipinos known as Philippine Scouts. Word came through to my unit at Port Melbourne that they were to be inducted into the U.S. Army. This produced a problem according to my book of *Army Regulations*. They were only five feet tall and did not meet the U.S. minimum height requirement.

Singapore and Rangoon had fallen to the enemy in mid-February. At home, $62 billion was allotted to defense and a War Production Board was established that stopped all nonessential building. The United States and Britain combined their forces under a joint Chief of Staff. As learned later, at the University of Chicago on December 2, a nuclear chain reaction (fission of U-235) was secretly produced under the direction of Arthur Compton and Enrico Fermi.

138

The Lakeside Unit of World War II
Fourth General Hospital, U.S. Army

When Adolph Hitler invaded Poland in September 1, 1939, the beginning of World War II, his strategy was to avoid war with U.S. at that stage if possible.

In the spring of 1940, with the war in Europe expanding, Torald Sollmann, dean of Western Reserve University School of Medicine, was asked by the U.S. Surgeon General, John C. McGee, to form a medical unit of doctors and nurses to be activated in case the United States was drawn into the conflict. The professional personnel were to be drawn from Western Reserve University, Lakeside and Associated Hospital staffs, to provide the personnel for an army general hospital of one to two thousand beds.

In the ensuing months, before the United States entered World War II, William C. McCally and Donald M. Glover volunteered and were appointed to head the surgical service. Joseph T. Hayman took the medical service. Olga Benderoff volunteered as Director of Nursing. Younger men and women volunteered for service in the various departments. Organizational meetings were held to familiarize us with army procedures and the unit existed on paper in outline form.

Background and Development of the Hospital Unit Idea

Wars in which Lakeside Hospital (University Hospitals) played a role.

1. War between the states (Civil War 1861–65)
   Home for Friendless, Lake St., Cleveland   1863–1865
2. Spanish-American War
   Lakeside Hospital, Lake St., Cleveland   1898
   Fifth Ohio Volunteer Infantry
3. World War I
   Lakeside Union I (Base Hosp. 4)
   Rouen, France   1917–1919
4. World War II
   Lakeside Unit II (4th Gen. Hosp.)
   Australia, New Guinea, Philippines   1942–1945

The Lakeside Unit World War I

Lakeside Hospital Unit I served in the first World War and was the first American contingent overseas in that conflict. This unit had taken shape in August 1914. Its beginning involved the Ambassador to France, a Clevelander, the Honorable Myron T. Herrick, U.S. Surgeon General W. C. Gorgas, and Professor of Surgery George Crile of Cleveland.

The Birth of Our First Beautiful Daughter, Jane Kathryn Weckesser

Kathryn and I had been living in an apartment on Cornell Road just south of Euclid Avenue in a one-room apartment with a Murphy bed that pulled down out of the wall at bedtime. It had been very handy to Lakeside Hospital, just through the alley and across the street, during my residency in general surgery, which ended July 1, 1940. Many other young doctors in training and nurses also lived there.

Katy worked as a nurse at Lakeside, and I was resident in surgery. We were on a limited income. My salary was fifty dollars a month, and Katy's was seventy. It was possible to eat some meals at the hospital. We had been married three years and decided to start a family in spite of the bad war news in Europe, with Hitler coming to power in Germany and building up a strong military force. Japan also.

The Lakeside Hospital Unit had been formed in May of 1940, and I felt it was my duty to volunteer in view of the danger to our country. The Surgeon General of the United States had asked Dean Soloman to form a unit of doctors and nurses for a 2,000-bed Army General Hospital.

When my residency was finished, I had opened an office in the Carnegie Medical Building, first with Dr. Wallace Duncun, and then sublet space from one of the medical men in the same building. My practice was soon quite busy.

In 1940 we had a hot summer. It was before air-conditioning, and Katy was quite uncomfortable in the heat. By this time we had moved nearby to 2320 Murray Hill Road, where we had a four-room apartment. Because of Katy's discomfort in the heat we put a cake of ice in a tub with a fan blowing across it to give her some relief from the heat.

Jane was born in the afternoon on September 30, 1941, and was a beautiful baby right from the start. She was three months old when I left

January 10, 1942. The intensity of the danger from Hitler and Japan was great. Hitler easily could have overrun Britain without our help. I am confident that Japan could not have been stopped and would have invaded Australia without our help. Jane was three years old when I returned from New Guinea in December 1944.

Returning now to the Lakeside Unit of World War II, in 1939 and 1940 Col. Charles A. Lindbergh visited Germany at the invitation of Adolph Hitler. In April 1941 Lindbergh resigned his commission in the U.S. Air Force when President Roosevelt criticized him for his position. The country was influenced by the opinion of this national hero and became largely isolationist. On December 7, 1941 this changed overnight.

Sequence of Mobilization

The Pearl Harbor surprise attack meant mobilization for the Lakeside Unit. The orders came by telephone from Surgeon McGee to Dr. McCally on Christmas Eve 1941, seventeen days later. "The fat was in the fire," McCally said as he notified us. This phone call was followed by a telegram listing the names of the unit members. With this, the group was mobilized and left the country. Written orders caught up with us several months later in Australia. We realized later how unusual that was. In the army the usual word is, "You don't move until you have your written orders." These were not usual times and formality had been dispensed with.

Departure from Cleveland

Summer 1941	Isolationism predominent in United States
December 7, 1941	Pearl Harbor attack.
	8:00 A.M. Hawaii Standard Time.
	1:00 P.M. Eastern Standard Time.
	Cleveland.
	U.S. Pacific fleet decimated at Honolulu.
	Tremendous loss of U.S. aircraft and more than 2,000 lives.
December 8, 1941	End of Isolationism.

	President Roosevelt addresses Congress.
	War declared upon Japan.
	Further attacks expected, possible invasion.
	Gen. MacArthur's air force decimated at Clark Field in Philippines.
December 10, 1941	British battle ships *Prince of Wales* and *Repulse* sunk in China Sea by Japanese bombs and torpedoes, proving superiority of bomber over battleship without air cover.
Christmas Eve, 1941	Lakeside Unit activated by telephone call from Surgeon General McGee.
Christmas Day, 1941	Hong Kong surrendered to Japanese.
January 9, 1942	Farewell party Wade Park Manor.
January 10, 1942	Departure 55th Street, Station, Cleveland.
January 11, 1942	Train stopped during day at Washington, D.C.

Fort Jackson, S.C.

January 12, 1942	Fort Jackson, South Carolina (5 P.M., 6 hours late).
	Combined with 56th General Hosp. Administrative Corps and 500 enlisted men to form Fourth General.
	Injections, long underwear, mosquito netting, bedding rolls. Hospital equipment crated.

Indiantown Gap

January 16, 1942	Entrained for Indiantown Gap, Pennsylvania, 6:15 P.M.
January 17, 1942	Arrived 11 P.M. in snow storm. Herded into 6×6 trucks to vacant barracks, no heat, sick from immunizations. Processed

142

throughout night with thousands of others.

Brooklyn Navy Yard

January 19, 1942	10:45 P.M. entrained for Brooklyn Navy Yard in ancient resurrected cars. (Everything pressed into service.)
January 20, 1942	5:00 A.M., Hoboken Ferry to Brooklyn Navy Yard.
	Joined by seventy-two Cleveland nurses, Webb Chamberlain, Val Jordan, Ike Hanger and Fred Rose plus forty-eight nurses from eastern states.
January 21–22, 1942	In port, Brooklyn Navy Yard. Unit members divided between USS *Barry* and USS *Kungsholm* at adjacent piers. Final checking of medical supplies. Boat drills. Life preservers. "Black-out" rules to be observed.
January 23, 1942	Sailed at dawn (6:00 A.M.) Convoy formed in outer harbor past *Ambrose* Flagship. Four destroyers, two cruisers with blimp overhead watching for German submarines. (Two more freighters sunk night before off East Coast.) Sealed orders, destination unknown, a seven-ship convoy in two columns zig-zagging down the Atlantic off the East Coast with escort vessels maneuvering on the periphery.
	The course was changed every few minutes.
	This tactic was employed during the entire voyage except during a heavy storm in the Tasman Sea.
	Drinking water scarce. A few warm soft drinks.
	Mess twice a day.

143

Embarkment—Seven Ship Convoy

( )
Santa Rosa
(*)
Kungsholm
( )
Santa Maria

( )
Argentina
(*)
Barry
( )
Crystabel
( )
Island Mail

Lost Convoy

January 25, second night out, off Cape Hatteras. Being O.D. I was in the dispensary about midnight when suddenly the ship's engines revved up and the ship began to vibrate. There was no word as to why. Glancing out into the night our sister ships to port were not visible. Word came a little later that we were in dangerous waters. With no further explanation this continued for the rest of the night. At dawn we could see that we had lost our convoy. There was nothing ahead of us, but the *Crystabel* and *Island Mail* were following faithfully behind.

With the blackout, our pilot had lost the small blue running light of the *Argentina,* our lead ship, causing our line of ships to separate from the others. When this occurred, we were without escort and the best defense against submarine attack under those circumstances was full speed ahead. It was now Sunday morning and we still had no escort anywhere on the horizon. Finally as a last resort, radio silence was broken (a risky thing) to gain contact with the balance of the convoy. Within a half hour, a destroyer appeared on the port horizon and took us safely back to our position in the convoy. Due to this mishap, we lost our position in the convoy. The *Crystabel,* which had faithfully followed us took our previous position and we followed the *Crystabel* with the *Island Mail* behind us. This was a demotion for our captain. We continued in this formation for the balance of the trip.

Panama Canal

January 26, 1942   Coast of Florida cited. Yellow Fever
                          inoculations. Weather hot. Diarrhea

144

	among men in hold. At night we traveled under complete blackout with only the blue running lights fore and aft on the ship. At dusk an announcement came over the loud speaker each evening in sort of a Bronx accent, "Cloos-s all portholes. Extinguish all lights. No smoking on the open decks."
January 30, 1942	Tropical weather. Hot and muggy. Typhus inoculations.
January 31, 1942	8:30 A.M. Colon Canal Zone. We wait our turn to enter locks. After passing through several, we entered broad, fresh water, Gatun Lake.

What a pleasant relief to have a fresh water shower! As we were tied up to the edge of the locks while the lock was filling with water, the side of our ship was only a few feet away from on shore civilian dock workers, then known as CBs, who to my disbelief taunted us by calling "Suckers", "Shark Bait," "See you in 1950." We took it for a while until Egeberg yelled back, "You sons of—why don't you leave this country club and go to war to protect your country?" That quieted them.

We were hurried through the canal. There was nervousness that another attack might come and our convoy offered an even greater incentive. Each lock of the canal had barrage balloons cabled above it to discourage dive bombers. Our own planes were in the air overhead for further protection. Entering the deep cut beyond Gatun Lake we were able to squeeze by a sunken Italian vessel that had been scuttled there with the intention of blocking our path. The enemy would naturally want to close the canal to prevent reinforcements from the east. The Pacific Fleet at Pearl Harbor had been nearly annihilated on December 7 but no aircraft carriers were in port. We reached Balboa on the Pacific end of the Canal and tied up for a night. Supplies were taken on. No leave allowed or expected. The algae in the water gave a luminescent glow to the wake of each ship as it passed in the night.

Pacific Ocean

February 1, 1942	By noon, with supplies on board, we leave Balboa harbor and head for the Pacific

Ocean past Panama City. In the blue Pacific the convoy resumes its zig-zag course to an unknown destination, although Africa has now been pretty well ruled out. We now had two cruisers and a destroyer as our Escort. Tetanus injections. Boat drills. Life preservers constantly worn or in hand. Large stack of life rafts stacked on deck.

February 3, 1942 — Stars extremely bright at night. The constellations very clear, "hanging right in the sky."

February 4, 1942 — We supposedly, according to rumor, are crossing the equator. Water in the toilets is supposed to swirl in the opposite direction in the southern hemisphere. With no other assignments, this was checked by many on board but our experiments could not verify it. The standard of deviation was quite high in the experiment!

February 8, 1942 — Weather very good. Drinking water rationed. Warm Cream Soda! What a delicacy! Orion brightly visible overhead at night and the Southern Cross visible.

February 10, 1942 — Unidentified plane at 26,000 feet. Everyone below deck to quarters. A period of suspense. Our guns fire repeatedly, including the three-incher, then silence. The event passes without further incident and we are again allowed topside. Was it an enemy plane? Zig-zaging continues. Gunnery practice. A balloon is set free and our guns fore and aft fire repeatedly while we are allowed on deck. The balloon drifts off into the distance, unhampered, out of site. War news read over loud speaker has been very bad during entire trip. It is no better. The Japs are advancing unchecked down the east coast of Asia. We don't know our destination, but who will reach it first?

February 14, 1942   Cooler. A bird in the sky. Clocks set back two hours.

Bora Bora

Mid-morning, the *Barry* veers to the north out of our convoy line, slows, allowing the *Island Mail* to proceed ahead to take our position in the convoy. The reason was not at first apparent, but when the *Island Mail* passed us, we then turned south.

We were making a left turn like former Cleveland street traffic. That maneuver apparently came from the sea. We were escorted by a destroyer and the convoy disappeared behind us. In a few hours we saw what appeared to be a mountain and then palm trees on the horizon as we got nearer. It was an island with white breakers about its periphery except at one area.

We headed for that area, turned to port through a channel and found ourselves in a beautiful harbor with the peaks of an old volcano all about us: Bora Bora, a deep-water snug harbor, the crater of the extinct volcano. Our former West Indies cruise ship the *Oriente,* now the *USS Barry,* after quick conversion did not have sufficient fuel for the entire journey. We tied up to a waiting tanker in the harbor and large fuel lines were passed across to us. Crew members of the tanker yelled to our men, "Where the—you been? We've been waiting on you." Well, that's nice, we're glad someone is glad to see us. But that wasn't all. It was exciting; there was much small boat activity on shore and suddenly the water on the free port side of our ship was filled with native outrigger canoes full of trinkets, grass skirts, bananas and other tropical fruit. Lively bartering takes place through the portholes of our ship with bed sheets tied together for bartering lines. The natives wanted cigarettes or clothes, we soon found out. I lowered a cake of soap on a line. The native did not know what it was. I had remembered my brother-in-law's experience with soap as a barter item in Germany in World War I and thought it would be a valuable item but that was not the case. He looked at it, tasted it, shook his head and sent it back up the line! No bartering with that! An old shirt readily brought me a grass skirt for Katy and a bunch of bananas. We were hungry with only two meals a day.

After an hour or so of refueling, our pleasant interlude at Bora Bora ended. With adieu and thanks to our tanker crew, we departed the lovely harbor and headed back to our convoy, which had been circling in the distance during our absence. We resumed our position in the convoy.

When Katy and I revisited the island in 1976 with Webb and Elizabeth Chamberlain it was still as pretty as it was in 1942. By inquiry we were able to locate a school teacher who was the lone radio operator on the island in 1942. He remembered the visit of the *USS Barry*. They were expecting a Japanese invasion at that time and were very glad to see Americans. We were one of the very first ships to visit the island after the American declaration of war.

Uncertainties

February 16, 1942	We are back in convoy. The weather is good. News over the loud speaker remains very bad. Singapore has fallen to the Japanese. The French liner *Normandy* has burned at its pier in New York with sabotage suspected. British losses at Singapore including prisoners estimated at 60,000 men.
February 18, 1942	Suspected submarine in vicinity. Depth bomb dropped by cruiser.
February 20, 1942	Cross international date line. Weather cooler.

Storm on Tasman Sea

February 24, 1942	Weather bad. Storm on Tasman Sea. Our ship pitches from the crest of one wave to the next. Things thrown about the old wooden ship took quite a beating on the crests of successive high waves until the course was changed to give a sensible

148

angular roll. Being in convoy, the
captain was not free to change course
until instructed to do so by the lead ship.

Australia

On February 25 we passed Cape Howe and entered Bass Straights, where the sea is not as rough. The next day we entered between the heads of the harbor at Point Lansdale into calm Port Philip Bay and soon the skyline of Melbourne was visible on the horizon. What a sight with the red-tile roofs of the homes! We docked at Port Melbourne in the late afternoon and remained on board for the night. What a relief. The 35 day journey had seemed endless but at least we were in an English-speaking country and were glad for that.

Debarkation in Melbourne

On February 27, we debarked and traveled to Royal Park by electric train. The city was full of much greenery and flowers. The people were very friendly and glad to see us. Their army had been fighting in the Middle East for the last two years and they felt very unprotected. We were a token force, mostly medical personnel, engineers and a squadron of pursuit pilots without planes, but more help was on their way.

Temporary Duty with Other Units on First Arrival

There was temporary duty away from the Fourth General for a number of officers:

In early 1942, there was:
    Darwin during Java Sea Campaign
    Jim Connelly—Ret. April 10
    Joe Kahn—Ret. April 23
    Carl Rundell—Ret. April 10

Port Melbourne Dispensary
   E. C. Weckesser—Ret. April 15
   William Gernon—Ret. April

Headquarters Toorak School
   Dave Chambers—Stayed with headquarters
   Roger Egeberg—Stayed with headquarters then GHQ
   Aide to General MacArthur Nov. '45 to Japanese surrender.
   John Thornton—Ret. April.

Tent Hospital in Royal Park

On arrival in Melbourne, our hospital was set up with one hundred cots in three marquee tents in Royal Park the first week of March, 1942 and we were taking patients.

Portable Hospitals

September 1942

Portable Hospitals, twenty-five beds each—
Buna Campaign

First Portable	**Second Portable**
Bill Hallaran	Tony Lazzari
V. Tichy	Carl Hammann
Elmer Maurer	Fred Rose
Jim Donnelly	Joe Morton

1943–44

Second Edition First Portable—Ataipe landing June 4
Ken Sharretts
Herb Johnson
Bill Markley
Graham Webster

Hospital ships

Tasman	**Maetsuycker**
Tony Lazzari	Tony Lazzari
Fred Rose	Fred Rose
Carl Hamann	

There was a large hospital building under construction just to the south of us toward the center of the city. This was to be the new home of the Royal Melbourne now on Swanson Street downtown. Under existing war conditions there was no way that this building could be occupied by its intended owner in the near future. Upper level decisions were made and the Fourth General Hospital was allowed to place its equipment into this partially finished building as it was completed. This building had a roof and was far superior to our tents. The Fourth General was assigned to utilize the Royal Melbourne Hospital structure along with an adjacent ten floor Nurses Home. About this time the Japanese were bombing Wyndam and Broom in Northwest Australia. Tokyo Rose was broadcasting over radio: "Hello Melbourne. Hello Melbourne. See you soon." The city was blacked out with all large windows boarded up downtown and protected with sand bags.

On March 8 Java fell to the Japanese. Entertained at the home of Dr. Frank Tate in Toorak included a buffet dinner for a large group and, after dinner, we were shown family movies of Gipsland, Queensland and the Great Barrier Reef. Excellent quality. He made a small movie theater in the rear of his home. He and Mrs. Tate were most gracious hosts. March 13 personnel moved to the nurses' home. The eighth, ninth and tenth floors were for nurses and the seventh floor was for officers.

MacArthur Arrives from Corregidor

On March 21st MacArthur arrived from the Philippines in HQ Melbourne. He took charge with the meager forces at hand. Prior to his arrival, plans for defense of Australia with trenches in Queensland, above Brisbane, was being entertained. He did not subscribe to this World War I tactic. Instead, air power was brought into play, and a leap-frog method of attacking the enemy developed. Groups were cut off, bypassed, and allowed to struggle with the jungle on their own, without supplies, while the main forces moved on. These tactics shortened the war greatly. MacArthur deserves much credit for this tactic.

April 6, 1942: Some patients admitted to the lower floors of Nursing Home.
April 10, 1942: Bataan surrendered. British cruisers sunk in Indian Ocean.

April 23, 1942: Colonel Starns in hospital with depression. Colonel McCally becomes C.O. Leo Walzer admitted to hospital with hepatitis from yellow fever vaccine.

May 6, 1942: Battle in Coral Sea. Losses heavy including aircraft carrier *Lexington.* Invasion turned back. Japanese soldiers have Australian invasion money.

May 18, 1942: Air crash at Essenden Airport. B17 crashlanded and caught fire. Nose gunner from Coshocton, Ohio burned to death. Could not escape. Crew of nine severely burned. Admitted as a group to Fourth General. Two Australian officers included. Treated intensively with fluids, IV and tannic acid, locally.

May 25, 1942: Colonel Starnes to States. McCally commanding officer.

May 31, 1942: A Jap sub in Sydney Harbor!

June 4, 1942: Maryland, Hopkins and Harvard General Hospital units arrived to go to Sydney and Brisbane.

June 8, 1942: Good News. Battle of Midway Island. Japs beaten back! Carrier *Yorktown* lost after valiant service.

June 13, 1942: Japs land in Aleutian Islands. Rommel driving across North Africa.

June 19, 1942: Churchill again visits Pres. Roosevelt.

June 22, 1942: Tobruk (North Africa) has fallen to Germans. Rommel has a sea port.

June 26, 1942: Rommel fifty miles from Egyptian border.

July 24, 1942: Japs land at Buna, east end of New Guinea.

July 26, 1942: Townsville bombed.

July 28, 1942: Japs moving south from Buna.

July 31, 1942: Dog fight over Darwin. Twenty-seven Jap bombers, seven brought down.

August 1, 1942: Darwin bombed.

August 5, 1942: MacArthur headquarters north to Sydney.

August 11, 1942: Battle in Solomon Islands—U.S. marines.

August 15, 1942: Marines holding landing on Guadalcanal in Solomons (Henderson Air Field).

September 10, 1942: Fire in tower of hospital.

September 17, 1942: Japs nearing Port Moresby. Marines holding Henderson Field, Guadalcanal.

First Marine Division from Guadalcanal

The patient load remained under one thousand for several months as units moved north during the latter months of 1942. MacArthur's headquarters, which had moved to Sydney, moved on up to Brisbane. The Fourth General remained in Melbourne and, early in January 1943, the First Marine Division was brought there from Guadalcanal. Admissions soared. Seven hundred patients were admitted in one day: malaria, typhus, dengue and all types of dysentery and skin diseases from the tropics. The census went to 2,200 and remained high until September of that year when the marines moved out. Over the next several months the census progressively dropped as the war moved northward and it became obvious that we would move nearer the front.

Move to New Guinea

Packing and clearing out the Royal Melbourne building to return it to its Australian owners was an extensive task. Much effort was made to clean and clear it completely, which took several weeks. The job was finally completed. Remaining patients were transferred to the 118th General Hospital in Sydney and a small station hospital that had been established in the barracks. Personnel were entrained at Melbourne on March 25, 1944, after two years and one month in that fine city where many friends had been made.

The trip north was made with four trainloads of equipment, which had to be reloaded at the New South Wales border and also at the Queensland border because of the different railroad gauges in the different provinces at that time.

Brisbane

Our troop train pulled into Brisbane in a heavy rain. The word came that we were expected, which only meant that some empty space was available, we had learned. In this case it was the Cricket Grounds, which did have tents with the sides rolled up and water standing in much of the area, but at least it was some shelter. The next phase of the journey was to be by ship, in order to take all of our supplies. In a day or so things dried out a bit and our quarters were more habitable.

Alcoa Polaris

We waited a week until finally the "victory ship" *USS Alcoa Polaris* arrived at the harbor and loading of our equipment began. The trip to New Guinea turned out to be an uncomfortable one in the hold of that vessel without air conditioning, with the bunks four high. Only a soldier who has been there knows what it was like. The intense heat and odors of the hold of the vessel caused many to be sea sick. This was too extreme for one of the radiologists, who took up lodging on top of a stack of life rafts on deck for better air. Here he spent most of the four-day voyage. We rounded the east end of New Guinea spending one night anchored in Milne Bay and dropping anchor in the harbor of Finschaffen on the Huon Peninsula of the northeast coast of New Guinea April 14, 1944.

Finschaffen, New Guinea

We were again near the front, the first general hospital in New Guinea. Finschaffen, with its good harbor and good American-built airfield, had become an important base for our rapidly advancing air force. Our hospital was set up on a smaller, previously enemy airfield on the southeast coat of the Huan Peninsula overlooking the Solomon Sea with New Britain to our northeast. Casualties from station and evacuation hospitals filled our beds as soon we could accommodate them, which was within a week. Tent wards were then tin-roofed wooden structures with open sides and concrete slab floors to deal with the deep mud from the tropical rains. These tropical rains were torrential and caused mud shoe-top deep around the compound and axle deep on the heavily traveled single road that paralleled the beach. A high mountain range paralleled the beach just a short distance inland. In addition to referred patients from smaller hospital units, we received direct casualties by air and ship from the invasions of Hollandia, Aitape and the Island of Biak. The war was moving rapidly in 1944 with our air superiority and MacArthur's leap-frog strategy, by-passing and cutting off isolated enemy groups and requiring them to struggle on their own with the jungle forces of nature.

Casualties

Our casualties had all sorts of bullet- and shell-fragment injuries, burns and fractures of all kinds. Our operating suite was set up beautifully by Ms. Gladys Haines and anesthesia was administered by nurse anesthetist Betty Boyer. Both were very dedicated to their tasks. The area was screened from the literal cloud of insects on the outside but occasionally one would get in. One of my associates, an excellent meticulous surgeon, Dr. John Thornton, had an unusual thing happen as he made an abdominal incision one morning. A fly did get into the operating room that morning and was most inconsiderate for itself as well as for Dr. Thornton and his patient. Just as Dr. Thornton was making the incision, the fly landed on the patient's prepared skin under his hand and was transected by the scalpel! It caused excitement and commotion for a short interval. Extreme care was taken to avoid insects in the operating room but the problem was horrendous and this one got in. With wound irrigation and antiseptics no ill effects occurred. It was before we had antibiotics.

In addition to surgical injuries there were tremendous numbers of dermatological casualties due to the hot, damp climate and probably the Atabrine then used for malaria prevention. Wards were filled with them. These were soon known by the apt name of ''jungle rot'' and demanded great amounts of special care. Malaria prophylaxis was oral Atabrine at that time, which gave us all an icteric, yellow complexion. Mosquito netting, over a frame above the cots and tucked in beneath the bedding was standard and mandatory. The hospital was set up on an old enemy airfield next to a rocky coral cliff which led down about twenty or thirty feet to the Pacific Ocean. The privations and intense strain of jungle warfare also produced many psychiatric problems.

With the many station hospitals available in the area, the Fourth General assumed its normal referral function in addition to receiving direct casualties. Patients were evaluated and returned to the States by air and ship as indicated, in order to keep sufficient beds open. In October, 1944 the hospital census was over 2,000 and adjacent station hospitals were taken over to provide more capacity.

The Snakes of Finschaffen

The enemies in Finschaffen did not all have guns. The intense heat, humidity, torrential rains, mud so deep that only four-wheel-drive vehicles could travel, jungle rot, malaria, and typhus, to name only the more

common ones, made things uncomfortable and in many instances dangerous. One other problem that caused consternation but fortunately, no
serious consequences to my knowledge, were the snakes, large, black
and, we thought, venomous. It was not long until we learned the coral
cliff in front of our tents at the edge of the ocean was literally a snake
pit. We had invaded their territory.

Like the Papua natives who worked for us, the snakes of Finschaffen
seemed inquisitive about what we were doing. After all, serpents are wise
according to an old adage of the Greeks. The serpent is entwined on the
staff of Aesculapius supposedly signifying knowledge and healing power.
Were the ancients correct about these reptiles? Do the serpents know
more than we think they do?

One morning I was operating on a soldier under spinal anesthesia
with the patient still conscious. He began to say and repeat something
about a snake. I said to the circulating nurse, "Please look at him, he
seems to have had too much morphine." When she got down to his level
and looked upward she saw a large snake coiled in the rafters just above
the operating table. The snake seemed to be quietly watching the operation. We completed the procedure without disturbing him but did not let
him see the next case.

Soon after our arrival in New Guinea we had gotten our generator
working and were watching a movie in the mess tent when someone
noted a snake slithering on the ground under feet. There was quite a bit
of excitement with people trying to stand on their folding chairs, a feat
not easy on the type we had, until the situation was brought under control.

Now the last episode involves me personally, in my tent, which was
shared with three others, one dark rainy night after the generator had
been turned off. There was no light to be turned on. Due to the hot humid
temperature one usually slept with no cover but, since toward morning
it frequently cooled off, I kept a light blanket rolled lengthwise on my
left so that it could be drawn over me if desired. The mosquito netting
that we all mandatorily slept under fit over a framework above the cot,
hung down and was tucked under the mattress on all sides. During the
day this was rolled up at the front. At night, after getting into bed, this
front portion was also tucked under the mattress so that all four sides
were tucked in to keep the mosquitoes out.

On the rainy night in question, I was awakened in complete darkness
by something slithering over my left thigh. Knowing one should remain
quiet, I did. It came upward so that I felt it going by my left ear at the

same time I could still feel it next to my left thigh. At this point I was awake enough to realize that the reptile had no egress. Slowly getting my right hand down to the front edge of the tucked-in mosquito netting, grasping it firmly, I made what I considered my most appropriate moves, upward with the netting and outward with me. It was successful.

There was no light and before I could successfully strike damp matches the intruder was gone, having only to slither out the edge of the tent and back to his coral cliff habitat below.

I took quite a ribbing on that incident. Some of my friends jokingly said, "Oh Weck, you had too much beer." However, I noted that these people more carefully inspected their cots at night before getting into them.

Papua Natives

The Papua natives who worked for us were an interesting group who felled trees and cleared land for our installations. They all or at least most of them had very flat feet but could walk for miles. Their footprints in the mud or dust, mostly mud, looked like bear tracks. An interesting episode occurred when we were able to get our compressor operating and made ice, frozen water. They had never seen ice in their tropical climate and were much intrigued by it. I remember them standing in a group looking at the ice cubes and when handed one they would chuckle and hand it quickly to the next person who was afraid of it and either handed it on quickly or dropped it to the ground.

Events of 1943

In 1943 the war effort of the United States and its Allies was building up. Things were beginning to change, to look a little brighter. The Battles of the Coral Sea and Midway Island had stopped the Japanese in their rapid uninhibited conquest southward in the Pacific. On the European front, see-saw fighting was taking place in North Africa. Rommel was advancing to the east but had been stopped short of Cairo. There was a polio outbreak in the U.S.

January 14, 1943: President Roosevelt met Churchill in Casablanca.

157

March 2–4, 1943: Battle of the Bismarck Sea a victory for Allies.

May 30, 1943: Attu, Aleutian Islands retaken by U.S.

July 10, 1943: Sicily invaded by Gen. George Patton's 7th Army and General Montgomery's 8th Army, French and Canadians (Carruth, 956).

August 15, 1943: Kiska, Aleutian Island retaken by Allies.

August 16–17, 1943: Wewack, New Guinea, Japanese air base bombed by General Kenny's air force.

July 19, 1943: Rome bombed by Allies.

August 17, 1943: FDR and Churchill meet in Quebec.

August 17, 1943: Sicily conquered (37 days after invasion) (Carruth, 540).

August 28, 1943: New Georgia Island taken by Americans.

September 3, 1943: Italian mainland invaded across Straights of Messina by Allies.

September 8, 1943: Italy surrenders.

September 9, 1943: Allied landing at Salerno, Italy.

September 11, 1943: Salamaua, New Guinea taken by U.S.

September 17, 1943: Lae, New Guinea taken by U.S.

November 2, 1943: Japanese stronghold at Rabaul.

November 22, 1943: FDR, Churchill and Chiang Kai-shek meet in Cairo.

November 28–December 1, 1943: FDR, Churchill, Stalin meet in Tehran.

December 24, 1943: Gen. Dwight Eisenhower named Supreme Commander of European Invasion Forces (Carruth, 543).

Mother, Ella Elizabeth Long.

Father, Christian Weckesser.

Grandfather, Henry
Jacob Weckesser,
circa 1909, age 73.

An artist's rendition
of Grandfather's
ship, the *New Era*.

Grandfather Emanuel Clifton Long, his daughter, Ruth Koeppen, reading, and probably grandson Robert Koeppen.

Grandmother Anna Bishop Secrist Long.

The nine living children of Christian and Ella Long Weckesser, 1932. Standing: Miriam, Elden, Sylvia, Ethan, Constant, Ernest, Ruth, Esther, and Louisa. Father Christian seated. This was twelve years after Mother Ella's death. An infant daughter, Bernice, had died of whooping cough in 1906 at age 18 days.

The Cunningham Sanitarium in the 1930s.

Aerial view of Cunningham Sanitarium in 1930s.

Letter from Dr. Lenhart with war clouds gathering, May 1940.

The beginning of World War II.

Members of the Fourth General Hospital Aus.

Surgical Staff of Fourth General Hospital, Finschaffen, New Guinea, September 1944. Seated: Kelly, Thornton, McCally, Glover, McGaw, Tooney, Blandford, Kauffman, and Foltz. Standing: Loeff, Jordan, unknown, Weckesser, unknown, Hamman, Couch, unknown, Briggle, unknown, Gray, Meschan, McNally, and unknown.

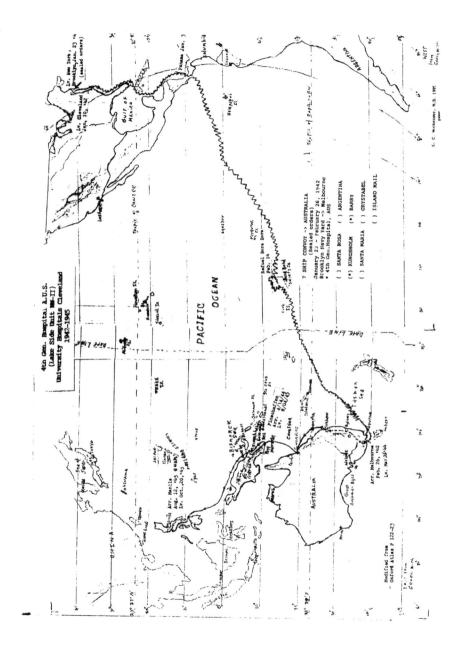

4th Gen. Hospital A.U.S.
(Lake Side Unit WW-II)
University Hospitals Cleveland
1942-1945

New York,
Brooklyn-Jan. 23 '44
(sealed orders)

Lv. Cleveland
Jan. 10, '42

GULF OF
MEXICO

Key West

Tropic of Cancer

Panama Jan. 3

Columbia

Galapagos
Is.

Tropic of Capricorn

PACIFIC
OCEAN

Equator

Honolulu Is.
Fanning Is.

Rafael Bora Bora
Feb. 14

Date Line

WAKE
IS.

Date Line

CHINA
Formosa

Manila Arr. Manila
Aug. 12, '45
Lv. Oct. 20, '45

SAIPAN
GUAM

BISMARCK
SEA

Finschhafen
Arr. 3/14/43

Coral Sea

AUSTRALIA

Great Australian Bight

Arr. Melbourne
Feb. 26, '42
Lv. Mar.26-44

Arafura
Sea

Timor Sea

7 SHIP CONVOY -> AUSTRALIA
(Sealed orders)
January 23 - February 26, 1942
Brooklyn Navy Yard -> Melbourne
• 4th Gen.Hospital, AUS

( ) SANTA ROSA   ( ) ARGENTINA
(•) KUNGSHOLM   (•) BARRY
( ) SANTA MARIA   ( ) CRYSTABEL
                    ( ) ISLAND MAIL

Modified from
Oxford Atlas P.122-3)

E. C. McKenzie, M.D. 1995

from
Greenwich

from
WEST
Greenwich

Aerial view, Fourth General Hospital, Finschaffen, New Guinea, 1944.

*Greetings from the Weckessers
Mary, Elizabeth, Jane, Nancy
Katy and Elden
1964*

Family post war of EC & KT.

FIG. 1. Mode of injury of Case J. M. B.

Severe penetrating injury of the rectum, large and small bowel, left chest, and iliac artery due to impalement on a metal flower stake. The patient was a ten-year-old boy. Multiple lacerations of the rectum, sigmoid colon, and two gaping lacerations of the upper small intestine were repaired and a colostomy, external opening of the large bowel, made on the abdomen. The pulses of both legs were normal. A side injury to the left common iliac artery caused severe hemorrhage on the seventh postoperative day. This and infections required reoperations following which he left the hospital and made a good recovery. He is fine thirty years later.

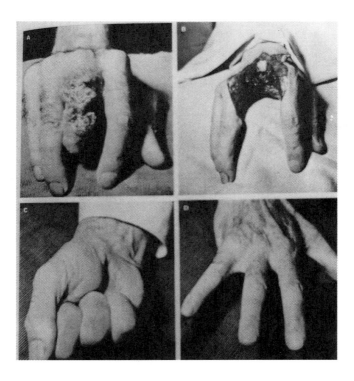

The right hand of a sixty-three-year- old dentist who had inflammation of his long finger for three years. He had held X-ray films with this finger for years during X-ray exposure. Biopsy showed squamous carcinoma. The entire finger ray was removed and the index ray moved over in its place. He continued practice with good function and was fine thirteen years later. From Weckesser, *Treatment of Hand Injuries.*

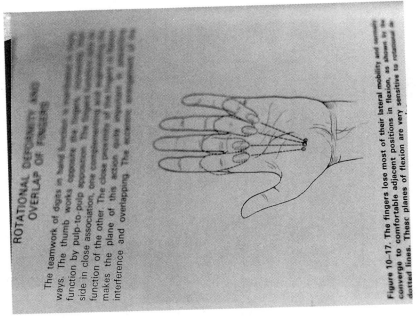

ROTATIONAL DEFORMITY AND OVERLAP OF FINGERS

The teamwork of digits in hand function is in two ways. The thumb works with each finger, function by pulp-to-pulp approaches. The fingers side in close association, tone complementing the function of the other. The close proximity of the fingers makes the plane of this action very critical to avoid interference and overlapping. The adjacent fingers act as

Figure 10–17. The fingers lose most of their lateral mobility and seem to converge to comfortable adjacent positions in flexion, as shown by a dotted lines. These planes of flexion are very sensitive to rotation.

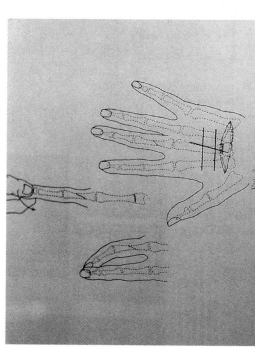

Fig. 3

Technique for rotational osteotomy. The osteotomy is made transversely at the base of the metacarpal through a transverse dorsal skin incision. The entire ray is then rotated to correct the deformity. (Approximately 25 degrees of rotation either way is possible.) Secure fixation is accomplished by Kirschner wires, two inserted horizontally through the distal fragment and one or both of the adjacent metacarpals and one vertically, across the osteotomy site. (The degree of rotation is exaggerated in this diagram.)

Rotational deformity of fingers. Weckesser, J Bone & Joint Surg. 47-A, p751-756 June 1965.

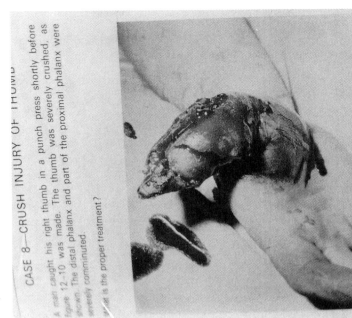

CASE 8—CRUSH INJURY OF THUMB

A man caught his right thumb in a punch press shortly before figure 12-10 was made. The thumb was severely crushed, as shown. The distal phalanx and part of the proximal phalanx were severely comminuted.

What is the proper treatment?

Figure 12-10. See Case 8.

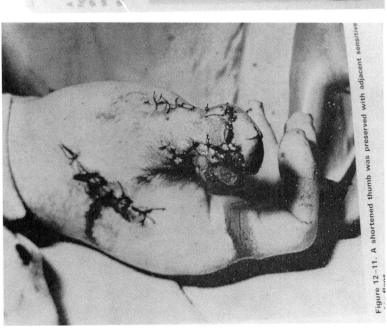

Figure 12-11. A shortened thumb was preserved with adjacent sensitive skin flaps.

Severe punchpress injury of the right thumb. A useful shortened thumb was preserved. From Weckesser, *Treatment of Hand Injuries*.

the additional necrosis of the palmar flap would have been difficult had a pedicle been employed.

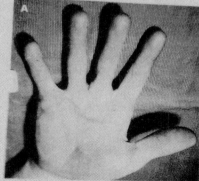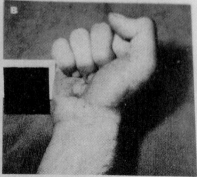

Figure 12-2. Condition of the hand of the patient in figure 12-1 eighteen months after treatment. The area requiring secondary grafting in the center of the palm is visible. The patient carries out his previous type of work. Loss of the normal palmar skin texture (dermal ridges) interferes with some functions; the patient complains that objects slip from his grasp more readily now than before the injury. This is not a serious complaint, however, and he has good use of his hand.

Severe avulsion injury to palm. Skin flap replaced, followed by skin grafting.

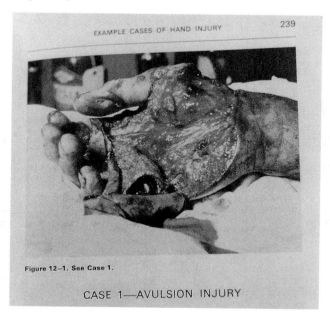

Figure 12-1. See Case 1.

CASE 1—AVULSION INJURY

Katy on the Home Front

After my departure from home, January 1942, Katy was able to engage a very nice elderly lady, Mrs. Florence (Nanny) Thompson, who lived a few doors away on Murray Hill Road, to look after baby Jane so that she could continue working at Lakeside Hospital. Emergencies and hardship bring out the best in people and make them cooperative and helpful to each other. Mr. John Minello who ran the grocery store at the corner of Murray Hill and Adelbert Road was very supportive in helping with groceries and supplies for Katy during the period of rationing (meat and sugar especially).

The wives of those overseas had a club in which they supported one another by comparing notes and exchanging information about what was going on. This was a great help to all.

While still in Melbourne, one of the men, Don Kelly, brought a patient back to the States and visited Cleveland for a few days. With the help of Dr. Chick Thomas in Cleveland some movies were made of the Cleveland families back home which the men had not seen for two years. When this film was shown on his return to Australia it was a moving emotional experience. Everyone had changed during the interval, the adults and especially the children. Our daughter, Jane, three months old when I left, was now two years old and would be three when I did return. We watched the film not knowing whose child you were seeing until you recognized something in the background that was familiar and then called out, ''That one's mine.'' Separation is always difficult, especially when so protracted. With the emergency situation of the war that existed there was no rotation of personnel set up or any possible in those first uncertain years. The outcome was much narrower than one likes to think. It was not at all clear who was going to win the conflict in the early days when initial reverses were extremely great for our country, which had been thinking in terms of outmoded isolationism rather than ever-necessary preparation for defense.

Battleships and Aircraft Carriers

The strategic position of the battleship in the hierarchy of naval vessels changed in 1941. The battleship had been the dominant man-of-war on the high seas for over one hundred years. It was the main unit about which battle cruisers and destroyers operated. It was designed for relatively close combat, usually within line of sight. Armor had been extensively increased and it was thought by some leaders that the modern battleship was essentially unsinkable, even by aerial bombs, especially with its own protective firepower.

The development of airplanes to carry bombs with greater destructive capacity than battleship shells and to carry them directly over targets, or torpedo them in from the side, was a challenge to the traditional battleship. These planes could be launched from a new type of flattop ship, the aircraft carrier. The practicality of this change was debated in high circles where the capacity of bombers to sink battleships was disputed. This dispute received nerve shaking evidence a few days after the Pearl Harbor attack when Japanese bombers sunk two of Britain's battleships, the *Prince of Wales,* brand new, and the *Repulse,* an older one, off the coast of the Malay Peninsula near Singapore on December 10, 1941. The loss of those two vessels alone without air cover was shocking to all Allies because it showed that battleships could be destroyed by aircraft delivering bombs and torpedoes. Winston Churchill later said, "In all of World War II, I never received a more direct shock." (Miller, 54).

Phases of World War II
Based on Dominance of Military Power

Phase I. December 7, 1941–mid-1943   In Favor of Enemy
The enemy had taken us by surprise when we were completely off guard, dealt us a severe blow with extreme loss of battleships, planes and personnel (no aircraft carriers). They next planned to destroy our fleet at sea. We were saved by our carriers, having them strategically placed by cracking the enemy code.

Phase II. July 1943–1945   In Favor of U.S. and Allies.

We had control. We had regained our strength. Our planes were faster, including the 6F6 Hellcat Fighter, and could now out-maneuver the Mitsubishi Zero, enemy fighter. Our aircraft carrier superiority had been reestablished by the Battle of Midway.

Our Aircraft Carriers

A Close Call December 7, 1941

The absence of aircraft carriers at Pearl Harbor on December 7, 1941, turned out to be most fortunate. Our aircraft carrier plane strength became of strategic importance. The loss of a single carrier on the fateful day of December 7, 1941 could have made a significant difference. The *Lexington* was hauling aircraft to Midway Island and the *Enterprise* was hauling planes to Wake Island, due back December 6, but held up by high seas. The *Saratoga* was in dry dock at Seattle, not Pearl Harbor.

The Battle of the Coral Sea, May 4–8, 1942

The first big test of power came approximately six months after the beginning of World War II. Enemy invasion forces had advanced uninhib-ited down the east coast of Asia through the Philippines, Malaysia, Malay Peninsula, Java Sea, Soloman Islands and to Rabal by January 23, 1942, and then the north coast of New Guinea. Their attempt to cross the Owen-Stanley mountain range on the Kokoda Trail and take Port Moresby by land bogged down due to the steaming, almost impenetrable jungle with steep cliffs, ravines, rushing mountain streams, malaria, other tropical diseases and stiff Australian resistance.

A sea invasion around the eastern tip of New Guinea was attempted by the Japanese fleet the first week of May. Our Navy learned of this intent through its Intelligence Service which had cracked the enemy naval code. This knowledge compensated partially for our limited number of surface ships following our heavy losses at Pearl Harbor.

A first stiff stand of World War II, at the battle of the Coral Sea, which prevented the invasion of Port Moresby, a stepping stone to the Australian mainland, was possible because of four important factors that also apply to the Battle of Midway one month later:

1. We still had Aircraft Carriers.
2. We had cracked the enemy's naval code.
3. The *USS Enterprise,* due to return to Pearl Harbor on December 1941, was held up by high seas.
4. The Panama Canal was open.

Admiral Chester W. Nimitz assigned Task Force 17, the *Lexington* and the *Yorktown,* under Rear Admiral Frank Jack Fletcher, to the task of stopping the enemy's southern advance, which up to this point had been uninhibited.

In the air battle of the Coral Sea that followed, the planes from our carriers, *Lexington* and *Yorktown,* met the enemy planes at sea. Enemy ships were never in sight of each other—the first sea-air battle of this type. Both sides suffered significant losses. Two large enemy carriers, the *Zuikaku* and the *Shokaku* were each seriously damaged and would be absent from the Battle of Midway one month later. Both the *Lexington* and the *Yorktown* were struck by enemy bombs and torpedoes. The *Lexington* had to be abandoned after the battle due to internal fires and explosions. The *Yorktown,* with a large hole in her side made it back to Pearl Harbor for quick temporary repairs. Port Moresby did not fall to the enemy, the first engagement in which the enemy in the South Pacific was repulsed in World War II. It was also the first sea engagement in which planes of aircraft carriers played the major role. The difference between success and failure was very small and it was the aircraft carriers, and the brave people on them under astute direction, that made the difference. The *Yorktown*, with a metal plate quickly applied, allowed her seventy-two planes to play a strategic role in the Battle of Midway before making the supreme sacrifice there from enemy bombs and torpedoes.

Battle of Midway Islands June 4–6, 1942

Looking back, years after the war, it is interesting to learn details of what was going on. At that time in 1942 in the Fourth Gen. Hospital in Melbourne, Australia, we were busy taking care of casualties from the Java Sea and New Guinea and knew little about the strategic battle of the Midway Islands until it was over. The enemy was trying to knock us out early, before we could recover to harness our tremendous industrial capability at home. The two battles to destroy our navy were the Battle of the Coral Sea and the Battle of the Midway Islands (Miller, 67).

	Enemy		U.S. and Allies	
Carriers	*Akagi* (Adm. Nagumo) *Kaga* *Soryu* *Hiryu*		*Enterprise* (Adm. Spruance) *Hornet* (Adm. Spruance) *Yorktown* (Vice Adm. Fletcher)	
Surface vessels	162	(N.W. Miday)	73	(N.E. Midway)
Battle ships	7		0	
Cruisers	+		8	
Destroyers	+		14	
Transports	12		–	
Submarines	+		20	

The enemy made its first strike at the Aleutian Islands at Attu, Kiska and Adak. This was to draw attention away from their main focus. There were many coded messages regarding ''AF.'' It could have been Pearl Harbor or the West Coast of the United States. It was thought by Admiral Nimitz to be Midway but proof was needed. Our cryptographer, Joseph Rochefort at Pearl Harbor, with an OK from Admiral Nimitz, instructed our people at Midway to send an open message back to Pearl Harbor that their water plant was not working (Miller, 79). A day later Rochefort sent a follow up message to Midway that a water barge was en route. A day later, an enemy message in code reported that ''AF'' was short of water! Admiral Nimitz correctly interpreted this report as evidence that the main focus was Midway Island and proceeded with appropriate action there with only minimal attention to the Aleutians.

Midway was as ready as possible on the date for the attack on ''AF.'' The island was manned heavily with anti-aircraft defense. The *Enterprise* and the *Hornet* were in rendezvous northeast of Midway, joined there by the quickly repaired *Yorktown* with seventy-two additional planes. The enemy would be approaching from the west, which was scouted closely for early detection of their approach.

When the air raid on Midway airfield came it was met by intense anti-aircraft fire. The ground planes were all in the air, in rendezvous. Due to this, the damage to the ground installations was not great and the enemy commander recommended a second attack. Admiral Nagumo, back on the enemy carriers, had his next wave of planes already on deck and armed with torpedoes for aircraft carrier attack. This caused consternation and intense confusion as a frantic attempt was made to rearm the enemy planes for an unanticipated task. This was augmented by the return of the original Midway bombing squadron for refueling (Miller, 70).

Admiral Spruance was able to time his attack of our U.S. planes from rendezvous, onto the enemy aircraft carriers, at this crucial time. Some of our bomber and torpedo planes had been previously sent to attack other enemy units. This served to occupy and distract enemy Zero fighters away from our bombers attacking the enemy carrier fleet. A most amazing thing then happened. In a short period of time our bombers and torpedo planes sank four enemy aircraft carriers!

The *Yorktown*, after dispatching many of those critical planes in the attack on the enemy carriers was itself struck by enemy bombs and torpedoes, which finally took her to the bottom. Admiral Spruance then wisely retired his fleet. He did not pursue the enemy to the northwest into a den of enemy battle ships! He had won the battle and still had two aircraft carriers, the *Hornet* and the *Enterprise*.

The balance of power at Midway, as shown above, was distinctly in favor of the enemy but less so than it would have been had the two large enemy aircraft carriers, the *Zuikaku* and *Shokaku,* been there. Seriously damaged in the Coral Sea battle, these carriers were in dry dock and missed the battle of Midway. Very important for the U.S. in the battle of the Midway Islands was the breaking of the enemy code so that in this encounter surprise was in our favor. In retrospect our victory in the Battle of Midway turned out to be the most crucial battle of the war and was the turning point of it in the Pacific.

Events of 1944

Invasion of European Mainland

On June 6, 1944 (D-day), the largest flotilla of ships (4000) and planes (3000) ever assembled in the history of the world was ready. The Allied (4 million) Troop invasion of mainland Europe began.

July 10, 1944: Saipan fell to the Americans in heavy fighting. Admiral Nagumo, who led attack on Pearl Harbor, is killed.

July 19, 1944: Democratic Convention, Chicago. FDR nominated for fourth term with Harry Truman as vice president.

July 25, 1944: German defenses at Normandy crumbled.

August 8, 1944: American drive toward Paris.

August 9, 1944: Guam fell to U.S. after fierce fighting.

August 25, 1944: Paris liberated (Carruth, 547).

October 20, 1944: U.S. landed in Leyte, Philippine Islands. MacArthur had returned as he had predicted on leaving in March, 1942. Japan began using kamikaze, suicide pilots (Carruth, 547).

October 23–26, 1944: Battle of Leyte Gulf. Heavy fighting. Japan suffered severe losses. Carrier *Princeton* lost. Japanese lost four carriers (Carruth, 547).

November 7, 1944: FDR defeated Thomas Dewey as president of the U.S.

December 15, 1944: The rank of Five-Star General of the Army created by Congress and bestowed upon Henry Arnold, Dwight Eisenhower, Douglas MacArthur and George C. Marshall (Carruth, 549).

December 16, 1944: Battle of the Bulge. General Von Runstedt broke through Allied lines and advanced into Belgium before being checked by Allied reinforcements (Carruth, 549).

Fourth General Hospital, continued

As the war continued to move rapidly northward in the South Pacific, more and more hospitals, including general hospitals, moved ahead of us once again so that gradually Finschaffen became a base for evaluation and evacuation to the States. By the latter part of 1944, replacement and rotation of our own personnel back to the United States had begun. By this time we had been overseas nearly three years and it seemed like eternity. Letters from Katy back home with daughter Jane were a frequent Godsend to know they were all right.

Rotation from New Guinea

By the early fall of 1944 things were beginning to look brighter for us. Our forces had destroyed many of the enemy's carriers and had air superiority in most places but it was still a long way back to the home base of the enemy. In this environment the north coast of New Guinea was bustling with plans for progressive invasions along the north coast of New Guinea leading to the retaking of the Philippine Islands.

Many of the Fourth General personnel were being returned to the States. In December 1944 Irwin Hanger and I had our turn.

In early 1945, William C. McCally, who had done an excellent job as commanding officer, was rotated home and his post taken by Donald M. Glover.

The Fourth General continued to function at Finschaffen until July 23, 1945, when the last remaining of its 46,100 admitted patients were transferred to the 119th Station Hospital and the Fourth General embarked for the Philippines on August 4, 1945. The atomic bombs were dropped on Hiroshima and Nagasaki during that voyage. The Fourth General was not assembled in the Philippines due to the end of the war by the surrender of the enemy on the battleship *Missouri* September 2, 1945. The Fourth General Hospital was absorbed by the Fifty-first General Hospital on October 20, 1945 ending forty-six months of overseas duty. Remaining personnel returned home in the weeks that followed.

During the two years in Melbourne, we cared for nearly 34,000 hospitalized patients and performed over 7,000 surgical operations. The Finschaffen period augmented this to a total of 46,100 admissions and 10,746 operations. This was during forty-six months of overseas duty, thirty-nine months of which the Fourth General took active care of patients.*

In the latter part of 1944 a camp had been set up at Finschaffen just a few miles south of the Fourth General for the processing of those with long overseas service, in preparation for their return to the States. Guy Brugler of our unit directed much of this and aptly named it Camp Utopia, which he thought was appropriate since the men were going home. However, with all the necessary preparation for the invasion of the Philippines

---

*In writing this section I was aided by the work of Bill Hallaran, Webb Chamberlain, Fred Rose, Olga Benderoff and Katie Deeds Hayman, Dave Weir, and Lew Bronson. It was written in 1991, on the occasion of the fiftieth anniversary of activation.

going on, ships and planes were not available to take the men home requiring them to wait for weeks not knowing if a ship would ever come. The men were separated from their units and felt forgotten. They no longer held responsible positions in their unit, and did not have assignments to keep them busy. They had been through emotional strain for a long while; their nerves were frayed. Morale became extremely bad, the worst that I encountered anywhere. Suicides occurred before the hoped-for homeward bound ships appeared.

The *USS Azalea City*

Finally, the troop ship, *USS Azalea City* (named for the city of Mobile, Alabama), came into port. Dr. Irwin (Ike) Hanger and I were being rotated home and were assigned medical responsibility for this ship back to the States. We left about the last week of November, 1944 without convoy for San Francisco making the journey in ten days. We were pushing right along in a straight line in contrast to our thirty-five day zig-zig trip over. On the way, about two days out of San Francisco, we were passed by the *USS Lurline,* which had greater speed. It was interesting to see it come up over the horizon, "out of nowhere" on our stern, pass us on our port side and disappear, out of sight, over the horizon ahead of us. It was traveling considerably faster than we. It and its troop passengers would get there ahead of us but we were happy knowing that we were right behind.

Landfall, San Francisco

Finally land appeared on the horizon and then the Golden Gate Bridge! When we sailed under it we knew we were back. What a wonderful feeling after nearly three long years, many times wondering whether this would ever happen. We passed the *Lurline* comfortably at its berth, turned north in the harbor past Alcatraz to Angel Island. We disembarked and were billeted in barracks. The young CO was going to keep us in quarters. We presented our case forcefully and he finally gave us leave to the city, where we went by ferry and then to the St. Francis Hotel! Ike and I took a room there and said, "Oh the luxury of walking on soft carpet once again!" The first thing was to call home and see if our wives were OK.

The ladies knew we were on our way. The St. Francis had a telephone room with telephone books for all the major cities of the country and some foreign ones. We first looked to see if we were still listed in the phone book. I found myself there but Ike did not. His listing had been changed. I was able to reach Katy on the phone and tell her we were safely back in the *Good Old* USA.

Troop Train to Camp Atterbury, Indiana

We and our troops from *Azalea City* were loaded onto a troop train heading east to Camp Atterbury, Indiana just south of Indianapolis. We would meet the ladies in Columbus, Indiana when we arrived! Just when that would be, no one knew. The troop train would discharge troops all along the route back in various cities and arrive at Camp Atterbury with the final group for the East. All the details were finally worked out and the train was under way. Ike Hanger and I were in charge. The railroads were very busy with freight and passengers heading west. Our train did not have high priority. In St. Louis we were placed on a siding, way out from nowhere, and our steam engine was taken away to pull another train. No information came as to what was going on. It was quite cold with snow on the ground and the cars were soon nearly freezing, at least we were. We were fresh from the jungles of New Guinea with little warm clothing. We tried to get help from the station master back across the tracks but there were no more engines available. Finally, after several hours, before we became frost bitten, they found an engine and on we went, with heat, to our final destination, Camp Atterbury Indiana. It was possible to get an occasional call through to our homes to let our wives know something of our position. The trip was taking quite a long time under wartime conditions and our many stops.

Camp Atterbury Reunion with Katy

Finally after about four days we arrived at Atterbury and had to be processed there and have new orders written. This was finally accomplished. We were on leave. Now to get to Columbus, Indiana, where Katy and Sally were waiting. There were no buses to Columbus for several hours. We were able to get one to a halfway point where we were stranded. "Climbing the wall," we finally were able to get a taxi for the balance of the journey. The intense anxiety after three years of separation under war conditions was very great. The room clerk at the desk greeted us warmly and told us our wives were waiting in rooms at the head of the stairs to the right and left. Up the stairs we went; I to the right and Ike to the left. With a slight knock, the door opens and I was about to throw my arms about Katy and to my surprise it's not her—unless she has changed greatly. It's Sally Hanger who until that moment I had never met. We had the rooms mixed. That correction was quickly made with no trouble at all and Katy and I were back together after three long years of separation. Katy was as beautiful as ever, but quite thin. The years of separation and uncertainty had been hard on her. We returned to Cleveland by crowded train having to sit on our luggage part of the way but happy to do so.

Return to Dear Old Cleveland

The apartment at 2320 Murray Hill Road was little changed during my absence showing Katy's warm touch as always. The adjacent buildings on Murray Hill Road looked a little older and even Lakeside Hospital down Adelbert Road appeared somewhat worn. The small grocery store at the corner of Adelbert Road looked about the same, reflecting the warm personality of owner John Manillo who had helped Katy with war food rationing. She told me he helped her get scarce items such as meat. This was something that made us grateful to him. It was cold and snowy, just before Christmas, 1944. This was the type of weather we had nearly forgotten, but with warm winter clothes it was invigorating. Jane was no longer a baby now but a three-year-old, running about and talking lively. It was difficult for her to be sure of me as her Daddy. The Daddy she had known was a photograph on her mother's dresser, "Daddy in New Guinea." She was not sure about this new entity. Was he more than an intruder? We had to try to get acquainted which would prove to be no small task. Soon after my return we were visited by my brother-in-law, "Uncle" Banks Rhine from Durham, North Carolina. He was passing through Cleveland and we asked him to spend the night with us. He was sitting on the davenport in the living room. I left for a moment and came back to the living room in time to see Jane standing in front of him, shaking her finger at him, saying, "You can stay, but you can't sleep with Mommy!'' After all, she seemed to be saying, since being pushed around by my father's return, let's get a few things straight in this house.

Katy and Jane

It was a warm homecoming in Cleveland with Katy, Jane and our Cleveland friends, as well as my folks in Doylestown and Katy's in Lima, Ohio. We got together with the families of those who were not yet home to give them the latest word about those still in New Guinea. This was a good added feature about the unit idea; other members can compare notes and exchange information. I think this feature was helpful to Kay during my absence.

Dr. Lenhart at the hospital was very cordial and welcomed me warmly. Dr. Beck was away in the service as director of the Fifth Service Command, which represented Ohio, Indiana, Kentucky and West Virginia. He soon played a very significant role in the balance of my army career as well as my future surgical practice. Dr. John Holloway was cordial but had noticeably aged. He had congenital high blood pressure, which caused his death in just a few years. All the other personnel at Lakeside Hospital were very cordial.

R&R, Florida

My orders from Camp Atterbury included two weeks of Rest and Recuperation (R & R) in Miami Beach, Florida for the two of us (Katy and me) starting the first of the year. Daughter Jane was left with Connie and Dorothy, my brother and my sister-in-law at Doylestown. We took off after the holidays in our 1940 Chevy, which Katy had given good care during my absence. We managed to get enough rationed gasoline for the trip. I think some coupons were included in my transportation orders. Rationing of fuel had been quite strict and of course there were no new automobiles during World War II due to all manufacturing being converted to defense, the building of airplanes, ships, tanks, all sorts of amphibious and land vehicles, to supply our forces and attack the enemy. This great manufacturing ability on our home front supporting our armed forces was an important and decisive factor in our victory.

Katy and I took off for Florida in our Chevy. We picked up the newly completed first portion of the Pennsylvania Turnpike from Irwin to Breezewood, Pennsylvania. This was a treat, a forerunner of the interstate highway system to come and a wonderful improvement for automobile travel. We stopped briefly with the Rhines at Durham, North Carolina and were warmly welcomed there, then on southward. In Brunswick, Georgia the brakes of the car gave out. Oh goodness, what now? I visualized an overall brake job to interrupt our trip. Katy said, "Maybe it needs a shot of fluid." I was of the opinion that the car still had mechanical brakes, but she was right and we were soon on our way and encountered no more problems. We arrived at our hotel in Miami Beach, the Warwick Hotel as I recall, and met two other couples from the Fourth General, Sally, Ike Hanger, and Mary Louise and Ed Harper. With them we made excursions to surrounding attractions in addition to enjoying the beach and sunshine. The time went very rapidly and was soon over. My orders said I should report to the army base at Charleston, South Carolina, which we did. It was now the third week of January 1945. This base was a bustle as an overseas embarkation point. Attention was all on the European Theater with units leaving in large numbers for that front, in preparation for the upcoming invasion of the European continent, which, we found out later, would occur on June 6, 1945.

Just having returned from a long overseas assignment in the South Pacific, I was somewhat out of place there and was assigned to a surgical ward awaiting specific orders. In time of need anything can happen in the army. I busied myself in the library with a report of the Coconut Grove Disaster, which had occurred in Boston several months earlier and with the methods of burn treatment used there. In the South Pacific we had been replacing fluids rapidly and using cleansing methods locally followed by tannic acid or vaseline gauze to the wounds proper. This was in agreement with the present report. Antibiotics were not yet widely available. Some penicillin was available for experimental use.

Col. Claude S. Beck

On about the third day it was a relief to receive orders to report to Crile General Hospital, Parma, Ohio. I was not forgotten after all. Claude Beck, my teacher and mentor, then director of the Fifth Service Command, was asking for me. Gladly, Katy and I headed off for Cleveland with a sigh of relief. Crile General Hospital was a new Army General Hospital just opening in Parma, a western suburb of Cleveland. It and a whole series of general hospitals were being opened by Surgeon General Norman T. Kirk in the continental United States to receive returning casualties from abroad. This one was honorarily named for Dr. George Crile, Sr. who gave much service in World War I and was responsible for the Lakeside Hospital Unit of World War I.

Events of 1945

The development of the artificial kidney by Dr. William J. Kolff in 1945 would turn out to be a life-saving mechanism for thousands of patients with kidney failure. Blood of the patient was brought next to a solution called perfusing fluid containing all elements of blood plasma except urea, separated by only a thin sheet of plastic. This thin sheet of plastic acted as a semipermeable membrane similar to that of the cell walls of kidney cells. The urea passed through the sheet of plastic into the perfusing fluid, which was then discarded and replaced by fresh fluid at each cycle. In this manner the urea was withdrawn from the patient's plasma. The perfusing fluid, which contained the urea from the patient's blood plasma, was then discarded. This discarded fluid was analogous to urine in regard to its urea content.

No one up to this time had realized that a special thin sheet of plastic could or would act in this manner. It was indeed a very valuable, useful observation. It provided a method of keeping people with kidney failure alive by using the artificial kidney at frequent intervals. This is now used to carry out kidney function for patients with kidney failure until a suitable kidney transplant can be obtained.

1945 was also an epochal year for all Allied survivors of World War II, a war that began suddenly for the United States on December 8, 1941 after the treacherous bombing of Pearl Harbor by Japan on the previous day. The United States had recovered from Japan's near knock-out blow and with our Allies had gone on to victory.

Casualties of World War II

The casualties of the war were tremendous and still occurring as the year began. Wounded men and women filled our military hospitals. When the war ended, the final total number of U.S. military lives lost in World War II was 292,100. Including the major Allied powers, the number was 10,560,000. The major Axis powers lost 4,650,000 making the total losses for both sides more than 15 million (Encyclopedia Britannica, 23:793.) The seriously wounded were many times that.

Death of Pres. Franklin Roosevelt

President Roosevelt died of a cerebral hemorrhage April 12, 1945 and was succeeded by Harry Truman. Hitler and the Axis powers were defeated.

Fortunately, none of our aircraft carriers were at Pearl Harbor on December 7, 1941. It was these vessels and the brave pilots who flew the planes that played a vital role in turning the tide of battle in the Pacific, preventing the invasion of Australia. Their effort was crucial in the Battle of the Coral Sea May 4–6, 1942, and a month later in the Battle of the Midway Islands, which turned out to be the turning point of the Pacific war in our favor. Atomic bombs were dropped on Hiroshima and Nagasaki bringing the war to an abrupt termination and preventing the great loss of life that would have occurred had invasion of the Japanese homeland been required. The thousands of American lives lost at Pearl Harbor on December 7, 1941 were more than enough. How the horrible conflict started should always be remembered in relation to the dropping of the bombs that ended it.

United Nations, International Bandits, Wars and Freedom

The United Nations, a cooperative world organization for peace was formed. A fine thing, but unfortunately, as long as international bandits continue to occur, it is probable that wars will need to be fought to protect freedom.

It is ironic that President Roosevelt did not live to see the successful end of the war. His strong American leadership was largely responsible for the victory. Hitler's defeat was twenty-five days after President Roosevelt's death and Japan's four months and two days later. The unconditional surrender of Japan on August 14, 1945, was a very bright spot in the lives of all Americans, as well as Katy and me. I was on an assignment at Camp Atterbury, Indiana. Katy and I had dinner that evening in a restaurant in downtown Indianapolis and the excitement was tremendous. It brought back my boyhood memories of the end of World War I on November 11, 1918.

Final Sequence of Events of World War II

January 9, 1945: U.S. 6th Army landed on Luzon, Philippine islands.

February 7, 1945: MacArthur reentered Manila.

February 3–11, 1945: Yalta Conference, Crimes, USSR. FDR, Churchill, and Stalin. Russia to enter war against Japan (Carruth, 548).

February 19–23, 1945: Marines take island of Iwo Jima in Pacific.

April 1, 1945: U.S. Marines invade Okinawa.

April 12, 1945: Pres. Franklin Delano Roosevelt suffers stroke and dies at Warm Springs, Georgia at age 63. Harry S. Truman becomes president of U.S.

May 7, 1945: Germany surrenders. Hitler commits suicide.

July 16, 1945: First atomic bomb produced at Los Alamos, New Mexico. Exploded near Alamogordo, New Mexico, without announcement.

August 6, 1945: Atomic bomb dropped on Hiroshima.

August 9, 1945: Atomic bomb dropped on Nagasaki.

August 14, 1945: Japan surrendered. (Katy and I were at Camp Atterbury, Indiana and had dinner in downtown Indianapolis that evening.)

September 2, 1945: Formal surrender was signed on board the battleship *Missouri* in Tokyo harbor.

September 8, 1945: U.S. forces enter Korea south of 38th parallel displacing Japanese.

September 9, 1945: Gen. Douglas MacArthur takes over post-war supervision of Japan.

Surviving Severely Injured Soldiers

Getting back to the hospital and our injured soldiers, there was a tremendous number of destructive injuries of all parts of the body among our injured men. More than in any previous war. The better understanding of shock and better methods of treatment, fluid and blood replacement, the development of vascular repair and the control of coagulation to allow successful vascular repair, add up to saving many more lives and extremities. Among those saved are many who in previous wars would have died or would have had extremities amputated. Stacks of amputated extremities outside operating tents did not occur in World War II as in previous wars. Lives and extremities were saved but many had severe associated injury to bones, joints, nerves, tendons and other structures that needed repair.

In regard to blood vessel repair, let us first consider the work of Alexis Carrel, M.D. with animals.

Blood Vessel Repair and Anastomosis in Animals

Alexis Carrel, M.D. (1873–1944)

In 1902 Dr. Alexis Carrel began his work on vascular repair in his native France shortly after graduation from medical school at the University of Lyon. He was stimulated to do this by the assassination of Sadi Carnot, president of France in 1894 (Edwards, 8). This French leader bled to death from a stab wound of his *vena cava,* which doctors at that time were not able to control. This inability impressed young Carrel, who took up the problem shortly after graduation from the University of Lyon.

In limited space there, Carrel was able to carry out experiments on animals and produce successful vascular anastomoses in dogs. He became proficient in avoiding hemorrhage and thrombosis at the site of union. On publication, his results quickly attracted wide attention. He needed more room to work. Adequate facilities were not made available to him at his Alma Mater, where promotion was on the basis of seniority.

In 1904 he migrated to Montreal in the French Province of Canada, where his native tongue was spoken. Word of his work, it is said, had preceded him there. On making rounds at the Royal Victoria Hospital, a patient with vascular injury was shown and he was told that a young man in Lyon was recommending vascular repair to which he replied, "That man is me." He was looking for a place to work and went next to Calgary, then San Francisco and finally to the University of Chicago, where he was given laboratory space at the Hull Physiological Laboratory. He worked there with a physiologist, Dr. Charles Guthrie. Both increased their skill in carrying out various types of animal blood vessel procedures.

Dr. Carrel wrote extensively about his results and on November 9, 1911 gave a report before the Clinical Congress of Surgeons of North America at Philadelphia. In this presentation he stated that his method of vascular anastomosis was developed during the previous nine years from the studies of Payr and Murphy. The causes of complications were studied and procedures devised to prevent stenosis, hemorrhage and thrombosis. He described his techniques and instruments to be used. Rigid asepsis was considered essential. Thrombosis was pointed out as following injury to the vessel wall, particularly the *intima.* He advocated that

192

vessels be handled with the fingers only and not crushed with instruments. "If a forceps be used, it must take between its jaws nothing but the external sheath," he said. Temporary hemostasis was obtained by smooth-jawed, spring Crile clamps and elastic straps with special care not to injure the endothelium, which he reverted to bring it together atraumatically. Tissues were kept moist with Ringers solution. Very fine silk sutures were sterilized in vaseline and kept coated with it, as were the operator's fingers to "prevent" soilage by fibrin ferment." Triangulation sutures were used and the fine suturing carried out with segments of the wall under tension to prevent stenosis. He had carried out all sorts of anastomoses between vessels, transplanting veins to take the place of arteries. He showed a photo of a small white dog, alive and apparently healthy two years after a section of its thoracic aorta was rejoined by a vein graft that had been preserved in cold storage before use. He stated that his technique could be safely applied to human procedures when it was carried out with perfection. He stated that his procedures could be applied to humans but he did not attempt that himself.

Carrel's fame continued to spread and in 1906 he was invited to Johns Hopkins by Dr. Harvey Cushing, who was impressed with his work and was about to provide space for him at Hopkins. Also at that time the Rockefeller Foundation in New York City was in the process of recruiting staff and he was offered a position there under the directorship of Dr. Simon Flexnor. He accepted. It proved to be an ideal setup in which he could work without economic worry. Additional procedures carried out.

Organ Transplantation

When blood vessel repair and reanastomosis became a reality, the road was opened for the transplantation of whole organs. It was thought by many people that it would also be necessary to reunite the vasomotor nerves of the transplanted organ before it would carry out its normal secretory functions. Carrel carried out a transplantation of a kidney from one cat to another in 1913 and observed that the organ secreted urine soon after. The organ from another animal worked fine for a number of days, then failed. Later this was shown to be due to rejection. He then worked with closely related animals with more success.

Organ Perfusion

This work was carried out with Dr. Charles Lindbergh in the 1930s. The fabrication of a workable perfusion pump was difficult with glass being the material with which to work, but the task was accomplished. Later, better ones were fabricated by other workers, with plastic, when it became available, instead of glass. With this technique organs could be kept alive for days by perfusing proper oxygenated nutrient materials through them.

Cell Culture

The growth of cells in tissue culture outside the body was a most amazing thing. Improving on a technique used by Ross Harrison of Hopkins, Carrel succeeded in 1933 by adding chick embryo extract to the culture cells for long periods of time. The periodic addition of the extract, along with proper nutrient materials and changing the fluid frequently to remove waste products, made it possible to keep cells alive in culture for indefinite periods. A culture of chick heart muscle cells was kept alive for 38 years. During the latter part of this time the culture was kept at the Lederle Laboratory after Dr. Carrel's retirement.

Carrel-Dakin Solution

During World War I serious gas gangrene infections were occurring in the wounds of French and American soldiers injured in the battle field. Dr. Carrel, then in the French army, set up an experimental field laboratory at Compieng Sp. With the aid of Dr. Flexnor at the Rockefeller Institute, Carrell obtained the cooperation of Dr. Henry Dakin, an excellent chemist. Dr. Dakin tested innumerable chemicals to find a material that would inhibit the growth of bacteria without injuring the tissues and finally came up with a hypochlorite solution, which, when irrigated into the wound, gave off chlorine, which was later used to purify water. This material and the irrigation technique with which it was applied actually worked and many soldiers' lives were saved. It was used after the war and was still in use in the 1930s when I first came onto the surgical scene. There were objections to it when it was first introduced, as usual, but it was proven to be of much benefit and served a long lifetime until replaced by the advent of antibiotics in the 1940s after World War II.

Man the Unknown

Man the Unknown is a very concentrated, mostly philosophical treatise written by Dr. Carrel between 1933 and 1935 in French, when he had become sixty years of age, after twenty-eight years at the Rockefeller Institute in New York City. His blood vessel work had brought him a Nobel Prize. Organ transplantation, organ perfusion, tissue culture and development of a very useful method of wound treatment by means of Carrel-Dakin solution had brought him much recognition and acclaim.

Dr. Simon Flexnor, director of Rockefeller Institute had been a guiding influence on Dr. Carrel. When he was preparing for retirement in 1935, he encouraged Carrel to put his thoughts on paper. He himself would reach the sixty-five year mark in 1938, but when that happened he expressed surprise when the rule applied to him also. For this, he was sometimes called "The spoiled child of the Rockefeller Institute." Due to the influence of Dr. Flexnor and other friends he proceeded with his writing.

When the book was published it was a tremendous success. It had fifty-five printings and was translated into eighteen languages. Being a scientist, Carrel was especially impressed with the material benefits that man had derived from science: * the development of power and machinery to do heavy work in industry and to carry people rapidly from place to place by rail, car and plane; the work-saving machines in the home to limit drudgery there; instant means of communication by telephone, telegraph and radio. Television was still on the horizon to be introduced shortly after World War II.

These were all material benefits or comforts that Carrel thought were softening us as a society and making us ignore our spiritual needs. He thought society needed strengthening of its moral fiber. He admired strength in individuals and thought we were protecting and preserving the weak. He wrote that discipline gives strength to men. The only way to obviate the disastrous predominance of the weak is to develop the

---

*He uses the term "man" throughout. From the context in which he uses it, I think he means "human individual."

strong. Promote growth of the fit. "Single out children who are endowed with high potential and develop them as much as possible."

In 1931 he had received from the German Ambassador to the United States the Nordhoff-Jung Prize for "improvement in methods of tissue culture elucidating fundamental questions regarding malignancy" (Edwards, 106). He was a loyal Frenchman but had admiration for fascist strength of purpose. Hitler had recently risen to power but he intimated that problems were deeper. He wrote that there was . . . "High development of the sciences of inanimate matter and an ignorance of life. Modern society had been built at random according to chance of discovery and to the fancy of ideologists without regard to the laws of our body and soul." This reference may have been to Hitler. It also probably referred to life in modern cities with the crowding, noise and air pollution there. He quoted Francis Bacon, "In order to be commanded, nature must be obeyed."

He wrote there was a glowing contrast between material progress and social disorder of the day. He thought civilization was tottering in spite of all its advances, that man was about to destroy himself unless changes were made. "Democratic ideology itself unless changed has no more chance of survival than the fascist or marxist ideologies." He expressed some doubt in the powers of science in only one regard, in that it dealt with the forces of intelligence. He thought that intelligence alone did not drive people to action like fear, hatred, enthusiasm, self-sacrifice or love. (If knowledge does not necessarily drive people to action, is it not more likely than ignorance to do so?)

Carrel thought that more profound knowledge was required to penetrate the mysteries of the mind since its functions were not quantified like those of other organs. He brought up the fact that we were built to survive on struggle.

Carrel is said to have had great loyalty for his native country, France, but was worried that the material developments of science were having an ill effect in making life too comfortable "at the expense of man's physiological development." In this regard his thinking may have been misinterpreted as agreeing with totalitarian ideas. He returned to France and attempted to again carry out studies helpful to the armed services in World War II, as he had in World War I. (The development of Carrel-Dakins solution for the treatment of infected war wounds.) Some reports were made in the media, but never proven, that he cooperated with the German occupying rulers. These accusations of collaboration with the occupational government are probably false (Malinin, 207; Edwards, 107).

Carrel gave opinions on many controversial things, like the place each of the two sexes and euthanasia, in addition to expressing his concern over the state of civilization for which he recommended the scientific method to gain answers to the problems. "Science brings a tottering civilization, for the first time in the history of the world, the power to renovate itself."

He was concerned that the upper third of the population was reproducing much less rapidly than the lower third. He was concerned about the number of criminals in the population and the expense of housing them, which is even more acute today. He suggested that possible ways of replacing prisons could be found by scientific study.

Carrel was interested in clairvoyance and telepathy and other metaphysical phenomena calling for more study and noted the work of my brother-in-law, Dr. J. B. Rhine in Durham, North Carolina. He expressed the opinion that miracles were rare but that they did occur.

He looked upon *The Science of Man* as a task force of the future to find answers to these questions. He called for superscience with multiple Aristotles, which are hard to find. In the late seventies, shortly before his death, J. B. Rhine funded a Foundation for Research on the Nature of Man in Durham, now directed by daughter Sally Rhine Hendrickson and son Robert Rhine. This was probably a response to the call of Dr. Carrel. Carrel's vascular work was all carried out before the advent of anticoagulation, which now gives added assurance of success especially in very small vessels. He died in Paris in 1944 at the age of seventy-one years. His many accomplishments during his active thirty-two years at the Rockefeller Institute are summarized here:

1. Perfection of a technique for blood vessel repair and anastomosis on dogs.
2. Organ transplantation.
3. Organ perfusion with Charles Lindbergh.
4. Cell culture in vitro (outside the body).
5. Carrel-Dakin solution for the treatment of war wounds in World War I (in cooperation with the French Government).
6. Experimental reversal of circulation in the extremities and necks of animals in an effort to improve the vascular supply of ischemic tissues. He showed that in animals, it could be done.

7. Writing a philosophical treatise, *Man the Unknown*, 1933–35—a call for broad scientific study of "man," including the mind.

Carrel was given the Nobel Prize in Medicine and Physiology in 1912 for his work on vascular repair in animals. However, his techniques were not employed by him or other surgeons of his day on human beings.

Repair of Vascular Injuries in Man

It is interesting to recall developments that eventually led to the successful treatment of vascular injuries in man. The control of hemorrhage had been a problem since the beginning of surgery and, for centuries, thinking was traditionally channeled along the lines of control rather than repair of blood vessels. What was responsible for the late realization that vascular structures could be repaired and, when repaired, would reconstitute themselves?

Progress depends upon bringing newly known bits of knowledge, new facts, together. It involves fitting new knowledge together, which is a slow process. There is confusion at the frontier of knowledge until enough facts are known to allow logical action. Where there is teaching against a procedure, the process is slowed even more. A pioneer is a person who takes the initiative, at some risk, to show that a thing can be done when enough knowledge, facts, have accumulated. A thing is never done until someone thinks it can be accomplished and tries it or, by chance, happens upon it.

The traditional attitude toward hemorrhage, since the beginning of surgery, was control of bleeding, ligation, rather than repair of vessels. Taking an operation from an experimental animal to a human being is a big step. Dr. Carrel, himself, did not take it. It may be said that he did not have clinical training. In the first decade of the twentieth century, surgical training in vascular surgery did not exist. No one was proficient in it. Operating on a human being electively to carry out an unproven procedure was and is unacceptable. The total responsibility for survival is on the shoulders of the surgeon, who is subject to criticism and even castigation in case of failure.

When dealing with trauma, the situation is somewhat different. The surgeon in this situation enters the scene after the patient has been seriously injured. His efforts for the injured patient are to prevent an untoward outcome from a process that is already under way. The entire burden of initiating the entire event is not his alone. This is one reason why many surgical advances have been made in treatment by taking care of the injured, especially in time of war.

In the case of the human heart the first successful dramatic surgical procedures were for the repair of stab wounds of the ventricles. Dr. Claude Beck did many of these in his early career. Elective procedures followed when valuable experience had been gained from treating traumatic wounds. The need for development of special equipment, proper restoration of fluid loss, correction and maintenance of electrolyte balance, anesthesia, prevention and treatment of sepsis and many other aspects of the problem are needed.

The practice of controlling hemorrhage by vessel ligation with no attempt at vascular repair persisted. The will to carry out vascular anastomosis was not in surgeons' minds. They did not think it would work. Vascular repair did become a clinical reality until the latter part of World War II and thereafter. In the case of the small vessels of the hand it was thought that thrombosis would certainly occur. It was not until the midsixties that it succeeded clinically, when antithrombotic agents were available.

Returning to the work of Dr. Claude Beck, his experimental work on adhesive pericarditis in the laboratory led to excision of the pericardium in humans suffering from restricted cardiac function following constricting pericarditis. This work later gave him the idea of bringing more blood supply into the ischemic heart muscle in humans by producing adhesions between the omentum brought up through the diaphragm and wrapped about the surgically scarified heart. Dr. Beck demonstrated new arterial connections to the myocardium after this procedure which was referred to as the Beck-I operation. At that time direct vascular anastomosis had been carried out by Alexis Carrel in larger blood vessels in dogs in 1902. With the 20/20 vision of hindsight, it is interesting to speculate why Carrel and why Claude Beck did not attempt direct vascular anastomosis in humans. He had a bird in his hand with the new vessels he had demonstrated from the omental grafts and chose to proceed on that line. He had to have been aware of Dr. Carrel's success in animals because that was widely known. Why did he not change to direct anastomosis? At that time, before anticoagulation, thrombosis of vessels the size of the coronary arteries led most certainly to thrombosis. His grafting method obviated that. For the larger vessels, I think I have alluded to the reasons why Dr. Carrel himself did not proceed with human application.

Benefit of Controlled Stress

Our bodies are made to respond favorably to stress as long as it is not too great. The necessity of challenge and some stress is necessary to keep

200

the tissues of our body healthy. This is well recognized for muscular development in athletes. It is actually true for all organs of our body. They all respond to stress; demand builds them up. But stress should be applied gradually so there is time for the tissue to respond. Actually, the converse is true. If we do not use an organ it loses its ability to respond. A patient required to spend a week in bed is fully aware of the extreme loss of strength that occurs. This is true of all living things. It may well be a factor in evolution not yet proven. Things do happen teleologically in our bodies. In philosophy this was thought not true; the teaching was that things did not happen because a necessity existed. Physiologically, in living tissues, it is true. My college professor is now long gone and I cannot tell him. Possibly he found it out for himself. When we exercise, our muscles become stronger.

Conversely, when we put a patient to bed for a long interval, the bones lose calcium and become soft and muscles atrophic; they become weaker. This was learned with wounded men in World War II and led to development of methods of avoiding prolonged bed rest, which had been the method of aligning bones by traction in bed.

It was carried further with early ambulation following abdominal surgery. In the treatment of wounded upper extremities and hands, immobilization was recognized as a calculated risk, avoided whenever possible and shortened as much as possible. A well-healed, stiff hand was and is a disabled hand. A good example of response to demand is the response of our tissues to a wound that divides our skin and structures below. The cells adjacent at the wound edges supplemented by cells from our blood stream multiply until they join with those of the opposite side to produce healing, a marvelous thing, all automatic, in response to demand. The force that causes this to happen, like the force that causes two cells to unite and form a new living being, is nearest to the ultimate in life, in my opinion. If this were worshiped, it could make a universal creed based on fact. This could obviate holy wars between creeds and do away with ethnic differences. The forces that make our bodies respond to demand, the greatest forces of all, are silent. When divided, cells that have lost their regenerative ability heal with connective scar tissue, which is usually the next best thing, but undesirable in highly mobile structures such as the hand.

201

Anticoagulation

Howell reported the discovery of heparin in 1918 (Howell, 328). He showed it would prevent the coagulation of blood. This was derived from beef lung and was purified in 1934. In 1937, nearly twenty years after Howell's discovery, Gordon Murray in Toronto used heparin experimentally and showed that its intravenous injection prolonged clotting time and prevented the thrombosis of injured veins in animals. This was a lag of nineteen years.

At University Hospitals, Cleveland, Dr. Fred Mautz was sent to Toronto in 1938 to learn Dr. Murray's methods. He returned from that trip with a supply of heparin, which was used successfully on patients at Lakeside Hospital, Cleveland.

A second report on the use of heparin by Murray appeared in the Archives of Surgery in 1940 and further verified his findings. He reported the successful use of heparin to prevent thrombosis following vascular repair of brachial and popliteal arteries in patients as well as its use following embolectomy. He also reported benefit in thrombophlebitis and pulmonary embolism. Following vascular repair, he advocated continuation of intravenous heparin to keep the clotting time elevated for ten to fourteen days post-operatively.

Coumarin, another anticoagulant drug, was next isolated from partially spoiled sweet clover. It could be given by mouth and was cheaper. This substance was found effective in animals and humans by Allen, Barker and Waugh. This gave a second anticoagulant drug available to prevent post-operative clotting. The stage was set for the advancement that followed in the latter years of World War II and after. As well as the many other advancements in medicine and surgery, it combined to save more lives of injured soldiers than in any other previous war.

Crile General Army Hospital, Parma, Ohio

With our return to Cleveland, I reported to Crile General Army Hospital, Parma, Ohio and was assigned to the Orthopedic Service. It had just opened a few weeks earlier in temporary wooden quarters, but was already swamped with cases.

Hand Surgery

A few months after my arrival at Crile General Hospital, I received word from Col. Claude Beck, director of the Fifth Service Command. He offered me a position in a newly forming branch of surgery, hand surgery, which was being formed in nine army hand centers in the United States. This carried with it an advancement in rank to Lieutenant Colonel and placed restrictions on my leaving the service before the cessation of hostilities. I accepted the offer. I had been a captain for three years, was a major one day, then given the rank of Lieutenant Colonel. The latter made up for some of the former delay, which had been a downside of the unit for the previous three years.

In World War II, due to the many advances in medical care, and especially vascular surgery, a larger percentage of severely wounded men were kept alive and their limbs not amputated than in previous wars. Vascular repair had been developed and was a limb saver, as well as a life saver. Many of the saved extremities had limited function from their injuries. When these men were returned to the zone of the interior, it was obvious that efforts were necessary to give them back hand functions so that they could be self-sufficient. Their life had been saved but it was still necessary to restore hand functions to give them back the ability to earn a living. Nine hand centers were set up in the zone of the interior of 1945 in the United States due to the efforts of Elliot Cutler and others in the military service. Dr. Sterling Bunnell of San Francisco, who had published a book on *Surgery of the Hand* in 1944 was made civilian consultant.

Wakeman General Hospital

I was sent to Wakeman General Hospital, Camp Atterbury, Indiana where I worked under a very fine person, Maj. Lot Howard for six weeks. Dr. Howard had been resident under and worked with Dr. Sterling Bunnell in San Francisco. He was in charge of a very large and busy hand service treating all kinds of extensive upper-extremity injuries. The service at Wakeman was under Col. Truman Blocker, a hard-working plastic surgeon. We were able to find a small apartment and Katy brought Jane down so that we were able to be together. It was a pleasant, productive experience.

The survivors of severe injuries to the upper extremity required extensive and specific treatments to regain strength and movement required for useful function of their hands. These were new requirements regarding war casualties that Surgeon General Kirk, and medical leaders including Gen. Elliott Cutler, then in Europe, and many others recognized. The surgeon general implemented action to supply the necessary facilities to carry out these procedures.

Special Features of the Hand

The hand is a strong, highly sensitive dexterous organ, the most mobile portion of our skeletal anatomy. Its normal function depends upon active movement of its small sensitive parts. This movement is provided by small muscles within the hand itself, augmented by large muscles in the forearm that give it great strength in addition to its great dexterity. The force of these large muscles is transmitted to the hand by means of tendons, which glide freely to transmit the force. This arrangement is an ingenious way of keeping the bulk of the hand small and yet providing great strength.

A very important feature of the many necessary fine joints of the hand is that they readily stiffen when immobilized. Ways needed to be developed to prevent this by recognizing joint immobilization as a calculated risk of disabling stiffening and keeping it at a minimum. Supervised movement was started at the earliest possible time. In addition to movement and strength, the exquisite sensation of the hand needed to be preserved and restored if the nerves were divided. All methods of nerve repair and grafting were carried out.

Use of the existing specialties in 1945, as they then existed, were not proper for the treatment of the extensively injured upper extremities that were being returned from the war zone with multiple severe injuries involving multiple systems. Regional specialization was needed with better understanding of wound healing, scar tissue minimization and replacement with healthy tissue where indicated. A bone graft could not be done in one department, allowed to heal, and then tendon and nerve work later performed in another department. In order to maintain proper movement, the structures packed together in the forearm and hand needed to be repaired at one time as much as possible by a surgeon capable in all these areas and mobility emphasized during the recovery period. This

204

was soon being greatly aided by special trained therapists who became experts in their field.

The procedures carried out in 1945:

Skin
Accurate gentle approximation of wounds
Fine sutures
Free grafting where necessary to hasten healing
Transfer of full thickness skin and deeper tissues by pedicle flap as required

Tendons
Special gentle repair
Nonreactive suture material
Early protected motion
Special dynamic (elastic) splinting

Nerves
Early accurate repair under magnification
Protective splinting with supervised movement
Nerve grafting

Bones
Accurate alignment
Free use of internal fixation to allow early motion
Grafting where necessary

Joints
Accurate repair of ligamentous injury
Special protective limited splinting, early passive motion
Replacement came a little later

Paralysis
Tendon transfers as indicated

Postoperative Care
Frequent observation
Limited joint and tendon immobilization
Early supervised movement

On return to Cleveland, the situation at Crile General Hospital was quite confused. The man in charge was greatly overworked. The chief of surgery gave me half of the service and later complimented me for my work. The final army report however, not written by him, left my name off the list. This worked to my detriment. According to Lot Howard I should have been included as a founding member of the American Society of Surgery of the Hand. If my credentials had been properly recorded, this probably would have happened. Instead I was elected a member in 1952. The important thing in the end was that the war was over and I had survived.

While working at Crile General in 1945 an ad appeared in the local paper regarding a house in Middleburg Heights, not far from the hospital. The owner, a returned Flying Tiger who had fought in China, offered a new house for rent to a returned veteran. We answered this ad and obtained the small new home where we lived for about eight months until he found a buyer for it.

The Death of Father

On June 7, 1945, six months after my return, while operating at Crile General Hospital, word came that Father had been in a serious automobile accident and had been admitted to the Barberton Citizens Hospital about thirty-five miles south. I left as soon as possible and within an hour was there. My sisters were surprised at my quick arrival. Father was in shock and breathing his last. Intravenous fluids were being given but that was all. He had been riding as a right-seat passenger in a pickup truck that was struck broadside from the right. Six-year-old nephew John Weckesser, who was riding between Father and Eldon Cleckner, the driver, was uninjured. Father had taken the brunt of the impact of the car coming from the right, at high speed. Death occurred just a few minutes after my arrival probably due to serious internal injury. He was unconscious and I could not rule out head injury in my quick examination. A decision had been made at the hospital that his injuries were fatal and I was unable to dispute it in the few minutes that elapsed. It was a serious blow to me. I had to accept it in spite of all my surgical training and experience, which was of no value in saving the life of my own father. He was buried a few days later in an oak coffin, next to Mother, who had preceded him in death by nearly twenty-five years. The burial was in the family plot at the south side of St. Michael's Cemetery. I had no idea that his death would be such a blow. It affected me for weeks after but life had to go on and it did. Katy and my family were a great comfort.

When our benefactor, the owner of the new little home in Middleburg Heights, found a buyer for his house, we were obliged to move. It had been a great help during all the uncertainties of returning after three years of war separation and coming back to different and changed conditions. After our return from Camp Atterbury in the late summer of 1945, through a friend, Dr. Richard Dickenson, we learned of a house in Cleveland Heights that was available to rent. This house was in an estate. Dr. Dickenson had taken care of the previous owner, a Mr. Allen, before his demise. Through the attorney, Mr. Ted Pratt, we were able to rent this fine old home and move to 2041 Goodnor Road in the late summer of 1945. We lived there about a year, during which time I finally wound up my army career, returned to civilian life and the practice of surgery at University Hospitals. Our second daughter, Betsy, was born there in February, 1946. In the early fall of that year, when Betsy was about six months old, we bought our first home at 2970 Coleridge Road. We were able to do this with a five thousand dollar down payment under the so called "G.I. Bill" which backed our purchase. It was a great feeling to own our first home.

Fourth General Hospital to Philippines—Final Transition

The personnel of the Fourth General Hospital finally began to be individually rotated back to the United States in the last months of 1944, as already told, after nearly three years of overseas service.

Col. William C. McCally returned early in 1945, at which time Col. Donald M. Glover became commanding officer and remained so until the end of service.

The Fourth General Hospital continued to operate at Finschaffen, New Guinea until departing there August 4, 1945, aboard the *USS Barnstable* en route to Manila, where it arrived on August 12. The atomic bombs were dropped on Hiroshima and Nagasaki on August 6 and 9 during that voyage, which made the Fourth General's intended use no longer necessary. The Japanese surrender occurred August 14 with the formal signing of documents on the battleship *Missouri* on September 2, 1945. This made further overseas service no longer necessary. Colonel Glover wrote in his final report, "There can be no doubt that long overseas service such as this—which is actually the longest overseas service recorded for any hospital since the beginning of the war—places an undue physical and mental burden on the personnel involved."

The Fourth General Hospital formed from the Lakeside Unit of World War II and the 56th General Hospital at Camp Jackson, South Carolina, January 12, 1942. Like an old soldier, it faded away into the 51st General Hospital in Manila, Philippine Islands, October 20, 1945.

The Hospital Unit Idea

Keeping people with special training together to perform special tasks is an efficient way to get things done, especially in the short term. An infusion of first-class talent is always desirable and helpful beyond denial. The use of highly trained specialty groups, like special teams in football, serve their purpose well. This is the unit idea. However, it can be wasteful of talent if prolonged. Each well-trained individual's capability for teaching and training others should also be utilized if the greatest benefit is to be realized. Weak points to be guarded against in the unit idea are unwise concentration of talent and lack of advancement for those involved.

Overall, the Unit worked well in World War II and much good was accomplished. For protracted assignments, judgement is necessary regarding interchange of personnel and reasonable advancement in rank.

Separation from the Army

In September 1946, I was separated from the army and Dr. Lenhart took me back on the staff at Lakeside Hospital with my office on the fifth floor. My practice was general surgery with emphasis on surgery of the hand. It was very good to get back.

Events of 1946

April 1 400,000 mine workers strike for higher wages.

April 11 A bill providing for government monopoly of atomic energy activities passed by Senate committee

July 1 Atomic bomb test held at Bikini Atoll.

July 4 Philippine Islands given independence from U.S.

July 30 U.S. joined UNESCO (United Nations Educational, Scientific and Cultural Organization)

August 1 The Atomic Energy Commission is created.

December 14 A gift of eight and a half million dollars donated by John D. Rockefeller, Jr. accepted by United Nations for purchase of property for permanent home of United Nations Headquarters.

December 31 State of hostilities was officially ended by President Truman but the states of emergency proclaimed by President Roosevelt during the war were not rescinded.

Our Second Lovely Daughter, Elizabeth Ann Weckesser

Our second daughter was born at MacDonald House, the Maternity Hospital of University Hospitals, Cleveland, February 20, 1946. She was a lovely baby delivered after a short labor to the delight of her mother and myself. We were living in a rented house on Goodnor Road, Cleveland

210

Heights. In November 1946 we would buy and move into our first home of our own at 2970 Coleridge Road.

Post–World War II Adjustments

In 1946, as the euphoria of the World War II's end wore off, there were many accumulated problems and readjustments being made in the country. Returning servicemen had to find their places back in civilian life and get reacquainted with their families. Workers on the home front had not been permitted to strike during the war. President Roosevelt had gotten no-strike pledges from the unions until the shooting was over. They now demanded higher wages, led by John L. Lewis and Walter Reuther. Their demands came in succession, auto workers, steel workers, miners and then the railroad unions. President Truman met their demands firmly, setting the pace with his straightforward, "The buck stops here" approach.

To settle a railroad strike that would have crippled the country, he signed an order in which the government seized the railroads on May 17, 1946. This broke the strike and alienated the unions. However, in 1948 he was reelected president of the United States in spite of his action.

A severe housing shortage was present throughout the country in 1946. This was accompanied by an office space shortage, which was present even at University Hospitals. There was a shortage of office space for returning doctors at Lakeside Hospital as well as living quarters in the community. Dr. Beck had to use a card table in a waiting room on the fifth floor for a short time.

Spiraling inflation became a problem when the OPA (Office of Price Administration) became inactive. Someone asked President Truman, "What about inflation, Harry?" He retorted, "I've got my eye on it." He undoubtedly did, but it became severe.

Buying a new car in 1946 was quite an experience since the auto industry had been committed to defense and needed time to switch back. New cars were just not available. After waiting about four months Katy and I were glad to take delivery on a new Chevy Sedan without bumpers. These had to be added later when they were available. We were very glad to get the new bumper-less car, which ran great. You just had to be careful not to hit anything front or back.

211

The Cold War, 1945—89

One of the most serious developments, following World War II was the worsening of relations between the West and the Soviet Union, as mentioned previously. A Negative Peace, an armed superpower stand-off between West and East, particularly between the United States and the Soviet Union, developed in regard to the Atomic Bomb and the danger of a nuclear holocaust from which there would be no winners. The world faced the danger of the most devastating conflict in history.

This so-called Cold War lasted forty-four years following World War II. The basic differences in the two forms of government, democracy and totalitarianism, were at stake. Each side had a passionate belief in its own type of government (Sharnik, 22) and mistrusted the other. The West thought that, from the actions and statements of its leaders, that the Soviet Union was bent on world domination. The seriousness of this mistrust was augmented by the threat of nuclear war, a threat that had never previously existed—the devastating destruction of a nuclear holocaust. In 1945, the United States alone had the bomb that it had used to end the war with Japan. In 1949 the Soviets exploded an atomic bomb of their own. This earlier than expected capability caused President Truman to order the National Security Council into action. It found sabotage by a technician at Los Alamos, the information being transmitted through Julius and Ethel Rosenberg in New York (Sharnik, 59).

There were now two great opposing powers; each would soon have the awesome atomic bomb and time would bring more. The effect was very sobering in all nations of the world and the intensity of the cold war increased. The finding of sabotage in a strategic place, which led to development of the atomic bomb by our competitive great power, frightened many people and had many effects. It was considered by many that this foreign power was intent on world domination. Sen. Joseph McCarthy carried the idea of finding seditious Communists in the government to an extreme. It became an emotional thing similar to the witch hunting of colonial days. The term McCarthyism came into being to indicate this. The basic different philosophies between free and Communist countries on methods of government for the conquered nations became very acute after the hostilities of World War II ceased. The Yalta agreement stated that these nations should choose their new leadership by popular vote of the people. This was not acceptable to Stalin, the Russian leader, who favored dictatorship. In 1946 the United States was the only country with the atomic bomb. Oppenheimer's plan to control atomic armaments was turned down flatly by Soviet Foreign Minister Andrei Gromyko.

Winston Churchill made a speech in Fulton, Missouri on March 5, 1946 in which he paraphrased the newly formed Communist governments in eastern Europe as an "Iron Curtain" across Europe. Stalin was not pleased.

The Russian Army had been the first to enter Berlin while the Americans had taken Leipzig and Dresden (Sharnik, 132). The Soviets were very interested in Berlin since the Nazis had invaded their country and caused much death and destruction there during the World War II conflict. This was an area of great difficulty. Finally, Berlin was divided into East and West sections. Cooperation between the Soviets and the Allies ground nearly to a halt with no provision for ground access to the Western sector, West Berlin. This lead to the "Berlin Air Lift" starting June 24, 1948 and lasting nearly a year. All supplies from the west were flown in during that period.

In March, 1947 President Truman announced what became known as The Truman Doctrine; "Support free people who are resisting subjugation by armed minorities or outside forces." With his leadership Congress appropriated aid to Greece and Turkey. The need in the other war-torn countries of Europe was extremely great. The people needed help. Aid was next organized under President Truman's leadership into what became known as the Marshall Plan, in honor of Gen. George Marshall, then secretary of state. On June 5, 1947 Congress appropriated twelve billion dollars to be distributed for this purpose over the succeeding four years.

In 1961 conditions in Berlin were a very sore point for the Russian leaders. The difference between free enterprise (market economy) and communism, with its remote, centrally planned economy, was obvious. Under the central planners, all sorts of tractors, cameras and numerous other items were being produced and stockpiled in warehouses, many of which became outmoded while in the warehouse. In the free market side of the city, things were being manufactured according to demand of customers. Models were changing rapidly as demands changed. The central planners were slow to change and dropped behind. My friends and my brother-in-law who traveled there said the difference between the two parts of the city was extreme. This of course was obvious to the people of East Berlin and they were leaving in droves to enter West Berlin where things were prospering.

The Berlin Wall Up

In order to stop this loss of citizens to prosperous West Berlin, the East Berlin government placed a physical barrier to pen the people in. The Berlin Wall was built August 13, 1961 for this purpose. The city was divided into two parts, the free west and the east behind the iron curtain. The free section prospered. People were rewarded for their work and ingenuity. And the east lagged behind. This condition persisted until the wall came down November 9, 1989.

Cuban Missile Crisis, October 1962

After the failure of the Bay of Pigs invasion of Cuba on April 17th 1961, President Kennedy knew that Krushchev and Castro were still cooperating. In August of 1962 there was evidence of increased activity in Cuba. On October 16, 1962 he was shown photographs of missile site construction there, less than one hundred miles from our shore. On October 22, 1962 he spoke to the American people on television telling them that these were offensive missile sites and that because further ships were en route from Russia, he had ordered a blockade. "All ships of any kind bound for Cuba from whatever nation or port will, if found to contain cargoes of offensive weapons, be turned back (Degregorio, 557). Things were extremely tense. Everyone waited expectantly. Katy and I were on the way to a medical meeting in Virginia and we listened to the announcements, which came every few minutes on our car radio during the trip. Negotiations between Khrushchev and Kennedy were under way. The vessels heading for Cuba suddenly stopped short of their destination. An agreement had been reached. Khrushchev would remove the missiles from Cuba if Kennedy would remove missiles from Greece and Turkey. President Kennedy accepted. He was a better negotiator than his predecessor. The tense crisis was over.

The unexpected changes in the Soviet Union leading to the end of the Cold War were a surprise to everyone, including our leaders. When the Soviet leader, Gorbachev, came to power in 1985 and became friendly, the first reaction was suspicion that it may be a trap to throw the West off guard. After all, they had shot down a South Korean airliner on September 1, 1983. It had strayed into Soviet airspace so they killed the crew and all 269 passengers, including Rep. Lawrence McDonald of

Georgia. Soviet medium-range missiles were being aimed at Western Europe and America from the Soviet Union (DeGregorio, 657). Pershing and Cruise missiles were being deployed with NATO in Eastern Europe to counteract this build up. President Reagan who, on the basis of these things and previous experience, considered the Soviet Union an evil empire, was not quick to change his mind.

What he did not realize, or at least what he could not be sure of was that the Soviet Union was in deep trouble economically on the basis of an inefficient and ineffectively planned economy, demonstrated by the austerity in East Berlin. Mikhail Gorbachev, the number two man of the Communist Party, had recognized the inadequacies of the planned economy of his country and seriously tried to change it in preparation for growth in the twenty-first century. When he came into power upon the death of Konstantin Chernenko in March 1985 Chernenko banners were quickly removed from public places (Beschloss and Talbot, 7). Gorbachev was facing the horrendous task of making the internal changes and convincing leaders to join him in changing the closed communist economy into a free one that could compete with the West.

Gorbachev's meeting on arms control with President Reagan in Iceland in October, 1986 produced little. Distrust was still great on both sides. The stumbling block was on-site inspections of missile sites, which is another way of saying mistrust. Gorbachev said that Reagan came empty handed. Suspicion was great on the American side.

When Pres. George Bush came into office, his advisors were also cautious about the Soviet Union. Also, Gorbachev had not demonstrated his stability as a Soviet leader. No American president had ever had to deal with a foreign leader who had less secure power in his own country. However, President Bush said in his inaugural address, "The day of the dictator is over, the totalitarian era is passing. We know what works: Freedom works. To secure a more just and prosperous life for man on earth through free markets, free speech, free elections and exercise of free will unhampered by state" (Beschloss and Talbot, 17). This was a great statement to which he might have added: Among people of good will with judgment to also work for the common good of their country which allows them the benefits of their labors.

Bush gradually developed a more secure feeling about Gorbachev after private meetings with him and consultation with other foreign leaders, especially Margaret Thatcher, "The Iron Lady of Capitalism." She urged him to proceed with the new Soviet leader saying, "You can do

business with him.'' Secretary of State James Baker and Edward Shevard-
nadze, his Soviet counterpart, were extremely helpful in working out
difficult details, especially with the transition to the second Soviet leader,
Boris Yeltsin. Glasnost was a new openness and official honesty between
the two countries that led to a partnership instead of just a Negative
Peace, Cold War, to avoid a nuclear holocaust. On November 9, 1989
East German citizens were allowed to leave East Berlin. The Berlin Wall
came down. At the Malta Conference, one month later, the fate of the
Baltic States was determined favorably for the West. The two leaders got
along well at this meeting. Bush indicated his acceptance of Gorbachev's
wishes for perestroika telling him that the world would be a better place
with it.

Perestroika

Perestroika, what is it? Gorbachev, in his book by that title, describes
perestroika as a restructuring, a complete overhaul of Socialism, as practiced in the Soviet countries. The book is written for the folks at home
as well as abroad. It was brought about by a study of the Central Committee Plenary Meeting March 1985, which also elected Gorbachev general
secretary. In his book, he states that the Soviet Union is living through
a dramatic period and has formulated this policy of restructuring to accel-
erate the country's social and economic progress, renewing all phases of
life. He speaks of a loss of enthusiasm among Soviet people, a lack of
receptivity to advances in science and technology and a lack of efficiency
in using scientific achievements. He thinks his people should regain a
spirit of purpose and work an extra bit harder. They should be aware of
what is being accomplished in socialism, ''From each according to his
ability and to each according to his work.'' With people protected from
the vicissitudes of life there should be no dishonest exploitation of the
advantages of socialism. The new direction for socialism is democratization in all aspects of society.

The change that has begun cannot be turned back. He states that he
does not agree with the Western idea that it is brought about by the sad
state of the Soviet economy, probably speaking to his own people, but
calls for economic progress with an eye to the twenty-first century. There
is no disenchantment with Socialism, he says, but speaks of dissatisfaction with how things have been going in recent years. In the mid-sevent-
ies, economic failures were more frequent and elements of stagnation

appeared with a slowing of economic growth. He states that Socialism has been under utilized on the seventieth anniversary of the revolution. After pointing out the advantages of socialism in providing security and jobs for all, Gorbachev states he is attempting, through the restructuring, to incorporate democratic principles to increase and replace lost enthusiasm.

The USSR is working for peace and cooperation in the world. "The world is one whole, one ship, Earth," he states. World range dialogue is needed. He wishes to cooperate sincerely and honestly for world peace by limitation of arms and weapons of mass destruction and avoidance of a spiraling arms race.

He states that they do not like certain aspects of American politics and way of life but respect the right of the United States as well as others to live according to their rules, laws and customs.

Gorbachev states, "We need democratization in all aspects of society. Perestroika can come only through democracy (Gorbachev, 32). He speaks to his own people quoting Lenin as saying: "Socialism and Democracy are indivisible. Socialism is capable of change. The changes undertaken require tremendous effort which can be achieved with perestroika and the openness and honesty of glasnost."

It is hoped that we in America can adopt some of the desirable things of socialism in a way that does not stifle initiative. Individual initiative has been the great driving force of our free society which has made it great. Freedom, completely unstructured and selfish with no thought for the group as a whole, can be destructive. We must guard against this. The continued success of a free society depends upon judgement being exercised by each member not to encroach on the rights of others. The welfare of the entire group must be remembered by each individual.

The changes set in motion in the Soviet Union by Gorbachev in 1985 aided by President Bush and his deputies in the United States and his consultation with the leaders of other free countries, had succeeded in ending the forty-four year 'Cold War' between the Soviet Union and the West. Bush said it best in his speech accepting his candidacy for a second term in August 1992, "Germany is united, the Soviet Union can be found only in history books. The captive nations of Eastern Europe and the Baltics are captive no more. The Cold War is over and Freedom finished first!" In spite of this, by a queer stroke of fate, he was not reelected. His first term, with all his negotiations abroad had taken much out of him, not leaving time for economic problems on the home front. He, like Winston Churchill in Britain after World War II, was turned aside by the voters when the emergency was over.

The Necessity for Governments

People living together in large groups very much need a government to carry out those functions affecting their group as a whole. The consequences of the absence of such a government has been demonstrated by the situations in Somalia and Bosnia. An overall government is necessary to maintain law and order, administer justice, provide safety, protection, general welfare and a host of other things, possibly health care or some aspects of it as is presently being considered. No form of government is perfect for everyone. We have witnessed the serious consequences of lack of effective government, anarchy, in Somalia this past year and seen the suffering starvation and death that has resulted. Each form of government has strong points and weaknesses.

Our country was founded by a strong vigorous independent people who took care of themselves and expected little from their government regarding their own personal life. Over time this has changed to include social welfare. This has carried with it a dependence on government for services that motivated people can provide for themselves. Help for the needy is necessary but should be provided with incentive to restore self-sufficiency. Steps are being taken in that direction.

Democracy, with its elected leadership, providing self-ruling has overall given a good account of itself during the past two hundred years in the United States. It has not been perfect, but it stacks up well with other forms of government. The widespread popularity of democracy among the peoples of the world speaks highly of it. One of its greatest, if not its greatest, attribute is the ability to change and to meet changing conditions being brought about by the governed. This requires an interested, altruistic and informed populace, interested in the country as a whole, constantly on guard against abuse and infraction.

Free enterprise has created prosperity by rewarding individual initiative, ingenuity, study, hard work and ability, which has been inspiring to others throughout the world. It allows for the accumulation of wealth, which has led to a very high standard of living. Levels of income in some

218

instances have gotten out of proportion to the value of the service provided. Selfishness and greed are factors to be guarded against. In contrast to this, like it or not, in China in the 1960s, among some of the young doctors there, it was interesting to see a reticence to attach their own names to a new method of microscopic blood vessel anastomosis in which they were involved. They gave the name of their province instead of their own names, which I thought was interesting. Their social upbringing had taught them to think of their province above their own name. We probably should ponder that. Statesmanship and patriotism are necessary to defend and keep a nation strong.

On the lower end of the scale, social responsibility must come into play for those down and out who need help. We must care for the less fortunate by providing help for them to get back on their own feet.

Planned economy has not fared well during the past seventy-six years in the Soviet Union. An eclectic selection could be good for both of our countries. I once heard Armand Hammer state "Socialism works when mixed with a certain amount of Capitalism." He cited Hungary as an example.

A Jewish Homeland

In 1947 a movement started to make a Jewish homeland in the Middle East, the biblical ancestral home of the Jews then occupied by an Arab majority who also claimed the territory. This movement was known as Zionism, named after a hill in Jerusalem. On May 14, 1948 David Ben-Gurion was proclaimed head of an independent state called Israel. Britain has been the administrator of this territory in the name of "The League of Nations" since World War I (Sharnik, 40).

Conflict between Israel and the Muslims and the Syrians continues today.

Chinese Civil War, 1945–49

When the Japanese were conquered at the end of World War II, civil war broke out in China between communist Mao Tse-tung and, nationalist Chiang Kai-shek, for leadership there. Chiang gained the backing of the

United States, but it was not enough. The communists under Mao persisted under severe hardship and finally won out proclaiming victory in September, 1949. Chiang Kai-shek was forced to retreat to the offshore island of Formosa, subsequently renamed Taiwan, which became a center for free enterprise, manufacturing and international trade, similar to Japan and South Korea. The Soviets and Communist China cooperated closely after 1949 until 1964. There was then an open break and they each went their independent ways. A boundary dispute was a part of the trouble between China and Russia, but this break, according to a Chinese friend of mine, was due to *hegemony,* a word not often used in the West. Its meaning, as used there, is influence, dominance or leadership. China, the longest continuous civilization in the world and the largest today, is noted for its independent way of looking at things and doing things. It is not easily influenced by outsiders.

Korean War, 1950–53

At the close of World War II in 1945, peace keeping American troops were retained in free South Korea south of the 38th parallel. North of the 38th parallel was Communist North Korea, allied with Communist China. In 1949 U.S. forces were withdrawn. On July 1, 1950 North Korea invaded South Korea. President Truman called General MacArthur to the aid of South Korea with the limited forces available, which were not adequate to stop the advance. After a two-month buildup General MacArthur made a strategic landing behind enemy lines and drove the North Korean army to the Yalu River, the southern border of China. He wanted to go beyond from a military standpoint but this was Chinese territory. It was a very delicate situation, and President Truman did not want to start World War III with China. After a conference on Wake Island with the general, which did not settle differences, President Truman finally exercised his power as commander-in-chief, firing the venerated General April 11, 1951 (Sharnik, 72). This was startling, not only for the general but for all of us at home. MacArthur came home a hero and spoke before Congress finishing with his famous statement, ''Old soldiers never die, they just fade away.''

The situation stabilized, the armies stayed in position and finally an Armistice was signed in July 1953 under Eisenhower's administration making the 38th parallel the dividing line between the two Koreas. The

Korean War had lasted three years at the cost of 35,000 American lives (Sharnik, 87).

The Vietnam War, 1964–73 (Nine Years)

In the fall of 1953 communist guerilla activities were also occurring in Vietnam, a French protectorate south of China. Things went from bad to worse and the French Garrison at Dien Bien Phu fell May 7, 1954. How Americans continued to be involved after the fall of the French Garrison at Dien Bien Phu is not completely clear. There was a general feeling at home among certain groups, that communism was on a road of expansion and world domination and needed to be stopped. President Eisenhower was of this opinion. Others were of the opinion that this was a civil war in Vietnam and that we should stay out when the French Garrison fell, especially after our recent bad experience in Korea.

Public opinion at home was very much divided and remained so, especially among young people of draft age. The antiwar movement among college students became very great leading to the burning of draft cards and even American flags. Wars are based on emotion, and need to be, in order to gain the proper cooperation and sacrifice that is required to win. This one did not have a clear-cut objective. Some young people left the country to avoid the draft. In spite of all these things, President Johnson, probably considering many factors that we do not know, continued to support the war effort in Vietnam. Our losses mounted. The Vietnam War continued to drag on through the rest of the Johnson administration and the first term of the Nixon administration. However, President Nixon, through Secretary Kissinger, had succeeded in opening the door to China, a very significant thing for which he deserves much credit. Americans were invited to a table tennis match in the summer of 1971. In February 1972, President Nixon himself visited Mao and Chou En-lai in Beijing. One week after President Nixon's second inauguration, on January 27, 1973 in Paris, France, Secretary Kissinger and Le Duc Tho signed a document ending the nine-year Vietnam War. It had cost 58,000 American lives and 2,000 missing in action (Sharnik, 237).

The Armistice for the Korean War had occurred July 27, 1953 under President Eisenhower during his first year in office. Let us now return to the events of his administration.

The Russian Sputnik, October 7, 1957

On October 7, 1957 Russia launched "The first artificial Earth Satellite," known as *Sputnik*, which circled the globe at 18,000 miles an hour every 96 minutes (Sharnik, 102). Our space program reacted vigorously as most Americans reacted with shock to realize that our competitors were ahead of us in space technology. Our first satellite was launched January 31, 1958, and our Mercury astronaut program announced a year later. On September 15, 1959, the First Secretary of the Communist Party Khrushchev, arrived in the United States and, on the invitation of President Eisenhower, made a coast-to-coast tour of our country. (Stalin had died in 1953.) There was friction; things were not good on this tour. At one point Khrushchev through a translator made the statement, "We shall bury you," which shocked the country. This may have been just a boast meaning that communism would outlast capitalism (Sharnik, 116), but Americans did not take it that way. After this awkward visit a summit meeting was arranged for Paris. Approximately two weeks before the summit meeting set for May 16, 1960, a United States U-2 reconnaissance plane was embarrassingly shot down over Russian territory. Ike defended the flight without apology at the conference (Sharnik, 119) and the conference broke up. Ike's invitation to Russia was cancelled. Khrushchev denounced the U.S. and its leaders and signed an agreement with East Germany regarding Berlin (Sharnik, 119). Four months later Khrushchev attended a United Nations session in New York City following which he courted Fidel Castro in Cuba (more below).

John F. Kennedy was inaugurated January 20, 1961. He was briefed on plans for an invasion of Cuba to occur April 17 of that year less than three months following his inauguration. Cuban exiles were to invade and make a bridge head on the beach. It turned out to be a case of changing horses in mid-stream for the young new president. He was the new rider who hardly had his feet wet. The exiles did what was planned for them but follow-up reinforcements were not properly arranged and the project became a fiasco. The Bay of Pigs invasion was a failure. Perhaps he relied too heavily on the planning of others. He was new and unfamiliar with all the circumstances and all the people he was dealing with. Coordination was not properly arranged.

Following the Russian *Sputnik* flight in October 1957, the U.S. stepped up its space program. In the early sixties we were preparing to put a man in space. In April 1961 a Russian by the name of Gagarin beat us to it. Alan Shepard was the first American to make a brief flight into space soon after the Gagarin flight and, in February 1962, our John Glenn circled the globe three times. A space program to put a man on the moon was inaugurated by President Kennedy. This would come to fruition with the flight of *Apollo 11* July 20, 1969, six months into the Nixon administration when Neil Armstrong became the first man to step onto the surface of the moon with the world watching by television. His historic words were, ''One small step for man, one giant leap for mankind.'' The United States had gone ahead in space.

Chest Surgery

The development of chest surgery depended upon many things including:

1. Relief of pain.
2. The understanding and control of infection.
3. The necessity to preserve respiratory exchange when normal respiratory function is interrupted with the chest open.
4. Understanding of the necessity for fluid replacement and the control of shock.
5. The training of competent personnel.

Ether had been used but not reported by Crawford W. Long in 1842 and demonstrated at the Massachusetts General Hospital by William Thomas Morton in 1846 by the inhalations of what turned out to be sulfuric ether (Garrison, 505). Following these observations by William Morton, Crawford Long and others on ether in the 1840s, the development of anesthesia for pain relief was on its way.

Antisepsis, Asepsis
Eighty Years before Antibiotics

Joseph Lister's paper in 1865, "On the Antiseptic Principle in the Practice of Surgery" (Garrison, 590) led to the next step forward regarding wound infection. Joseph Lister, a young man in Edinburgh, Scotland, had graduated in medicine from the University of London thirteen years earlier. He had become intensely interested in putrefaction and suppuration, influenced by the work of Pasteur on the fermentation of wine. Lister's father, a wine merchant in London, may have called his son's attention to Pasteur's work.

Lister's epochal paper was published the same year the bloody American War between the States terminated, the year Pres. Abraham Lincoln was assassinated. Lister's work with carbolic acid to control the growth of germs in surgical wounds was epochal, the forerunner of aseptic surgery, which made possible elective surgery on our peritoneal and pleural cavities as well as all delicate structures of our body. The cells of our body are able to make many corrections spontaneously. Surgery

224

comes into play to help nature when situations get out of hand, when the cells of our body need help.

Lister's work showed that:

1. Suppuration in surgical and traumatic wounds resulted from the growth of microscopic organisms introduced from without.
2. These organisms could be controlled by carbolic acid according to his method.

As is usual with new ideas, his work was received with skepticism but his antiseptic methods were sound and gradually became accepted and expanded to asepsis (avoidance of the introduction of organisms).

With some understanding of suppuration, a large barrier to the surgical entrance of the peritoneal and pleural cavities of the body was removed. Surgery of the peritoneal cavity for the treatment of diseases of the abdominal organs came soon after but that of the pleural cavity lagged behind. The physiology of respiration had not been worked out. It was not understood how respiration could be continued when the chest was open. Sauerbruch in 1903 developed an elaborate negative pressure chamber in which the body of the patient was within, head outside. Willy Meyer developed a positive-negative pressure apparatus (Blades, 164) but both were cumbersome. Chest surgery then mainly consisted of the treatment of conditions of the chest wall and *empyema,* where the lung and pleura were sealed by adhesions. Then came World War I, in which wounded men had large open chest wounds which were treated by sealing the chest wall, when this was possible, and using sealed pleural drainage. The demands of war were a stimulus to further development of chest surgery during World War I, which became intensified in the following years.

Positive Pressure Breathing

Positive pressure breathing somehow received a bad name around the turn of the century. It was said to be injurious to the alveoli. Presumably the pressures used were too great. In 1918, Bevan, one of the leading surgeons of that era, said, "Endotracheal anesthesia has little place in practical surgery" (Blades, 165). This held back advancement for years; even in my era in the 1930s, when endotracheal tubes became available,

225

this idea persisted. Because of these objections the thoracic cavity had no particular attraction for surgeons until the development of safe positive pressure breathing with endotracheal tubes in the mid-thirties (Blades, 163). Required anesthetic techniques were developed. Radiographic improvements for better diagnosis were also an important stimulus to advancement.

After World War I the treatment of tuberculosis by collapse therapy and by thoracoplasty gave further experience in operating on the chest. This experience led to development of techniques applicable to other conditions. In 1933 Evarts Graham performed the first successful pneumonectomy for cancer of the lung. The patient was alive and well twenty-two years later. With maintenance of respiratory function with the pleural cavity open, by positive pressure anesthesia, the path was opened for surgery on all organs within the chest cavity. From here on developments were more rapid.

The training of personnel to carry out the new procedures that became possible was progressive in centers throughout the country. By this time it was no longer necessary to go abroad for advanced surgical training.

Cardiac Surgery

Cardiac surgery, referred to as the last frontier of surgery by Claude S. Beck in the 1930s, had a very slow beginning. With this powerful organ the physiology of the circulatory system had to be well understood with fluid and blood replacement available in quantity. The first successful procedures were emergency procedures for stab wounds of the *myocardium* (heart muscle). In this circumstance the surgeon is not responsible for the original wound, which takes some weight from his shoulders. Rehn recorded success with a patient under these circumstances in 1907 (Blades, 164). In 1923–24 four cases of mitral stenosis were operated upon electively by Elliott Cutler and Claude Beck at the Peter Bent Brigham Hospital in Boston just before Cutler came to Cleveland as professor of surgery at Western Reserve University in 1924. Approach was made by inserting a small knife, later a valvulotome, through the left ventricular wall after exposure of the heart through a median sternotomy incision. The sternotomy avoided opening the pleural cavity. Ventilating mechanisms for the lungs with the chest open had not been developed.

Mautz at Reserve made a good one in 1938. Souttar of London reported successful finger fracture of a stenotic mitral valve in 1925 (Blades, 172).

Revascularization of the Myocardium

Revascularization of the myocardium was undertaken by Claude Beck in the early thirties. He had been working with pericardial adhesions, which restricted the function of the heart pump by limiting its activity. He noted brisk blood supply between the restricting pericardium and the myocardium, heart muscle, when removing the thickened pericardium. Recognizing these adhesions as an added source of blood supply to the myocardium, he decided to make adhesions with a soft pliable organ, omentum, brought up from the abdomen to surround the heart with its blood supply intact. He proceeded to utilize this technique with success in patients with cardiac ischemia (diminished blood supply) after heart attacks.

He was, in all probability, aware of Alexis Carrel's work with blood vessel anastomosis. Carrel had presented his work at Hopkins in 1906 at the invitation of Harvey Cushing. It is probable that Beck through coronary vessels were too small to remain potent after vascular repair. This was before the advent of heparin and other anticoagulants that were developed in the late thirties. He developed two procedures to make adhesions between the myocardium and the omentum and demonstrated vessels crossing from omentum to myocardium by injection techniques.

Direct blood vessel anastomosis with anticoagulation, however, eclipsed his long and determined efforts in the 1960s. He devised two operations using omentum, which he wrapped about the heart after scarification, which would probably still be used if direct anastomosis had not been successful.

Retrospect speculation with its 20/20 hindsight vision makes one wonder why Dr. Beck, in his search for methods of increasing blood supply to the myocardium, did not go to direct anastomosis. He knew of Alexis Carrel's successful use of direct anastomosis for larger vessels on dogs. Conventional thinking before the advent of anticoagulation was that small vessels would thrombose. Furthermore, he had made the observation himself, dissecting off adherent pericardium during his operations for "constricting pericarditis," that very brisk bleeding occurred from the myocardium and showed that vessels had crossed over to the myocardium from the pericardium. This was his observation and he worked hard to perfect it by wrapping the heart with omentum and showed that this procedure brought new vessels to the myocardium.

When a researcher is intensely occupied with a project, it is possible to overlook an alternative method. In fact, his primary interest may make him particularly vulnerable to this type of error. An example of this occurred in 1892 when Thomas Edison was working with direct current and making all sorts of marvelous observations about it. Simultaneously, generators were being installed at Niagara Falls, New York to harness the tremendous energy of the Falls. Transmission of this current to Buffalo, New York some twenty miles away required several booster stations for direct current transmission. Edison, acting as the consultant, held up the project for some time, insisting that direct current be used until straightened out by George Westinghouse. Tesla had introduced alternating current, which could be converted to high voltage and transmitted without significant loss, the method in use today.

Events of 1947*
Harry S Truman

It is the second year after the end of World War II. President Truman has been in office two years. Many post-war adjustments are still taking place. The miners' strike of 1946 is settled with a large wage hike for the workers.

General George Marshall becomes Secretary of State. Truman asks Congress to approve aid to Greece and Turkey to avoid the spread of Communism. This was granted in May. This doctrine, supporting free people to make their own choice, becomes known as the Truman Doctrine.

The Cold War between the communist countries, especially Russia, and the democracies is intensifying. The Pacific Islands, formerly under Japanese control, are placed under U.S. Trusteeship by the United Nations Security Council. The United States ceases mediation in the Chinese Civil War. Mao, the communist leader, appears to be gaining on Chiang Kai-shek, who has been backed by the United States.

There are widespread telephone strikes.

Britain proposes partition of Palestine. Both Arabs and Jews object and the question goes to the United Nations. Both groups have claims to the territory and this dispute continues in 1997.

The Texas City Disaster

A freighter explodes in Texas City, Texas, killing 500 people. This terrific blast occurred when a shipload of nitrate fertilizer exploded. Water was used to quench a fire in the hold. The water is thought to have caused a chemical transformation of the fertilizer into an explosive nitrate compound. The role of the fire was primary.

A plan to help rebuild devastated Europe is launched which becomes known as The Marshall Plan. Three hundred billion dollars is allocated by Congress for the war-ravaged countries. Congress passes the Taft-Hartley "Employer's Rights" Act over Truman's veto.

---

*This chapter was done by memory, augmented by World Almanac, (522), Gordon and Gordon (257), and Carruth (558), and Daniel (739).

William Odum flies around the world in seventy-three hours. The Dow-Jones average fluctuates between 184 and 166. Unemployment is 3.9 percent. Admiral Byrd departs for South Pole.

Henry Ford dies.

Veterans are enrolling in colleges in record numbers under the "GI Bill of Rights." This helps returning soldiers greatly in making loans for education available to them. The Presidential Succession Act is signed by Truman designating the Speaker of the House and President of the Senate as next in succession.

New York City has its greatest snowfall in history, 25.8 inches. A severe hurricane from the Gulf of Mexico caused severe damage in Florida, Mississippi and Louisiana killing 100 people. Howard Hughes completed a huge plane with four engines on each wing called Spruce Goose, which was barely able to become airborne. For the first time the World Series baseball game was broadcast on television.

Third Beautiful Daughter, Nancy Carol

November 25, 1947, our third daughter, Nancy Carol Weckesser was born to us at University Hospitals to the great satisfaction of Katy and me. The home on Coleridge Road was still adequate and the growing family was happy there.

Two of my mother's sisters, Aunt May Long and Aunt Ruth Koeppen, with her husband Uncle Erwin Koeppen, visited us from Williamsville, near Buffalo, New York. They wanted to see a major league baseball game and we all went down to see the Cleveland Indians play at the stadium. It was a fun visit for all. Aunt Mary Long (also called Aunt May) became a little short of breath walking back to our car in the parking lot, which was some distance, but being very independent, would not let us help her or even stop to rest.

Television At Home

In the summer of 1947 when home television sets became available at reasonable prices, Katy and I invested in one made by General Electric. We were then living at 2970 Coleridge Road and the children were small. It was an immediate hit with the young people, who especially liked a children's program called Howdy Doody, which was good clean entertainment. The program became synonymous with television for them. They called it Howdy Doody Television. That old vacuum tube set is still in the basement.

The broadcasts for adults developed very rapidly. It also had great impact in the home, with graphic images supplementing the audio of radio. The television room in the home is now offered home movies and graphic news events that previously were only available in newspapers and at the cinema. The American family now had graphic news, entertainment, personal interviews with political leaders—all available in their own homes. New responsibilities were brought with these new additions to the home. Not all adult news is suitable for young children. With television the home was no longer isolated from the outside world. Interesting as this was for adults, the influences on children needed to be considered. Mothers especially had a greater burden in this regard. More judgement was required to determine what the child should see and hear at a particular age.

The media became king. A young nephew said to me, in partial jest, "Throw out the books and we'll all watch television!" This was a joke. Seriously, we still need the printed word that can be studied in detail to be sure of meaning. We still need the printed word to guide us in difficult tasks and give us understanding in complicated situations and for permanent records. It is easier to subjectively watch than think for ourselves but the latter is most important. Television's great advantage is in bringing more information to us so that more understanding can occur among people and better decisions can be made. The wide range and value of television, with proper supervision and controls, can be utilized without adversely affecting our children if it is kept under control as all good parents know.

Return to Civilian Life

1947 is my first full year back in civilian life after four and a half years of military service. I am getting my feet back on the ground back at University Hospitals after the long war hiatus. Office space is very scarce. Dr. Lenhart took me back as instructor in surgery in September, 1946. My rank rose to assistant professor 1949, clinical professor 1964, professor 1978 and emeritus professor 1983, then retirement. On my return in

1946, things were very crowded with all returning veterans. I shared an office on the fifth floor of the building. I was an attending surgeon, licensed to practice surgery by the state and, as such, legally responsible for what went on. I was assigned to ward supervision on the staff service, overseeing the residents there. That job is a one-to-one relationship with the resident, primarily, in addition to other duties. It is the responsibility of the attending surgeon on the General Surgery Service to double check what is happening with each patient. It's an interesting relationship in which the young person who has had several years of training is watched closely in the beginning to determine his judgement and ability and given more and more responsibility as he becomes proficient. It requires tact and judgement. The object is to help the young doctor as he or she needs help and then let the person go ahead on his or her own when capable. Each young person is different. We discuss each of the patients together and make decisions regarding the operative procedure indicated after diagnostic studies. He or she is supervised and yet the resident is allowed to proceed on his or her own as soon as capability is demonstrated. During ward rounds there is quizzing to find the resident's depth of knowledge and sometimes make suggestions as to reading material. With the rapid increase in new knowledge, it is very stimulating to discuss things with bright young minds who many times have fine ideas on the subject. It is frequently a learning experience for all involved and at the end of the service the resident becomes capable of proceeding on his or her own with confidence. The process as it progresses is similar to a father-son or-daughter relationship. At first you are wanted very much, in most instances, and then later you are wanted to go away, actually. It's a delicate balance, which you try to handle with tact, and usually works out fine, sometimes much easier than others.

Patient Care, Teaching, Research, and Publication

In addition to ward activities with the residents, in a teaching hospital, the visitant asks the resident to present cases at meetings where subjects are discussed in detail before groups of doctors. The duties of the visitant in a teaching hospital can be divided into three parts as follows:

1. Patient care of high quality.
2. Teaching as described above.
3. Research for new knowledge. Publication of results.

Research and Publication

For the clinician this type of endeavor can be of two types, publishing reports in medical journals giving experiences and results of actual patient treatment, or carrying out experimental laboratory work on animals to gain new knowledge.

Pneumo-Arthrograms

My first post-war paper was written with Dr. Wilbur McGaw and published in the *Journal of Bone and Joint Surgery* in July 1945. It involved work done in Melbourne when we were taking care of many soldiers with knee injuries. It involved injecting oxygen, later carbon dioxide, into the joint to visualize the small cartilaginous structures in the joint to see if they were torn or injured. This was a new procedure that we developed to help with diagnosis. The plain x-ray pictures of the knee did not outline the small cartilaginous structures. When the gas was injected into the joint, it made them stand out so that one could see when they were torn. It was very helpful.

War Amputations

The second paper was on the treatment of war amputations under field conditions when vascular repair was not possible. This was written in

New Guinea and published in *The American Journal of Surgery* in November 1945 after I returned to the States. It dealt with the great danger of serious infection at that time, especially under field conditions, and the desirability of leaving the wounds open for safe drainage until close post-operative observation was possible. It was prior to the introduction of antibiotics.

The third paper was on "Reconstruction of the Distal Portion of the Thumb" in June, 1948 early after my return to Lakeside Hospital. It described a method of rebuilding the end of an amputated thumb of a young man by means of bone grafting and the transfer of healthy tissue from the abdominal wall, which restored most of the thumb function though sensation in the pedicel tissue was reduced.

Intraabdominal Adhesions

I spent two afternoons a week in the dog laboratory carrying out experiments there in an effort to answer patient care problems. My subject of study in the beginning was the problem of unwanted adherence, growing together, of tissues in areas of the body where normally free gliding occurs. This was and still is a serious problem. It exists in the peritoneal and pleural cavities and about tendons that transmit force from muscles to joints some distance away when strength is needed in areas where there is no room for the bulk of muscles. The prime example of the latter is the upper extremity and particularly the hand.

Compound E, Cortisone

First, in regard to peritoneal adhesions, efforts were made toward intestinal adhesions in the peritoneal cavity following injury and infections such as appendicitis and diverticulitis. Normally the intestines glide freely over one another due to a delicate, fragile layer of flat cells that form their peritoneal surface covering, which is the lining layer of cells within in our abdomen. This layer is readily injured, which is followed by adherence during the healing process. The injured tissues grow together instead of staying separate as they were normally before injury. These adhesions can interfere with normal function and can lead to life-threatening intestinal obstruction. Methods were needed to avoid them and overcome them if possible. Prevention is always the best remedy and every precaution is needed during surgery to prevent injury. This teaching is emphasized to all the young people in training and is very effective during surgical procedures. However, accidental injury and infectious processes destroy peritoneal surfaces, producing adhesions and the surgeon is presented with the problem already present. While we were working on this problem, Compound E,—Cortisone,—became available. It slowed the healing process and we turned our attention and found some encouraging results.

Working with dogs, a standard injury was produced on the peritoneal surface of the small intestine in a number of animals. Half of these animals were given no special treatment. They were the controls. Their abdomens were closed and they were observed. The other half were given injections of Cortisone into the peritoneal cavity during the healing period. On re-operation several weeks later the degree and number of adhesions were compared in the two groups of animals. We found fewer adhesions in those animals that had Cortisone injections that began preoperatively and continued after operation, but no animals were completely free of adhesions. Local application to the wounded area was more effective but had limited application in patients. From a practical standpoint, the drug had some effect but was not of great benefit.

We were trying to prevent a very fundamental process, wound healing, which in this case was occurring between structures that normally have a smooth gliding peritoneal surface and move freely over one another. The healing process is the same throughout the body. Collagen is produced and draws the wounded tissue edges together producing scars. In most areas of the body this is a favorable thing, but not so in the case of gliding mechanisms such as those on the surfaces of intestines and tendons. Said differently, scars, although sometimes unsightly, do not seriously interfere with function usually except in those areas where tissues normally glide back and forth.

Heparin

We next took up the use of a new drug then, Heparin, to prevent the formation of clots that are involved in the early process of wound repair and scarring. This was effective but the danger of post-operative hemorrhage was a serious complication that limited its use.

If we could not prevent adhesions, perhaps we could control them so that the danger of intestinal obstruction was diminished and that took us to the next part of our study, plication of the small intestine—sewing it together in a uniform pattern so there were no bands about which the bowel could strangulate. This indeed was of benefit and we wrote several papers on that procedure as described below.

Plication of the Small Intestine

If adhesions among loops of intestines cannot be prevented, can they be controlled so that they present less hazard of intestinal obstruction? A doctor in Indianapolis, Dr. Noble, had presented this idea in a surgical journal. We next worked on this method in our animals and reported our results in the *Archives of Surgery*. The idea here was to sew the small intestine together at its base so that it was already adherent in a regular back and forth pattern from top to bottom so that it could not twist or loop into obstruction. We found that this method worked well in animals and also in human patients. This was a particularly good method to use in patients who had very severe adhesions over an extended area of bowel. The technique was named *Intestinal Plication.*

Functions of the Hand

First let us consider the tremendous functional capacity of this sensitive most mobile portion of our skeletal anatomy. I'll give a list and you can add to it. "This tool of the brain" was what Dr. Bunnell used to call it.

Grasp
Dexterous manipulation
Communication
Sensation, touch, cognition
Reassurance, The touch or clasp of a hand

Sensation of the Hand

Of all these important functions of which you are aware, I would give special consideration to sensation since it is no extremely valuable, so meaningful, and essential to normal function. Our fingertips are the eyes of our hands even for those of us who have vision. Our hands are such a special part of our body, yet we tend to take them for granted until something happens to one. Having cared for many people with injured hands and arms it makes me cringe to see a person driving an automobile with a hand out of the window. The individual is not thinking about possible injury. I'd like to remind him or her of the great risk involved.

The sense of touch in our fingertips is extremely acute. Test this yourself. Bend a paper clip open and then into a large U. Next press the two ends together so they are two millimeters apart. (If your ruler is in inches, make the distance 1/16th of an inch; that is approximately the same.) Also have the two arms of the U as near parallel as possible. Now place the two ends of the paper clip lightly against the tip of your index finger. Can you tell it is two? If not, broaden the ends just slightly until you can. Now place the two ends of the clip against the back of your hand. Is it still two or just one? For most of us it is the latter. Now with your eyes closed, test progressively from mid-palm out to your index fingertip once again and note at what location you first are sure you recognize the two ends. Now just for comparison test your lips and then last of all, the tip of your tongue!

What is going on here? We are testing two-point discrimination and it is by no means uniform over our entire body surface. In the hand , the fingertip is usually most sensitive. The lips are quite sensitive and the tongue also. Why do we not have the exquisite sensation of our fingertip all over our body? I do not know of course, but the required size of the brain could be a consideration. The supreme intelligence probably considered it unnecessary and actually gave us something better in that our senses, like muscle function and bone strength, become greater with use. Also we should always remember the converse, if we stop using a function of our body, it deteriorates. The saying is, ''If you don't use it, you lose it.'' This is a true admonition. We are wise to continue to exercise all parts of our body with moderation. If we have medical problems, the advice of our doctor is essential to prevent throwing more burden on any part of our body than it can tolerate. However, it is a truism that we should exercise to the limit of our tolerance to prevent deterioration of function, and this includes the brain. It is something well known that needs more emphasis. Medical consultation is not necessary if we are in good health but is mandatory before physical exercise if we are not. One should be on the safe side.

Prevention of Adhesions about Tendons

A great part of my life following World War II was given over to treatment and reconstruction of injured hands. Preventing adhesions about tendons after injury is best considered along with joint stiffness in the hand. The hand has a plethora of tendons subject to injury as well as a plethora of small joints that stiffen readily. Why does the hand have so many tendons? In order to supply strength with limited size for dexterity. The intrinsic muscles of the hand are small to prevent the organ from being too bulky. The large muscles of the forearm would take up too much space in the hand itself and are conveniently placed out of the way, so to speak, in the forearm, with their force transmitted by way of tendons that act as living cables applying strength to the wrist and joints of the fingers.

Since the hand carries out many things that the brain conceives, it tends to be where the action is and is frequently injured. The gliding surfaces of the tendons are very delicate and readily injured, similar to the gliding surfaces within the abdominal cavity. Healing in any part of the body is by production of collagen, which leads to scar tissue. In most areas of the body this works fine. The scar tissue contracts and the epithelium closes over the surface and all is usually fine in most parts of the body but frequently not the hand. Scarring prevents the to-and-fro motion of tendons and the movement of joints, two most important aspects of hand function.

We considered the possibility of placing an inert substance between the tendon and the surrounding sheath to prevent adhesions. The problem was to find an inert substance. In 1947 fibrin film became available. This was made from blood, which is normally accepted by the tissues of the body, and thin sheets of it were tried in animals. It was still reactive. We published our results in 1949. When blood coagulates, it no longer is an inert substance. The body treats the clotted blood as a foreign body. We found that out the hard way, by trial-and-error experiment.

Prevention of adhesions following tendon repair, as well as prevention of joint stiffness, received great attention by many bright minds throughout the country and abroad after World War II. Much progress was made and is still being made. The achievement of good function after flexor tendon repair is still a great challenge and requires special care and techniques by those versed in the field and even then success is not always forthcoming depending upon the extent of injury and many other factors.

In summary, present techniques include the following principles:

1. Early direct repair of tendons by an experienced operator.
2. Use of as near an atraumatic technique as possible.
3. The least reactive suture material possible.
4. Special strong gathering suture techniques to withstand early movement.
5. Special post-operative care starting next day:
   a. Protective splinting to reduce strain on repair.
   b. Assisted passive movement, preferably by a trained therapist, starting the day after operation to physically prevent the bridging of adhesions. Early active motion in a few days with the joints in relaxed position.

Joint Stiffness and Injections of Triamcinolone

Early movements postoperatively also act to prevent stiffening of joints, which is also extremely important. Work carried out in our lab showed that local injections of triamcinolone, a Cortisone derivative, into the tissues about the joint also diminished joint stiffening, especially when complete immobilization was necessary. This was also helpful in addition to early movement when the joint was not completely immobilized.

Patient Care

In addition to supervising care of patients on the ward service I saw private patients in my office on the fifth floor several afternoons a week. These consisted of patients with general surgical problems, abdomen and extremities as well as problems of the hand. I was soon very busy. It was wonderful to be back.

Events of 1948*
Harry S Truman President of U.S.

In China, the Communists gain on Chiang Kai-shek, who is being backed by the U.S.

---

*This section was done from memory augment by Gordon and Gordon (266), Wenborn (287), and Daniel (740).

239

Coal miners strike over pension rights.

Russia condemns Marshall Plan to help war-torn countries of Europe.

We apparently are helping too much!

Russia bans all allied land traffic to West Berlin.

The Berlin air-lift is instituted, which carries all supplies to West Berlin for one year.

The UN passes a Palestine Partition plan, creating Israel.

Egypt, Syria and Transjordan attack Israel.

U.S. recognizes Israel.

Chinese Communists declare Republic of North China.

Soviets close U.S. Consulates in Moscow and U.S. reciprocates.

Allies disagree with Soviets on handling post-war Germany, which is divided into East and West.

Tojo is hung for war crimes.

President Truman is elected to continue as president of the U.S. for four additional years, by defeating Thomas Dewey. It is a surprise upset.

The *Transistor,* a tiny clever, economical device, was developed in America. It very soon became a replacement for the fragile, cumbersome, costly vacuum tube in most electronic devices. This led to the development of tremendous numbers of miniaturized electronic things that no one had dreamed of previously. It made possible the age of automation. It allowed an electrical signal to be activated when a light beam was interrupted. From this type of activation, electrical currents could be made to do all sorts of things automatically in sequence.

Television was introduced to the public in 1947–48, just after the end of World War II, and rapidly became popular. It was an electronic development that had been predicted. In fact the last radio that we had purchased before World War II had a place to add it. Television viewing screens had required further development at that time but became available in 1948 in black and white and the new media with vision as well as audio rapidly became very popular. Color would follow in 1950.

Energy and Matter

Some simple definitions of energy and matter make a good beginning in an effort to increase our understanding of electricity and electronics, which have had such a tremendous impact on our lives. To demonstrate these two things let us think of children playing softball. The ball they play with is something that they see, feel, throw, catch and knock around. It is "matter." All solid objects are matter. They are motionless, stationery, unless acted upon by an outside force. Spontaneous intentional movement is usually a sign of life. An inanimate object does not move unless force or energy is applied to it in some way. Energy is the force that can move matter, or objects, from one place to another. The children move around, throw and knock the ball around by muscular contraction. Moving objects about is physical work, in this case play, requiring energy. Carrying a pail of water or a stack of books about is another example of actions which require and tire us out.

Matter's a broad term that includes all substances in our universe, all things that we can touch, see and feel which tend to remain the same, although some are much more stable than others.

Energy, on the other hand, which we hear so much about and pay for every month in our heating and electricity bills, is harder to describe because it is not visible. Only the effects of it can be seen and felt, but we are all familiar with it. Energy can also be thought of as a power, the force to get things done, to move matter around. Gasoline and electricity are common sources of energy. But in the children's ball game, the players run with vigor to control the ball and run the bases. This type of energy is due to muscular contraction, something that only living things have. In the evening after a hard day's work we are tired; our energy level is low. In the morning after a good night of rest we are invigorated and have much energy, especially when we are young. In physics, energy is considered the force necessary to move matter, or in other words, to do work. Electricity has been developed into one of our greatest work horses, and the control of electrons, electronics, has given us automation, one of the greatest boons of the twentieth century.

With the cracking of the atom in 1945, it was shown that matter and energy are related and that matter (uranium 235 in that case) was converted to the awesome energy of the atomic bomb. Knowledge of the relationship between matter and energy is not complete. It is still expanding.

Electricity—History

Lightning in the sky, associated with thunder storms, was looked upon with wonder and frequently with fear by human beings since very early times. To the Persians and many primitive people it was looked upon as an indication of divine wrath.

Benjamin Franklin

In the middle of the eighteenth century, 1752, Benjamin Franklin is supposed to have carried out, dangerously for his own safety, an experiment with a kite in the sky during a thunderstorm. He demonstrated, at risk to himself, that the flash in the dark clouds during a storm immediately preceding thunder, lightning, produced a spark between the kite line and a key that he held in his hand!

The historical observations related below have to do with electrical induction. This is the electrical disturbance that occurs in the vicinity of a flowing electrical current—the influence that an electrical current exerts on its surroundings when it flows through a wire, for an example. The recognition of electricity and its presence in lightning, as shown by Franklin, was an astounding observation. The recognition of this and its further understanding during the eighteenth and nineteenth centuries led to the development of the electrical generator, which converts mechanical energy to electricity and sends it to the electric motor, which converts electricity back to mechanical energy.

Electromagnetic Induction

Knowledge of electromagnetic waves and electrical induction, controlled by the laws of nature, was slow in developing. It was long known that plants and vegetation required sunlight for growth. It finally was recognized, when I was in college, that sunlight consisted of electromagnetic waves that bring light and energy from the sun and thus make life on Earth possible. Further discovery and understanding of electromagnetic waves has given us almost unlimited benefits. These include artificial light, radio, television, microwaves. X-rays, Gamma rays used for health purposes, radar giving vision through clouds, fog and even darkness, as well as many other conveniences still developing.

First, the significant observation by Luigi Galvani in 1786: While he was dissecting the leg of a frog in his laboratory at University of

Bologna, an associate was working nearby with a static electricity generator. A spark occurred between his scalpel and the sciatic nerve of the frog when the electric generator discharged a spark, causing the leg to jump. Since a spark was involved with the twitch of the leg, and lightning had been found to be due to sparks in the atmosphere, he decided to determine whether lightning would cause the same result. To test this idea, he hung freshly killed frog legs on a brass hook which he fastened to a wire fence just ahead of an approaching thunderstorm to see if they would twitch when the lightening flashed. Much to his amazement, the legs twitched violently whenever they came in contact with the fence. Not understanding what he had observed, he called it "Animal Electricity." This curiosity was recorded and went unexplained.

In 1820, Hans Christian Oersted, a Dane, while giving a demonstration before a class, noted that a compass needle, when placed parallel to a wire carrying an electrical current, turned perpendicular to it. This was evidence that a current flowing through a wire had lines of force about it. Thirteen years earlier he had placed a compass needle perpendicular to a similar wire and had noticed no change when the current was turned on but had not tried it parallel! The trial-and-error method is a slow process. How near a brilliant person can be to a significant observation without making it! In this case it took thirteen years.

Reason and theory can be helpful in this type of situation. Intent effort on another line of thought can sometimes be distracting. Fortunately for Oersted, he made the observation later by chance before his class but still did not recognize its significance. This observation showed that the passage of an electrical current through a conducting wire sets up a magnetic field, which runs in a circumferential way about the wire.

A year later, Andre Marie Ampere in France noted that two parallel wires carrying electrical currents had an effect on each other. If the currents of each traveled in the same direction, they were attracted, and if the current flowed in the opposite direction, repelled. The stage was set for making electromagnetic fields by means of electrical currents but no one had a way of producing sustained electrical current at this time. Incidentally, the use of the word current to describe electrical flow is interesting. Electricity was not understood and was thought to be some kind of liquid instead of a flow of electrons as we now know. Hence its flow then was likened to that of a stream of water, a current.

The Electric Generator and Motor

In 1830 Joseph Henry in America, and a year later Michael Faraday in London, each showed that moving a wire through a magnetic field produced a temporary electric current in it. This was the discovery that electromagnetic induction could produce electricity. The production of an electric current by mechanically passing coiled wires through a magnetic field that changed appropriately made possible the electric generator. *Mechanical energy from a waterfall or a steam engine could be converted to electricity* by this means.

Reversing the process, passing an electric current through a mechanism similar to that which had generated the current, turned the generator into an electric motor to do work.

With the use of induction, coils of wires spinning through a magnetic field in an electrical generator, mechanical energy could convert to electricity.

Love Canal

The plan of developer William Love at Niagara, New York, in the late 1880s was to use this idea for generating electricity near a new model city that he was developing about seven miles from the Niagara River. He planned to bring water from the river to the Niagara Escarpment just adjacent to his new city and have it turn generators for his Model City. This would have been fine except that alternating current was discovered by Tesla at about this same time. It was found that alternating current could be "transformed" to high voltage and transmitted at high voltage, through wires to remote sites, with very little loss, where the voltage could be lowered properly and used to run motors that worked at the new location. This is what made William Love's Canal at Model City, New York, obsolete in 1892, while it was still under construction.

His idea, before electrical transmission had been developed, was to divert water from the Niagara River to his new city, seven miles away and have the water fall over the Niagara Escarpment near his new city. Alternating current and the electrical transmission of energy was not known when he started but was found out before he finished. He also ran into more rock than expected during the excavation for the canal.

244

The enterprise was a failure in the 1890s and his abandoned canal was later used as a toxic waste dump, which became apparent in the 1960s.

Thomas Edison

Ninety-seven years after Galvani's observation, Thomas Edison, in 1883, while working with his electric light bulbs first noted that a second wire within a bulb, not connected to an electrical source, developed an independent electric current when current flowed through the light bulb filament. He recorded this and patented it but did not recognize its importance. It was known as the "Edison Effect," a curious thing (Asimov, 379). This and Galvani's, Ampere's, Henry's and Faraday's observations were instrumental in using induction in the development of the electrical generator and the electrical motor.

Electromagnetic Waves

In 1888 Heinrich Hertz observed that a spark across a gap in a wire attached to a wire coil made a second spark occur across a similar gap in a similar adjacent wire and wire coil when the two were not physically connected to each other (Asimov, 390). This was what had occurred in Galvani's laboratory 102 years earlier and in the second unattached wire in Edison's light bulb five years earlier. Hertz studied the phenomenon, found it repeatable and is given credit for the first recognition of manmade electromagnetic waves transmitting energy through space caused by the surging of electrons in the first coil. The energy of surging electrons in the first coil was transmitted between two wire coils, with no circuit connection between the two. The waves were found to be very similar to light waves, differing only in wave length and frequency. It was soon learned that the transmitting and receiving mechanisms were better if long strands of wire, antennae were used, that these could be placed far apart and that transmission of the signals was at the speed of light.

Electromagnetic waves transmitting energy in this manner had been postulated mathematically by the Englishman James Clark Maxwell in 1855–64 (Asimov, 348). He worked out mathematical equations regarding the lines of force in magnetic fields and about wires carrying electrical currents (Asimov, 277, 328, 390).

From a practical standpoint, these "man-made" waves constituted a whole new method of transmitting energy, electromagnetic energy. They were first and rightfully known as Hertzian waves but due to their radiant nature and the wide radius of their spread, the name radio waves was applied in the United States. In England they were known as wireless waves. That they needed no wire or other conductive substance through which to travel seemed amazing. However, it was soon realized that they were like light waves, which had been bringing energy from the Sun since the beginning of our universe.

Several decades were required to realize the full capabilities of these new "man-made" waves. Their first development for transmission of sound, music and voice in the teens of the twentieth century was so successful that the receivers themselves became popularly known as radios.

The following list includes some of the functions of electromagnetic waves today:

1. Energy, light waves from Sun to Earth, to which our eyes are sensitive, giving us vision.
2. Communication, wireless, radio, television after World War II.
3. Radar (RAdio-Detection-And-Ranging). Object detection beyond line of vision, in darkness, beyond clouds and fog.
4. Maser (Microwave-Amplification-by-Simulated-Emission-Radiation).
5. In medicine, diathermy, laser (Light-Amplification-by-electronic Simulated-Emission-Radiation), and other sophisticated equipment.
6. Physics and chemistry, astronomy, telescope, microscopy.
7. Cooking, microwave ovens.
8. Other.

It is interesting to consider the overall spectrum of electromagnetic waves on the basis of their wavelength and frequency to see where the various kinds fit it.

Much had to be learned before man could bring about the transmission of sound and visual images by electromagnetic waves. The list of important names in bringing this about is long including Hans Christian Orsted, James Clark Maxwell, Andre Marrie Ampere, Michael Faraday, William Sturgeon, Joseph Henry, Aleksandr Stepanovich Popov, Guglielmo Marconi, Edward-Eugene Branly, Oliver Joseph Lodge, Albert Wallace Hull and many others (Asimov, 65). Additional length of wire for the antenna was found to increase the intensity of transmitted signals and to aid in their reception. Later disk-shaped antennas were used to beam signals to a definite target.

Morse Code

Prior to Hertz's recognition and description of electromagnetic waves in 1888, Morse Code, dot-dash messages, had been transmitted electrically over wires since 1844. This involved sending an electrical impulse over a wire by pressing a telegraph key at the transmitting end which in turn caused a key at the other end of the line to click. The interval between successive key strokes varied. It was either short, a dot, or long, a dash. The Morse Code of dots and dashes (binary system) transmitted the letters of the alphabet to the other end of the line. In this (now considered) rather slow way, messages were transmitted from one station to the next electrically, which was much quicker than any other known method at that time.

Wire telegraphy was widely used for many years. The clattering of telegraph keys at any railroad station was mysterious and intriguing when I was a boy in the teens of the twentieth century. My older brother, Ethan, knew the Morse Code and could interpret the messages for us while we sat waiting for trains at the station.

The Telephone

Alexander Graham Bell transmitted speech over wires in 1876, by converting human voice into fluctuating electrical currents that waxed and waned similar to sound waves. These were converted back to sound at the other end of the line giving us the indispensable telephone that we all still depend upon today.

The Crystal Set Radio

One of the earliest radio receivers, when I was a boy in the early 1920s, was a "crystal set," which could actually receive messages by placing a small wire, a "cat whisker," on a special crystal connected to a receiving antenna. This method rectified, or converted, the signals to direct currents, which were then converted back to sounds in the earphones that we took turns wearing. The electric currents, surging electrons, in a transmitting antenna produced the electromagnetic waves that traveled to the receiving antenna, where they again set up electrical currents, which were then processed in our receiving set.

The crystals in the crystal sets were soon replaced by more sophisticated DeForest vacuum tubes, electron tubes, which were more reliable. The vacuum tube was a great improvement over the crystal of the crystal sets and led to the practical development of radio transmission. However, the vacuum tube was bulky, fragile, slow to start up and short lived; and it required much power. It had a heating element that necessarily warmed the cathode to make it function by sending out a stream of electrons. One had to wait to let the set "warm up" when it was first turned on.

The Transistor

In 1947–48 the transistor, an "electrical valve" to control the flow of electrons, was developed to replace the cumbersome, fragile vacuum tube. This used a small current to control a second larger current and had very wide application. It could convert an alternating current to a direct current as did the crystal in the crystal set. The two currents in the transistor are used in such a clever way that the resistor portion of the mechanism, which does not usually carry a current, is made to do so when the first current flows, hence the name "tran-sistor." The value of this electrical valvelike little marvel has been tremendous. It was brought into being by the work of Walter Brattain, John Bardeen, and William Shockley at Bell Laboratories in New Jersey. Interestingly, it is an improved version of crystalline molecular structure similar to the crystal of the crystal set. It is small, even tiny, solid and sturdy, needs no heating element and very little power, yet does the same thing as the vacuum tube. This tiny mechanism that allows a weak current to control and alter a larger current can transform the alternating current of a radio or television signal into direct currents, which can then be converted back to sound or light. It also can be made to make currents stronger, to amplify them when that is desired. Weak signals can be picked up and strengthened, if desired, before being sent onward or converted back to sound.

Tiny transistors have made possible all sorts of small electronic mechanisms that we have today. Unfortunately, the discovery was allowed to get out of the country for a time. The Japanese picked up the ball and ran with it, but hopefully we are now back in the race.

The Computers

Like an epidemic, computers have come upon the scene for recording, storing and transmitting information and have taken over almost all aspects of the field. what are these things and why are they so popular? We have a tendency to throw up our hands much as the scribing Monks must have done when the printing press was invented five hundred years ago. They do remarkable things and are not going to go away. They are here to stay. They are understandable. Read below. The monks made it and so shall we.

The computer by converting thought and data to electrical impulses, offers an advanced method of recording, combining and communicating that has as many advantages as the printing press over handwriting. We humans have been using our five senses to convey thoughts and ideas from one to another since our beginning. Now the computer gives us a new electrical, "electronic" method of doing it quickly, efficiently and compactly. Electrical impulses travel at the speed of light through conducting wires, or as electromagnetic waves through space similar to sunlight. Recorded electrical impulses are fragile but we recognize that and make back-up records. Also, we can make permanent records. We do not lose the security of the printed work. We still have that. We simply have the electrical impulses run our printers, which make permanent printed records for us. Since electrical impulses in our computers are readily erased and changed, the work of editing is greatly simplified.

Comparison of Typewriter and Computer

We have said earlier in the introduction that the computer has given us an electronic method of recording, storing, editing and rapidly transmitting ideas and data. For further understanding, let us compare the typewriter and the computer.

When the A key of a typewriter is pressed, a letter A is physically imprinted on paper as the A "key head" physically strikes the paper over an inked ribbon leaving its imprint. In this way the typewriter converts thoughts to printed letters, words and numbers on a paper page. The computer, on the other hand, does not do this. When we press the A key on a computer key board, positive electrical charges are made on two of eight tiny wires within most computers. (Positive and negative is also referred to as 1 and 0.) Two of the eight tiny wires are then positive and the other six are negative in an established sequence. This tiny "electronic" recording of A is a "byte" of information made up of eight infinitesimal "bits" each representing a positive of negative charge on the tiny wires referred to. The bit is the smallest unit of memory within the computer. The positive or negative charges are two different recordings, so the binary system is used instead of the decimal system. Each letter or number that we press on the keyboard charges and records the little wires in the computer in a different sequence of positive and negative, 1 or 0. The computer very cleverly stores these positive and negative charges in their important binary sequence at specified locations on a hard or floppy disk within the machine. They can be recalled to the display screen of the computer at will by pressing a certain key or combination of keys, or by clicking a mouse. When on the screen, editing, changing the information, can very readily be done and the next document then stored, printed or copied as desired.

These infinitesimally small electrical charges are stored in huge quantities in neat rows within the machine's memory so that they can be accurately recalled. The computer mechanism takes care of this for us. These bits and bytes of information can also be copied and stored on tapes and disks of many types outside the computer as well as on hard disks within it. The information, thus stored in meaningful sequence, is readily manipulated, moved about, corrected, edited within the machine or, being bits of electrical charge, transmitted at the speed of light about the earth and even into outer space.

When we want to see our stored information we bring it up on the computer screen where it is converted back to words that we can read or edit. When we want to print it we feed it into a special printer that mechanically converts it back to printed words on paper. The technique of widespread electronic methods of recording ideas and data with instantaneous manipulation and transmission has allowed unparalleled development, from which we have all benefitted.

As already mentioned, the electronic recordings are fragile and must be carefully protected to prevent loss. They are erased, such as by electromagnetic fields and extremes of temperature, and backup copies are constantly necessary. The idea of doing away with hard copies of documents presently carries hazard and is risky. A permanent record, printed word of contracts, agreements, bank balances and deposits, seems necessary to me as things now stand. In addition to loss, great care must be taken to ensure privacy, which now is at additional risk. With electronic messages being whisked about, there is more opportunity for clandestine interception. This must be kept in mind and safeguards used for privacy.

Thoughts, ideas, and solutions to problems can be combined in computers in very clever ways that are called macros. Complicated tasks can be joined together with this technique to greatly simplify them for future use. These can be recalled by pressing a designated key or sequence of keys, which is much more efficient than laboriously going through the whole thought process each time it is needed. The possibilities in this regard are almost unlimited. Computerized tomography in radiology is an example. The so called CAT scan for radiological diagnosis makes transverse cross sections of our body! These are a great aid in diagnosis. This valuable diagnostic procedure is not possible without special high capacity computers.

Transmission of a message, a printed letter, halfway around the world in less than a minute by facsimile (fax), is an amazing thing. I recently had occasion to talk to a botanist in Papua, New Guinea about getting some tropical nuts for seed to be planted in the large new atrium at University Hospitals, Cleveland. If the trees grew, they would make a nice memorial to commemorate the service of the Lakeside Unit II Fourth General Hospital, Army of the United States in New Guinea during World War II, 1944–45. In order to get requested information back to my New Guinea friend quickly, a letter was faxed back to him. It required fifty-nine seconds of telephone time for the entire page to be transmitted to him. It was 2:00 P.M. Friday my time and 4:00 A.M. Saturday his time when it was sent. I did not waken him. His fax machine should have printed it out in his office bothering no one. With fourteen hours difference in time and the international date line taking away one day, it should have been on his desk when he arrived at his office on Saturday morning, if he worked on that day. The telephone charge was for fifty-nine seconds to transmit a one-page letter halfway around the world. The speed of electricity is almost as quick as thought, sometimes faster. One wonders about other similarities between computer and brain function; knowledge which the future may bring.

First Computer

In 1944 IBM built its first Mark I electronic calculator at Harvard and in 1946 the Electronic Numerical Integrator And Calculator (ENIAC) was built at the University of Pennsylvania. Each was enormous weighing nearly thirty tons but could do 5000 calculations a second (Wenborn, 293). The great feature about these machines that made this possible was the ability to convert the data into electric charges as we have just discussed. The new-fangled things were ungainly in size but the tiny transistor changed that. The transistor carried out all the functions of a vacuum tube as we have already discussed. Now, with radio and television in the late twentieth century, small laptop and notebook computers are available but more fragile and harder to repair than desktop computers. Frequent backup copies on floppy disks are strongly advised.

Events of 1949*
Harry S. Truman President of U.S.

Secretary of State General Marshall resigns and is succeeded by Dean Acheson.

Department of Justice brings suit against AT&T to separate it from Western Electric.

Salary of U.S. president raised to $100,000 plus $50,000 expense allowance.

President Truman is inaugurated for his first elected term.

John L. Lewis calls two week walkout of United Mine Workers.

April 4—North Atlantic Treaty Organization (NATO) formed by United States, Canada, Great Britain, France, Belgium, Norway, Denmark, Luxembourg, Iceland, Italy, Portugal and Netherlands, in Washington, D.C. Ratified by Senate, July 21.

Discovery of cortisone from Adrenal glands found helpful for many things including arthritis.

May 12—Berlin blockade lifted by Soviets. United States withdraws last of its troops from Korea.

Aid to Nationalist China stopped.

Gen. Omar Bradley named Joint Chief of Staff.

August 25—First transmission of color TV.

September 21—President Truman signs Mutual Defense Assistance Act, providing aid to NATO members in case of attack.

U.S. Communist Party leaders found guilty of advocating violent overthrow of U.S. government under Smith Act.

Permanent United Nations headquarters in New York City dedicated.

Einstein presents theory of relativity.

Rodgers and Hammerstein's musical, *South Pacific* is presented.

Soviet Atomic Fission, Espionage, and the Rosenbergs

On September 23, 1949, the Soviet Union detonated an atomic fission bomb. This was at least three years earlier than expected (Daniel, 746).

---

*This chapter was done from memory, refreshed and augmented by Wenborn (295).

253

Espionage was suspected and eventually proven. Ethel and Julius Rosenberg were convicted and executed June 19, 1954.

Coleridge Road, Family

1949 was my third year back in the department of surgery after World War II. We were living in our own home at 2970 Coleridge Road, Cleveland Heights, which we had purchased two years earlier with the aid of the "GI Bill of Rights," which was a government-funded bill guaranteeing credit to banks for loans to help returning veterans become reestablished. With that backing we were able to buy this nice three-bedroom home in a good middle-class neighborhood. It was very helpful. We had many friends from the university in the neighborhood. It was just a few minutes down the hill to University Hospitals, which was handy for night calls that a young doctor must take.

Katy and I now had three lovely daughters, Jane, Elizabeth and Nancy, seven, three and two years old respectively and were comfortable there. My work at the hospital was going well. I was teaching interns and residents, doing research in the laboratory and seeing private patients for income and had become quite busy. Dr. Lenhart had increased my teaching title to assistant professor of surgery. In the laboratory I had been doing research on intra-abdominal adhesions and on the extensive loss of small intestines and methods to increase absorption in the shortened bowel. I had published three papers in the surgical literature and was carrying out studies on prevention of adhesions about tendons following injury and operation as already told.

Events of 1950*

The Cold War between free and Communist countries, particularly the Soviet Union, was heating up.

January 21—Paul Larsen named first chairman of Civilian Mobilization Office to upgrade Civilian Defense in case of Nuclear attack.

Civilian defense became an urgent priority throughout the States, including the city of Cleveland, Ohio.

The Hydrogen bomb, developed by the Atomic Energy Commission, was announced by President Truman. This was a bomb of fusion of hydrogen atoms (small atoms) into helium with the release of huge amounts of energy, in contrast to the splitting of uranium atoms (large atoms), as in the first atomic bomb, with the release of tremendous amounts of energy.

Senator McCarthy

In February Sen. Joseph McCarthy charged the State Department with harboring Communists and revealed a list of suspects. He then headed a Senate Subcommittee of Investigation. He appeared to respond to a very troubling thing. Rosenberg and other espionage had occurred, giving the Soviets our atomic secrets leading to their atomic success in 1949. His method of approach to the problem may have been overly vigorous. (See "Events of 1949")

Discovery of the heaviest known element, Californium, announced by researchers at United of California, Berkeley.

Brooklyn Battery Tunnel, longest in United States, opened in New York City on May 25.

Supreme Court bars segregation of black university students.

Korean War

June 25—Korean War (1950–53) begins as North Korean troops invade South Korea across the 38th parallel. The UN orders withdrawal.

---

*This chapter was done by memory, greatly assisted by Wenborn (295) and Gordon and Gordon (748).

President Truman authorizes U.S. Navy and Air Force to aid South Korea with backing of UN Security Council. U.S. Congress asked for $10 billion for rearmament.

Gen. Douglas MacArthur was named Commander of UN troops in South Korea. On August 4, 62,000 reservists called up. President Truman seized railroad to prevent strike. Former secretary of state George Marshall became secretary of defense. On September 26, UN forces recaptured Seoul, South Korea. On September 29, UN forces reached thirty-eighth parallel and crossed it northward. On October 20, UN forces under MacArthur captured Pyongyang, capital of North Korea. On November 1st, an assassination attempt was made on President Truman at Blair House by Puerto Rican nationalists, Washington, D.C.

Communist Chinese Troops aided North Koreans.

On December 5, UN troops retreated from Pyongyang. President Truman announced a ban on U.S. shipments to Communist China.

Dr. Carl Lenhart Retires, 1950

Dr. Carl Lenhart, professor of surgery Western Reserve University and director of the department of surgery University Hospitals, Cleveland, retired. He was succeeded by Dr. William Holden as director of the department. This changed my relationship at the hospital and I opened a private office at 10465 Carnegie Avenue at Carnegie and 105th Street, which was one of two buildings at that intersection that housed many of the local doctors practicing at University and St. Luke's Hospital. It was approximately a mile from University Hospitals and about three miles from St. Luke's Hospital. I sent patients to both but primarily to University Hospitals, the main general hospital, still known as Lakeside Hospital, a carry over of its name from its previous location downtown on Lake Erie prior to 1931. My practice had become quite busy in both general surgery, abdomen and neck extremity with special emphasis on surgery of the hand. My war experience in the latter gave me a leading position in hand surgery in the community.

American Society for Surgery of the Hand

I became a member of the newly formed American Society for Surgery of the Hand in 1952. I should have been a founding member of that organization in view of my extensive work at Crile General Army Hospital in Parma 1945–1946. I carried one half the clinical load there for over a year as associate chief of hand surgery, until the hospital was turned over to the Veterans Administration in September, 1946. I was very much appreciated in the department of surgery at Crile General Hospital but that was apart from those leading the group forming the society. Consequently I did not receive the honor of being invited as a founding member of the new organization formed in Chicago. My mentor, Dr. Lot Howard from San Francisco, was sorry and said it was an oversight.

Fourth Lovely Daughter, Mary Grace Weckesser

On the home front, daughter Mary Grace arrived May 22, 1950 to complete our family of four lovely daughters. The house at 2970 Coleridge Road was crowded. We liked the house and the location in Cleveland Heights, which was handy to the hospital, but it was now too small. We had an architect draw up plans for an addition that fall and gave much consideration to an enlargement. At Thanksgiving time, Katy and I took our family to her mother's, Mrs. Grace Tuttle's, in Lima, Ohio for the holiday, a distance of one hundred and eighty miles. It was a pleasant drive and the children looked forward to Grandmother's house. We sang the song on the way. It was a happy time. The turkey and Grandmother's pies were delightfully enjoyed with Katy's sister Dorothy, her family, cousins and Aunt Cecil. Katy also enjoyed seeing her friends of former years.

The Big Snow of 1950

On the Friday after Thanksgiving, as I was filling the car with gasoline, preparing for the return trip to Cleveland, the man at the station said, "Did you hear about Cleveland?" The answer was, "No, what is it?" "The city is paralyzed with two feet of snow." On checking radio reports, this was not only true but it was still snowing and people were warned not to try to drive, the roads were impassable. It was also snowing in Lima with an accumulation of several inches. Plans had to change. After some telephone calls I obtained a railroad ticket to Cleveland through Toledo and Kate drove me to the local train station. As the train was pulling out I saw poor Katy stuck in a snow drift in the parking lot of the Lima station. It was a helpless feeling but I knew she was capable of handling the situation.

The train was held up in Toledo but by evening it pulled in to the Terminal Tower at Cleveland. Katy had fortunately given me a scarf for my neck, which was lucky as it was very cold. There was one bus finally which ran through the deserted snow-stacked streets out Carnegie Avenue to East 105th Street where it stopped. Nothing was running beyond and there was no traffic on the streets. Everything was "snowed in." I walked the three to four miles to Coleridge Road, very thankful for the scarf and finally arrived home through deep snow in darkness. The house was O.K. and next day I shoveled out the drive and helped a neighbor do the same. Distress brings out the best in people. The hospital was isolated. Taking care of emergencies only, the doctors stayed there in the building until gradually the streets were cleared enough to let traffic move.

In a day or so I went back to Lima by train and brought the family home. That was the great snow of 1950, about which all victims have tales.

Larger Home, Coventry Road

When we were back together after the big snow, we learned that our friends, the Carol Dundons, were moving to California and their house was for sale. This one had five bedrooms! Why add on to the smaller house when this one had ample room, was adjacent to Shaker Square, in a good school system, Shaker Heights. We bought it and moved to 2708 Coventry Road in January 1951.

Surgery, 1951

Dr. Austin Chinn and I made an analysis of the mortality of upper intestinal tract bleeding among patients admitted to the hospital with upper gastro-intestinal bleeding in order to define the indications for operation. We studied 322 cases admitted to the hospital with this diagnosis over the previous fourteen years with particular attention to the role of blood loss in the cause of death among the forty three who died. With our findings a protocol for the treatment of acute gastro-intestinal hemorrhage was set up. The patients were admitted and evaluated rapidly to determine the extent of blood loss and observed that some patients had been treated conservatively too long. There were two groups that needed early operation: those who did not respond to an intensive fluid replacement, and those who stopped bleeding and then developed signs of recurrent bleeding.

This was published in *The Annals of Internal Medicine* in February, 1951 and was well received.

Events of 1951

*February 1—UN accuses Communist China of aggression against Korea.

March 26—Twenty-second amendment to the U.S. Constitution limits the term of President of US to two terms.

March 14—Seoul, South Korea recaptured by UN forces.

March 24—General MacArthur threatens China with bombing.

April 4—Supreme Headquarters Allied Powers (SHAP) established in France, Gen. Dwight Eisenhower.

April 5—Julius and Ethel Rosenberg convicted of passing atomic information to USSR in 1944, which lead to early possession of nuclear bomb by Soviets. Both sentenced to death. Executed June 19, 1953. The Communists are operating from bases north of the Yalu River and MacArthur threatens to attack.

April 11—President Truman relieves General MacArthur of his command to prevent extension of Korean war into China. The commander in chief had exercised his Supreme Command. General MacArthur returns to the U.S. a hero and speaks to Congress urging action versus Communist China. His concluding statement, "Old soldiers never die, they just fade away," is a dramatic end to his distinguished military career.

July 10—Peace talks between UN and Communist China. These lasted two years. Fighting ended July 27, 1953.

November 25—Floods in Mississippi basin.

September 4—First transcontinental television broadcast of president's address. Japanese Peace Treaty signed by forty-nine nations in San Francisco.

October 10—First transcontinental dial telephone service begins.

December 20—First atomic generator placed in operation in Idaho.

At home, our experimental study on treatment of extensive small bowel loss in dogs was completed. Our findings with resection of the vagus nerves were negative and the procedure was not recommended for

---

*This chapter was done from memory and Wenborn (298) and Daniel (754).

use in the treatment of patients. Our results were reported in *Experimental Surgery.*

Cleveland Skating Club

The children were growing. Jane was ten years old and it seemed appropriate for them to have a place to exercise and meet friends. We, the family, joined the Cleveland Skating Club that was nearby. Katy and I skated for a while but it was mainly for the children and they took to it readily. I remember taking Jane, Betsy and Nancy there in the late afternoon and helping them get their skates on. I left them there while I went to the hospital to do an operation. When I arrived back, expecting to see them still holding onto the rail, it wasn't so; they were all out on the ice having a fine time. Each of them became quite proficient and were cute in the annual skating carnivals. Betsy's name was posted on the bulletin board for quite some time giving her figure skating accomplishments. Jane and Nancy also did very well and Mary soon caught up. Cousin Tom Schaffer visited from Piqua, Ohio and one of the girls let him wear her white skating shoes on the ice. It wasn't long until someone called him a girl which almost led to ''fist i' cuffs''! It was soon straightened out when all realized that boys wear black shoes.

Events of 1952

*March 2—Supreme Court rules that 'subversive persons' can be barred from teaching in public schools.

March 20—Japanese Peace Treaty ratified by Senate.

April 2—Ambassador to Soviet Union appointed. President Truman takes over steel mills, Youngstown, Ohio to avert strike.

May 23—Railroad owners regain control of lines.

May 26—United States, France, Great Britain, West Germany sign peace treaty in Bonn.

June 2—Presidential takeover of steel industry ruled unconstitutional by Supreme Court. Strike again in effect.

June 14—*Nautilus,* first atomic submarine dedicated by President Truman.

July 7—Dwight Eisenhower nominated for president of U.S., Richard Nixon, vice president, Republican Connecticut.

July 21—Democratic Convention nominates Adlai Stevenson for president and John Sparkman vice president.

July 25—Puerto Rico becomes Commonwealth and placed under U.S. jurisdiction.

September 23—Vice president candidate makes successful "Checkers Speech" on TV to defend himself vs. illegal activities.

November 4—Eisenhower and Nixon elected.

November 16—Hydrogen bomb testing announced completed at Eniwetok, Marshall Islands.

Family Trip West

Family takes auto trip west with camping trailers to Yellowstone and other national parks. The children, Jane, Betsy and Nancy, eleven, six and four years of age respectively, went along. Mary, age two, stayed home with Aunt Ruth, my sister. We were accompanied by brother Connie and Dorothy Weckesser and two of their boys, John and Tim who had their own similar type of trailer. The Badlands of South Dakota, the mountains, Yellowstone and Glacier National Parks were all enjoyed. On the way home we visited sister Miriam and Randy Whaley in Indiana

---

*This chapter was done by memory, greatly assisted by Wenborn (301) and Daniel (758).

at Purdue University for a nice visit. It was a strenuous trip for the adults but the parks were interesting. It was nice to see relatives but, all in all we were tired—but we enjoyed it.

Events of 1953*
Dwight Eisenhower, 1952–60

January 20—Dwight Eisenhower inaugurated as president. Soon lifts blockade of the island of Taiwan. Thirteen communist leaders in New York convicted of plotting to overthrow U.S. government. Controls on salaries and wages lifted. Joseph Stalin dies.

April 1—Congress establishes Department of Health Education and Welfare.

June 19—Julius and Ethel Rosenberg executed for revealing atomic secrets to Russia during war.

May 11—Tornadoes kill 124 in Texas.

July 27—Korean armistice signed in Pyongyang.

July 29—U.S. bomber shot down by Soviets off coast of Siberia.

August 7—Refugee Act admits 214,000 foreign nationals.

August 5—A hydrogen bomb is exploded by the Soviet Union less than a year after the first hydrogen bomb explosion by the U.S.

August 18—United States, Great Britain, France invite Soviet Union to peace conference in Lugano, Switzerland. Soviets refuse to attend unless Communist China included.

September 26—Military and economic aid pledged to Spain for air and naval bases.

October 1—President Eisenhower uses Taft-Hartley Act to prevent dock workers' strike. President Eisenhower meets with representatives of Britain and France in Bermuda to discuss atomic information.

December 9—GE announces it will dismiss all Communist employees. George C. Marshall wins Nobel Peace Prize for his Marshall Plan of economic aid to postwar Europe.

Back at home, our work on the control of "Peritoneal Adhesions by Intestinal Plication" was published in *The Archives of Surgery* in October, 1952 and another article on "The Effect of Cortisone on Adhesions" with Charles Hubay and William Holden was published in Surgery, Gynecology & Obstetrics Journal in January 1953. No animal was

---

*This chapter was done from memory, greatly assisted by Wenborn, (301–32) and Daniel (761–63).

266

completely free of adhesions in this study. The adhesions were less if the drug was given preoperatively and in large doses. It had some effect but practical use was not established.

Ulcerative Colitis and Cancer with Dr. Austin Chinn

A study of 118 cases of ulcerative colitis admitted to University Hospitals between 1932–1950 made with Dr. Austin Chinn showed an incidence of 3.4 percent carcinoma. The affected patients were thirty-five years old or less. Among those who had their disease at least ten years the incidence was 9 percent. This indicated that the ulcerative disease in these young people had a serious risk of malignancy. Unless the ulcerative disease could be corrected, removal of the large intestine was indicated before the malignant changes occurred. This was a significant finding and became quite well accepted. (There is some evidence now that the transplant drug cyclosporine may be helpful in ulcerative colitis.)

Doylestown Weekend Cottage

With our growing family, whose friends took them to country clubs we considered joining one but there was a desire to have a place in the country of our own. It was my thought also that rural property would increase in value and be a better investment. After searching many places, we finally purchased from brother Ernie acreage in the old orchard property one mile south of Doylestown, Ohio. This is where I had spent my boyhood. We had a cottage built there at the top of the hill overlooking the broad beautiful Chippewa Valley to the southwest. The red barn of Grandfather Weckesser's farm was visible across the valley, about five miles away but quite recognizable, which added to the attraction.

Actually, the area at the top of the hill had become heavily wooded. Enough trees were bulldozed out to open up the view. When we first saw it, the view was greater than Katy and I had anticipated. It seemed to me that eternity was right across the valley to the southwest beyond Grandfather's farm. I used to tell friends that, pointing across the beautiful valley. They would look at me quizzically, but did not disagree.

Events of 1954*

January 21—*Nautilus* first nuclear powered submarine launched.

February 2—President Eisenhower announces the detonation of a hydrogen fusion on Eniwetok Atoll in 1952.

February 18—Berlin Conference of Big Four Foreign Ministers, US, GB, France and Soviets fail to reach agreement on government for Germany.

February 23—Dr. Jonas Salk develops Polio vaccine for school children. A wonderful accomplishment.

March 8—U.S. and Japan sign mutual defense agreement.

March 24—Second hydrogen bomb test on Marshall Islands announced by Pres. Eisenhower. Destruction 500 times greater than that on Hiroshima.

April 8—Early warning radar construction announced by U.S. and Canada in view of the growing Cold War between free Allied countries and USSR.

Army McCarthy hearings held regarding subversive elements.

May 7—Dien Bien Phu in Northern Vietnam falls to communists.

May 17—Racial Segregation ruled unconstitutional by Supreme Court.

July 2—Senator McCarthy charges CIA infiltrated with Communists.

June 15—Further aid to France in Vietnam refused.

August 2—Senate committee formed to investigate charges of misconduct vs. Senator McCarthy.

August 11—Red Chinese threaten to attack Taiwan held by Nationalist Chinese under Chiang Kai-shek.

September 6—Ground breaking for first atomic power plant, Pittsburgh, Pennsylvania.

September 27—Senator McCarthy censured by Senate Committee.

December 2—U.S. and Taiwan sign mutual defense treaty.

100th Anniversary of Grandfather Weckesser's Arrival in USA

It would be one hundred years since November 13, 1854, when Grandfather Henry Weckesser was shipwrecked at Deal Beach, New Jersey on

*This chapter was done by memory, augmented by Wenborn (303) and World Almanac (523).

his arrival in America and just barely escaped with his life. The majority of the passengers drowned but he miraculously survived. It seemed appropriate to mark this event with a Weckesser Reunion on the 4th of July of that year and give thanks for his survival. Much planning was carried out by Katy, me, and many people and this was done at the new cottage overlooking the Chippewa Valley with Grandfather's farm in the distance. A pointer was nailed to a small sassafras tree pointing to his red barn. So that the young ones could sight along the top of the pointer to the barn, a glacial boulder, of which there were many around, was placed for the children to stand on. They were told that the stone on which they were standing had been delivered early, quite early, ten thousand years earlier during the glacial age! The weather cooperated and the event was a success according to the one hundred and fifty people who attended.

Events of 1955*

January 1—U.S. starts aid to Southeast Asia.

January 29—President Eisenhower's news conference broadcast on television, a first.

February 9—Senate ratified mutual security pact with Nationalist China, Formosa.

February 12—U.S. agrees to help train South Vietnamese Army.

June 6—Ford Motor signed pact with auto workers including increase in wages and reserve funds for those laid off.

July 18—Disneyland opened in Anaheim, California.

July 29—U.S. announces plans to launch orbiting satellites in 1957.

September 26—New York Stock Exchange loses 44 billion dollars. Bus segregation declared unconstitutional.

December 5—AFL and CIO merge.

December 12—Billy Graham opened National Headquarters in Washington, D.C.

December 26—Severe floods in California. Traffic deaths Christmas Holiday: 609. Cleveland Browns defeated Rams for NFL title.

IBM introduced 700 line of computers in challenge to Remington Rand.

Marilyn Monroe was starring in Hollywood.

Our last paper on the effect of cortisone given intra-peritoneally was published in the *Archives of Surgery* in October 1955. We found the local application through a small catheter left in the abdominal cavity at operation more effective than other means of administration.

"Clasped Thumb"

Next we had an interesting series of five cases of "Clasped Thumb," in which small children held their thumbs in their palms tightly clasped by their flexed fingers. Normal babies hold their thumbs in their palms part of the time. We found that among thirty-six newborn infants in the nursery at

---

*This chapter was done by memory, augmented by Daniel (768), World Almanac (523), and Wenborn (305).

University Hospitals, fifteen (42 percent) held their finger clasped over their thumbs part of the time. It was not uncommon thumb posture of newborns in the nursery. It was also noted that the infants periodically released the grasp on their thumbs allowing the digit to come out of the palm and assume its normal position opposite to the fingers. The newborn infant begins to use its thumb in grasp at about three to four weeks of age usually.

In the five cases that we treated, this had not happened. In our five cases the thumbs had remained clasped under the fingers. From our experience we advocated the application of plaster casts holding the thumb out of the palm when this was noted. If the thumb is thus freed early enough, it will usually assume normal function if its tendons are intact. If it does not after a six to eight week trial, surgical restoration of tendon function must be considered. Plaster cast immobilization gave excellent results in three of our patients. The other two required surgery. In most congenital anomalies, the earlier treatment is begun the better. Our recommendation was to reserve operation for those who did not respond to a preliminary casting. In my opinion this was sound advice. Our results and recommendations were given at a meeting of the American Society for Surgery of the Hand in Los Angeles, California on January 28, 1955. The paper as then published in *The Journal of Bone and Joint Surgery* in October 1955. The value of the presentation was in pointing out that early plaster immobilization with the thumb in extension, freed from the over pull of the fingers, was successful in giving normal thumb function in three of five patients. Tendon restoration procedures were reserved for those children who did not respond.

Katy and I traveled to the west coast on the California Zephyr train to give that talk. At that time, train travel was a real pleasure, especially that one. The trip itself was a comfortable experience. In addition to our small but pleasant compartment there was an observation deck above to more readily see the beautiful scenery we were passing through. With that kind of travel, one's enjoyment started when you boarded the train. Meals were served by reservation. There was no waiting in line. The train stopped at the Grand Canyon on the way back, we laid over a day there and explored that beautiful site from the south rim. It was a very comfortable, pleasant train trip. The train took longer but it was a relaxing, comfortable experience starting when we entered the train in Chicago. Kathryn's mother kept the children for us while we were away. During our stay at the Hilton Hotel, Los Angeles, General MacArthur arrived for the dedication of MacArthur Park in his honor. This was four years after he had been relieved by President Truman of his command in Korea. Katy had a very close view of him and was very impressed and pleased. He was a great general in my opinion. We both admired him.

Ventricular Fibrillation

This is a very dangerous abnormal condition in which the individual muscle fibers of the heart muscle contract at random rather than in unison. The heart muscle appears to quiver rather than contract. When this occurs there is no effective pumping action and blood circulation ceases. Brain cells are seriously damaged if this condition persists more than five minutes without cardiac resuscitation.

Normal cardiac contraction can be restored by effective artificial respiration and applying a high voltage shock to the heart. The shock makes all muscle fibers contract at one time following which they relax at one time and are ready to make the next contraction in normal unison. Originally the shocks were applied directly to the heart. In 1960 the technique of external shocking was developed.

Dr. Ransone

On June 21, 1955, I was coming in the back entrance of Lakeside Hospital. Dr. Albert T. Ransone, a member of the staff, was standing at the Protective Service desk on the opposite side of the corridor talking to one of the protective service officers there. As I was coming in the door I saw him suddenly collapse to the floor. I quickly crossed the corridor to his side as he lay on the floor. His heart had stopped beating. He was pulseless, apneic and becoming cyanotic. He was hurriedly lifted onto a patient cart and quickly transported down the hall to a room in the emergency ward, a short distance away, while given artificial and mouth-to-mouth respiration. This was switched to face mask in the emergency ward until an endotracheal tube could be inserted. Slapping and compressing his chest did not restore a heartbeat. The work of Beck and Mautz on resuscitation at that time was by open-chest compression of the heart. (The closed-chest method was developed five years later.) When his heartbeat did not return and his pupils became dilated, I opened his

272

left chest quickly between the fourth and fifth ribs. The ventricles were fibrillating. His heart was then compressed directly by hand to maintain his circulation while respiration was maintained by face mask and endotracheal tube. A protracted period of manual cardiac compression followed. There was no rib retractor in the emergency room and the pressure on my wrist was great. Dr. Frank Barry came by and gave me some relief. Dr. Beck arrived and the defibrillator was brought from the dog lab in the Medical School. With the electrodes directly on the heart a shock was given in an effort to restore normal ventricular contraction by producing contraction of all the ventricular muscle cells at the time of the shock. In fact all the muscles of the body contracted throwing his head forcefully back, known as opisthotonos, and producing rigidity of his entire body. The first two shocks were not successful, but with a third stronger one (3A for 2 seconds, 110 volts A.C.), after moistening the electrodes with saline, his heart muscle stopped quivering and began normal contractions. This was after a period of artificial manual cardiac contractions of nearly an hour. His chest wound began to bleed following restoration of normal rhythm and larger vessels were clamped and ligated as the chest wound was closed.

There had been doubt prior to this experience that normal rhythm could be restored following a heart attack. Dr. Carl Wiggers, professor of physiology, had produced ventricular fibrillation in dogs by ligating their coronary arteries and had found it necessary to remove the ligatures before he could restore normal rhythm in his animals. Dr. Claude S. Beck had carried out the first successful ventricular defibrillation of the heart in the operating room in 1947, an outstanding accomplishment. This case, Dr. Ransone, demonstrated that defibrillation could be done successfully after a heart attack. It was followed by the development of closed-chest resuscitation as stated later.

Doctor Ransone's heartbeat remained strong and vigorous. He regained consciousness during the night. In the morning we were all amazed and many wondered what he remembered of his brush with death. He had had no pulse or normal respiration for approximately an hour after his attack. Dr. Beck was particularly interested in this aspect but unfortunately the patient could give us no insight into the "hereafter." He did not remember anything of it and was confused as to what had happened.

He left the hospital on the eleventh day and recovered completely and lived a normal life for twenty-eight more years. He returned to practice and referred a patient to me for abdominal surgery before retiring to Florida where he lived normally and comfortably until the age of ninety-three years.

Christmas cards were received from him for many years. The 1984 June issue of *The Ohio State Medical Journal* recorded the date of his death as February 2, 1984 at age ninety-three. I corresponded with his trust officer in Florida who told me that he had a cheerful attitude and was up and around until the end. As I reported in *The New England Journal of Medicine,* "He slipped away quietly one morning while sitting in a chair in his own home listening to his housekeeper read to him." He had enjoyed twenty-eight years of good life after conversion from ventricular fibrillation to normal rhythm by a strong electrical current applied directly to the heart, the first such conversion following a heart attack at University Hospitals, Cleveland.

This technique of converting ventricular fibrillation of the heart muscle, which kills the majority of people who die after a heart attack, to normal contraction by applying a strong shock has been refined and developed. W. B. Kouwenhoven and those working with him in Baltimore in 1957–60 perfected the technique of restoring circulation by compressing the chest anteriorly to compress the heart and also applying the shock to the anterior chest, which simplified things a great deal. Stronger currents are used with this method, which no longer necessitates opening the chest for cardio-pulmonary resuscitation as I did for Dr. Ransone. The "closed technique" is now in wide usage throughout the world by doctors, resuscitation technicians and lay people and has saved thousands of lives. The technique of supporting life by chest compression and mouth-to-mouth respiration is something that all should know and be able to carry out until the 911 technicians arrive. Always send someone to call 911 while cardiac compression and mouth-to-mouth respiration is being given. The 911 technicians have the equipment to do the shocking of the heart when it is necessary. You can keep the patient alive by mouth-to-mouth respiration and intermittent compression of the front of the chest. This gets enough "oxygen for life" into the lungs of the victim and the intermittent compression of the chest provides enough circulation usually to carry it to the brain and other organs until the technicians arrive. There is also another reason to go ahead. Sometimes the heart is in standstill and will restart beating when the chest is compressed or slapped.

Second Family Trip West

It had been three years since our first trip West in our camping trailers. In 1955 the family took a second trip West. This time we traveled a little better in a closed trailer pulled by our white Ford Station Wagon. Katy and I went with the four girls and Kathryn's mother, Mrs. Grace Tuttle of Lima, Ohio. It was a little crowded sleeping at night with double-deck bunks, and was not luxury travel, but we had fun and the trip was a success. Brother Connie with his wife Dorothy and two of their sons, John and Timothy, accompanied us with similar equipment.

The plan of this trip was to see places that we did not visit in 1952. We headed for Glacier National Park in northwest Montana. Mrs. Tuttle had a pen pal in Buffalo, Wyoming whose name was also Grace Osborn, the same as her maiden name. We found this lady without difficulty. Mrs. Tuttle and she had a nice visit after which we traveled on.

In the Glacier National Park we had some steep pulls for our car and the weather was hot. On one mountain road, we developed a "fuel lock" in the car's engine due to the high altitude and the heat. The gasoline had vaporized in the fuel line between the tank and the carburetor and the engine stopped. Other drivers were having the same problem. By letting the engine cool we finally were able to get going again.

The scenery and views in the park were marvelous. Pitching camp at night, worked out satisfactorily. We were able to find camping areas which had water and comfort facilities where we frequently could connect up with electricity. One night we were awakened by a noise at the door and on glancing out saw a large brown bear turning things over in search of food. The day before when we stopped, the children had gone to some play swings a short distance away and I looked up to see two bears crossing the path between us and the children. My concern, as I rushed over was lessened as I saw the bears heading down to the trash area away from the girls. The bears were going for their evening ransack of the trash cans for food. We quickly got the children back onto home base where they were willing to stay. The trip continued northward through Calgary and further into Alberta to Banff, beautiful Lake Louise and Jasper. This was the turning point from which we headed back eastward through Edmonton, Alberta where we arrived late in the afternoon and had a good dinner at a nice restaurant.

The evening was pleasant and we decided to travel on eastward to Elk Island, a Canadian National Park, a distance of about twenty miles further eastward where camping facilities were marked on our map. It was dark when we arrived in this isolated area but by following signs we were able to find the park and pulled our trailers into an open area off the road for the night. The children ran around outside, to get rid of some of their energy while we were setting up for the night and all seemed to be going well. There was something undesirable on their shoes when they came in which was carefully wiped off. We settled in for a good nights rest.

When we awakened in the morning the nature of the substance on the children's shoes the night before became apparent; politely described as "intestinal residue of large animals." We had camped with a herd of buffalo! I went outside to survey the situation and as I approached the group, the leader snorted and pawed the ground and I said "OK mister, we are not going to dispute your position." We then withdrew quietly and orderly back into our cars, then onto and down the road to the first outpost for breakfast.

Our journey then continued through Saskatchewan and Manitoba. Eventually we crossed back into the USA at International Falls and back home through Minnesota, Wisconsin and Michigan to Ohio. We all stood up well, including Mrs. Tuttle, and arrived gladly back in Cleveland tired but happy. Connie and Dorothy with their two boys had a similar experience. We had all seen a lot of beautiful country and had interesting experiences.

Events of 1956*

February 6—University of Alabama enrolls first black student.

March 20—End of 156-day Westinghouse strike.

April 2–3—Tornadoes in MI, WI, OK, KA, MS, MO, AK, and TN kill many people. $15 million damage.

April 19—Grace Kelly marries Prince Rainier III.

May 2—Methodist Church calls for end of segregation.

June 30—TWA Constellation and United DC-7 collide over Grand Canyon, 123 killed.

July 26—Egypt nationalizes Suez Canal.

August 1—Salk Polio vaccine available to public.

August 20—Eisenhower and Nixon nominated for second term and elected on November 6.

September 25—First transatlantic telephone cable became operable.

October 26—Seventy nations sign Statute of the International Atomic Energy Agency.

November 13—Supreme Court invalidates Alabama bus segregation law.

Salk Vaccine

The Jonas Salk vaccine for the prevention of poliomyelitis was a wonderful advancement in 1956 for all, especially children. This required the injection of the vaccine under the skin. The medical profession took this up seriously throughout the country. In Cleveland the Academy of Medicine set up injection stations throughout Cuyahoga County, which were manned by volunteer doctors and nurses to give the treatments. People were allowed to make monetary donations to cover the cost of the vaccine, which they did freely. It was appreciated much by the people of the community and was a great satisfaction to those who donated their services.

---

*This chapter was done by memory, greatly assisted by World Almanac (523) and Wenborn (307).

Sabin Oral Sunday

The Academy of Medicine enhanced its standing in the community greatly with this effort and again in 1962 with the "Sabin Oral Sundays" program when the oral preparation became available due to the work of Dr. Sabin as mentioned later.

Surgery

In January 1956 I presented my results on freeing adherent tendons in the fingers and thumbs of patients, injecting hydrocortisone into the wound through a tiny catheter at the close of the procedure and then having the patient move the finger early after operation. The to-and-fro movement of the tendon after operation was used to prevent the regrowth of the adhesions. The exercises were supervised to encourage the patients to make the movements. After operation it is customary for a patient not to move operated fingers because of pain. During that early time, the adhesions reoccur and the operation fails. Our results were quite favorable and we presented them at a meeting of the American Society of Surgery of the Hand in January, 1956. Among nineteen operations on digits of the hand, 84 percent were benefitted significantly. (37 percent excellent, 16 percent good, 31 percent fair, and 16 percent poor). The cortisone not only delayed the reformation of adhesions to the freed tendons but cut down on post-operative pain and thus encouraged movement.

This was a new thing and as usual drew criticism. One man from Kentucky said I was expecting an awful lot from two cubic centimeters of hydrocortisone. Dr. Koch from Chicago, at that time one of the leaders in hand surgery, said my work was very interesting and Dr. Posch from Detroit supported it strongly. Tendon grafting was an alternate procedure to the tendolysis (tendon freeing) that I was advocating. I continued to have favorable results and it was taken up by others.

Events of 1957*

January 5—Eisenhower Doctrine offered protection to any Middle East nation seeking aid against communist aggression. This was an extension of the Truman Doctrine of his predecessor. It was approved by Congress Mar. 7.

January 20—Eisenhower and Nixon were inaugurated for second term. The ceremony carried on National Television for first time.

April 29—First nuclear power reactor dedicated at Fort Belvoir, Virginia.

May 2—Death of Sen. Joseph McCarthy.

May 24—Rioters mob Embassy in Taipei.

June 27–28—Hurricane kills 531 in Louisiana and Texas.

August 29—Civil Rights Act establishes Civil Rights committee providing penalties for violations.

September 4—Arkansas National Guard prevents black students from entering high school in Little Rock.

September 19—First underground atomic explosion at Nevada proving ground.

September 20—Militia removed Central High School in Little Rock, Arkansas but rioting continues.

September 25—Eisenhower orders Federal troops to Little Rock.

October 4—USSR launches *Sputnik* earth satellite.

November 1—World's largest, Mackinaw Straits suspension bridge opened connecting upper and lower Michigan.

October 25—President Eisenhower suffers minor stroke.

December 5—U.S. tests Atlas Intercontinental Ballistic Missile.

Sputnik

The launching of the *Sputnik* earth satellite by the USSR on October 4, 1957, had a sobering effect in the United States. The Russians had beaten us to it and indicated that they were leading in space. This lead to spurring our Space Program into greater action requiring the allotment of more funds to it.

---

*This chapter was done from memory and Wenborn (309) and World Almanac (523).

The launching of *Sputnik* was a significant scientific achievement for Russia, a "home run" for them in the game of space travel, so to speak, and a prodding stimulus to a surprised U.S. scientific community. Americans witnessed this object in their sky as it rotated about the earth; something that had never happened before, which roused some apprehension. We were at our cottage on the weekend. The family went out onto the tennis court in the darkness to see it as it streaked across the sky from east to west, readily visible. The airspace above us, we had thought belonged to us out to eternity and here came this bright foreign object high over our heads passing through our sky.

Events of 1958*

January 3—United States Air Force forms Strategic Air Command with intermediate range ballistic missiles.

January 27—U.S. and USSR sign pact encouraging exchanges in education, sports and technology.

January 31—Explorer I First U.S. satellite launched at Cape Canaveral.

March 17—VanGuard I satellite launched by U.S. Navy.

April 28—U.S. begins atomic tests at Eniwetok Atoll, Marshall Islands.

July–October—Five thousand U.S. Marines sent to Lebanon to protect government there.

June 29—Bomb explodes outside Bethel Baptist Church in Birmingham, Alabama.

July 29—National Aeronautics and Space Administration.

August 5—U.S. *Nautilus* atomic submarine makes world's first undersea crossing of North Pole.

August 25—Pensions granted to presidents of United States.

September 2—National Defense Education Act gives government back student loans for education in science.

September 30—Governor of Arkansas closes four high schools in Little Rock.

October 6—Atomic submarine *Seawolf* completes two-month underwater voyage.

October 12—Synagogue bombed in Atlanta, Georgia.

October 31–December 19—Meeting of United States, Great Britain and USSR discussing suspension of nuclear testing.

December 10—First domestic jet airline passenger service in U.S. opened between New York and Miami.

On January 31, 1958, the United States launched *Explorer I* at Cape Canaveral and there was national satisfaction.

The launching of an earth satellite in January of 1958 by the United States gave further comfort to Americans in regard to our space program. Unbelievable things were happening as demonstrated by the feat of the atomic-powered U.S. submarine *Seawolf,* which made a first passage

---

*This chapter was done from memory, plus Wenborn (311).

under the North Pole. Atomic power gives extra energy for feats of that nature. From a practical standpoint, the development of jet airline passenger service between New York City and Miami, Florida was a great accomplishment. The jets were much faster and would speed up service greatly.

The Emblem of Medicine

The symbol of the healing art of medicine has long been the stout Aesculapian Staff. It has one serpent twined about a stout staff said to have been carried by Aesculapius, the Greek God of medicine. Accurate dates in mythology are not possible. He is not mentioned in Homeric poems, which date back to 1000 B.C. (Garrison, 187). His cult enjoyed a lively age as god of healing in the early Hellenistic Greek period. (Encyclopedia America 113:432). In this period serpents were considered to represent wisdom, rejuvenance, longevity, fertility and healing according to Greek mythology. They were kept at Aesculapian temples. The Aesculapian staff has been depicted with only one serpent, however.

The more symmetrical and possibly more artistic staff with two serpents entwined about it with wings above is the Caduceus, the wand of Hermes (Mercury) in later Roman times. In Rome at that time Mercury was the patron of trade and commerce. The two became confused. This confusion is addressed in an article of mine entitled "A Symbol of Trade for the Emblem of Medicine?" written in 1958. The meaning of the two symbols is pointed out and their usages listed.

Events of 1959*

January 3—Alaska enters union as 49th state.

January 8—U.S. recognizes government of Fidel Castro Cuba.

February 10—Severe tornado, St. Louis.

March 5—U.S. signed mutual defense pacts with Iran, Pakistan and Turkey.

April 7—Oklahoma repeals prohibition.

April 15—Secretary of State John Foster Dulles resigns due to cancer.

April 25—*St. Lawrence Seaway* opens.

May 3—American Unitarian Association and Universalist Church of America merge.

May 20—John Foster Dulles receives Medical of Freedom, dies May 24.

May 20—Citizenship restored to 5,000 Japanese who renounced it during World War II.

May 22—Brig. Gen. Benjamin O. Davis, Jr. U.S. Air Force becomes first black general appointed to this rank.

May 28—Two apes launched into space.

June 9—Submarine *George Washington* capable of firing Polaris missile launched.

June 18—Supreme Court rules that Arkansas law used to close Little Rock schools unconstitutional.

July 9—Two American soldiers killed in South Vietnam by Communist guerrillas.

July 15—Steel workers strike twenty-eight companies.

July 21—*Savannah,* first atomic-powered merchant ship launched at Camden, New Jersey.

July 23—Vice president Nixon begins two-week tour of USSR.

August 7—NASA launches *Explorer IV* satellite Cape Canaveral.

August 12—Demonstrations at Central High School, Little Rock.

August 21—Hawaii enters union as fiftieth state.

September 1—Nikita Khrushchev, Soviet Premier, arrives in U.S. for six-day transcontinental tour! Some fireworks.

September 11—Secretary of Agriculture to distribute surplus food to impoverished.

---

*This chapter was done from memory plus Wenborn (313) World Almanac (523).

September 14—Londrum-Griffin Act designed to curb racketeering in labor organizations.

October 9—President Eisenhower invokes Taft-Hartley Act to break nationwide steel strike.

November 10—*Triton*, largest atomic submarine, launched in Groton, Connecticut.

November 21—U.S. and USSR sign agreement for two-year exchange in science, culture, and sports. Guggenheim Museum opens in New York City. Television now in millions of homes.

Severely Injured Hands—Reconstructed of Sensitive Grasping Mechanism

This was a study that gave me experience with the terrible problem of destructive injuries of the hand, which had destroyed prehension. It was presented at the annual meeting of the American Society for Surgery of the Hand held in Chicago on January 24, 1959, and published in *Clinical Orthopedics,* Volume 15, later that year. This paper, which reflected my experience with this terrible problem, was very well received. The various types of prehension that the normal hand provides were pointed out. Methods of restoration of functional use of the deformed hands was shown. The deformities were extreme. Functional grasp was restored, not cosmetic appearance. With their extreme loss of digits the emphasis had to be on the former so that the worker could carry out the functions of daily living and return to useful employment when possible. In summary, any opposable and motored sensitive portions of the hand can frequently be useful for grasp. Examples of this are shown in the photo section.

The ability especially of children to learn to utilize remnants of the amputated hand is outstanding and should be remembered by all doctors giving initial care. Case 9 shows a man in his forties who suffered an amputation of the right hand at age seven through his carpal, wrist, bones and forearm. The photo shows him tieing his shoe, holding the shoelace with his right hand remnant flexed in this manner. Another young lady, also at age seven, who lost all digits of her right hand except the thumb and index finger is shown playing the violin. With the benefit of transferring tendons to bring the two remaining digits of her right hand together for strong grasp she was able to hold the bow for the violin securely.

284

She had played the piano but shifted to the violin and became very accomplished with the instrument. She fingered the strings normally with her normal left hand.

Now many amputated portions of the hand can be reattached when damage to the amputated part, especially the vessels and nerves, is not too great. This is a benefit of vascular and nerve repair techniques developed during and after World War II.

Surgery, 1960

The American Society for Surgery of the Hand met at the Palmer House Hotel in Chicago in January 1960. We had a preliminary one-day meeting at the University of Iowa held at the Children's Hospital on January 21. Dr. Tidrick presented the problem of joint changes in severe burns of the hand. The stiffening of the joints associated with immobilization must be guarded against with extra care and supervised movement exercises in saline baths. The tendency is to hold the joints motionless because of discomfort. It is a large and very important part of burn treatment of the hand, the most mobile portion of our skeletal anatomy. Extreme effort must be made to maintain mobility.

A wide variety of cases was presented followed by active discussion. Guy Pulvertaft from Derby, England gave his techniques for dealing with the problem.

We then flew back to Chicago for the two days of scheduled meetings at the Palmer House in downtown Chicago. Tendon healing was dealt with, describing the latest techniques to get the tendon to heal end to end together without becoming adherent to the surrounding tissues. This had been and still was a most vexing problem. If the tendon is caught in scar tissue it cannot transmit force distally to move the joints beyond. This problem has no easy answers but the most favorable approach is to use protected, guarded movement very early. It has to be done under strict supervision and sometimes with local block anesthesia to accomplish the objective of letting the tendon heal end to end without growing fast to adjacent tissue. Roller, compression injuries were discussed as well as the problems of pain and swelling, which also lead to crippling due to joint stiffening. Cross-finger flaps bridging tissue from one finger to another to provide skin and pliable tissue to cover an injured joint were extensively discussed with the problems of syndactyly, children born with two or more fingers joined together, which prevents the normal function of digits. The question was whether to operate early or later. As much as possible should be done for the preschool child to correct obvious abnormalities. If not they can cause embarrassing comments by classmates.

Events of 1960*
John Fitzgerald Kennedy, 1960–63,
Assassinated 11/22/63

1960—An election year. Things are squaring off for a hot contest between Democrats and Republicans in the November elections.

Racial problems continue in the South.

February 1—Black students stage sit-in at lunch counter in Greensboro, North Carolina.

January 4—Longest steel strike in history ends.

January 19—U.S. and Japan sign a mutual defense treaty.

March 15—A disarmament conference of ten nations in Geneva, Switzerland.

April 1—The first weather satellite, *Tiros I* is placed into orbit by U.S.

May 1—Downing of a U-2 over USSR. U.S. admits it was an intelligence mission.

May 7—Eisenhower and Khrushchev, both strong leaders, do not get along.

May 11—President Eisenhower does not apologize for U-2 missions. This leads to angry response by Khrushchev.

May 16—Paris summit canceled by Khrushchev. The *Triton* nuclear submarine made the first undersea voyage around the world. Hurricane Donna killed thirty people as it ravaged our east coast from Florida to New England and sugar imports from Cuba were reduced severely.

June 12—President Eisenhower starts an eight-day trip to Philippines, Taiwan, South Korea and Alaska.

June 2–13—Broadway theaters closed by actors' strike.

July 6—Senators John F. Kennedy and Lyndon B. Johnson nominated at Democratic convention for president and vice president.

September 17—Mobs attack U.S. Embassy Panama in a dispute over flying American and Panamanian flags.

---

*This chapter was done by memory, aided by Wenborn (315), World Almanac (524), and Carruth (625–28).

November 8—John F. Kennedy and Lyndon B. Johnson, president and vice president were elected by a majority of only 120,000 votes, the smallest margin ever.

November 30—Anti-integration riots occur in New Orleans.

December 28—A United DC-8 and a TWA Lockheed Constellation plane collide in mid-air over New York City in a fog killing 132 persons. A most horrid accident with debris and body parts landing in the city below.

In this election year, young Sen. John F. Kennedy, Democrat, was the first candidate nominated for the presidency of the United States. Within a few days Vice President Nixon, Republican, declared his candidacy having served as President Eisenhower's vice president for eight years with a good record in foreign policy. He also had a good record against un-American activities. It was to be a hot contest. On September 26, the first of four televised debates between presidential candidates Kennedy and Nixon took place. These debates were thought by the viewing audience to be a great success, and have become the method of choice for campaigning.

Downing of U-2 Plane

The downing of one of our U-2 observation planes over the USSR in May caused additional stress on the already severely strained relations with the Soviets. This was made worse when President Eisenhower refused to apologize. Eisenhower and hard party man Krushchev did not get along well (as already mentioned). In addition to cancelling the scheduled Paris summit meeting, he began further cooperation with Fidel Castro in Cuba that would lead to a very serious missile crisis two years later.

Family Trip to Europe

1960 was the year the family decided to take a trip to Europe, to see the big cities, tour the countryside and Germany to visit the place of origin of Grandfather Weckesser. Much planning went into this trip. At that time there was an advantage to buying a car in Europe, driving it around as desired and then shipping it to America. Not being particularly interested in large automobiles and preferring smaller economical cars, arrangements were made to buy a French Peugeot to be picked up in Paris on a certain date. We planned to fly to Paris, pick up our car there, drive southward through the French countryside, down into Italy, then Switzerland, Austria, Germany and wind up into England. It was a very ambitious journey. Katy and our four daughters were all excited about it—Mary, Nancy, Jane, and Betsy, with some exception on the part of Jane, our eldest who had just graduated from Shaker Heights High School. She would have preferred probably to do other things, but also consented to go, which made a party of six.

The planning for the family trip was a large task. Kathryn handled it with dispatch but it took a toll and she wound up in the hospital on the week we planned to leave. The trip had to be delayed two weeks and then off we went for a shortened version of it omitting Italy and England. The story is very nicely told by Kathryn Tuttle Weckesser:

Europe with the Weckessers, by Kathryn Tuttle Weckesser

Wednesday, July 13th.
We thought the day would never come—but here it is. Everyone up early, flying about. Cameras, grips, coats, jackets? Everything seems to be in the car, even our lunch that Grandma packed. Dutchess is excited, thinks she is going along, we say goodbye, wave a kiss to Grandma and out the driveway at 9:30 A.M.

The day was warm with intermittent rain and heavy traffic on the turnpike, so we ate our lunch while driving. Stayed at King of Prussia, Pa. at a Howard Johnson Motel. Nancy and Mary had a swim before dinner and another before going to bed. This is the life! To bed early, all are tired after the excitement of getting on our way.

Thursday, July 14.
Up at 8 A.M. Dad and Nancy have gone for breakfast for us. Came back with two poached eggs for me and rolls and milk for the girls. Raining hard as we started for New York, via New Jersey Turnpike, Holland Tunnel, and Battery Tunnel to Idlewild. It has rained all day and there is heavy fog. The road was flooded in one place but we got through. Checked in at Idlewild, we were all impressed with the fabulous beautiful buildings. KLM had everything in order, we sit together, so started on in the pouring

rain to the Walter Benedicts at Baldwin, Long Island to leave our car. Arrived about 3:30 P.M. Walter was glad to see us, Peggy was off at a children's camp. Visited with Walter and we all put on clean clothes. Walter drove us back to the airport and took the car with him. We are really on our way.

KLM certainly has a smooth running organization, had a Bon Voyage telegram from the Auto Club. Boarded the plane at 8:30 P.M. Jane, Dad and Nancy next to the window were in front of Betsy, Mary and myself. Took off at 9 P.M. with a great roar and then the plane settled into smooth noiseless flight. Very thrilling. A handsome young Dutch steward gave a demonstration of the life jacket, oxygen mask and "ditching" procedure. It is dark now and supper is being served. Any kind of drink you want and a wonderful meal. Lights out at midnight, pillow and blanket for each of us. Everyone napped and awakened to a beautiful sunrise (11:30 A.M. our time). Served breakfast and we saw a glimpse of the Irish coast. Amsterdam in 1/2 hour. 3,000 feet altl., 600 miles per hour, 6 1/2 hours for the trip!

FRIDAY, JULY 15th

Arrived Amsterdam at 9 A.M. The landing a little scary, loud noises and shaking of the plane as the power was reversed, we held hands in our seat and said a prayer, and rolled smoothly to a stop. Dutch farmers were making hay between runways. All out! A beautiful sunny day and officials barely glanced at our papers. We were transient so not allowed out of the station. Had tea and mailed "Arrive Safely" postcards. KLM flight to Paris at 10 A.M. Couldn't find Jane right away, but she was reading. This trip was more to the children's liking. We stayed low and were able to see the countryside. Had a jolly French steward who joked with the girls in French and served lunch. I guess it's a good thing I'm on a diet. Arrived Paris 12:30 P.M. You get a really good idea how big the city is from the air. Presented passports and identification cards to the immigration officials. Customs opened no bags and asked no questions. We got into a taxi but the Frenchman put up a terrible fuss. Apparently he could only take five and there were six of us. Out we get and into another. The driver knew his way to Hotel Lenox.

We had reservations at this Left Bank hotel on the advice of good friends, the husband being an Episcopal minister whom we trusted. Our driver pointed out places of interest on the way, made quite a point of the Dior Salon! Madame Pelloile at Hotel Lenox had rooms for us and came out to help with the baggage. Up winding steps to the second floor where we had three rooms. Floor to ceiling windows, red plush covered furniture, shabby but clean. Marcel, the husband, in a long blue apron, cleaning and smiling at the same time. We unpacked and then walked several blocks for tea at an outdoor cafe. We are all so tired we can hardly believe we are here so back for rest, at least for the old folks.

Walked to a small clean restaurant, Le Ministers on Rue de Bac. The food was plain but good and we had no trouble with the money or ordering so decided to take the Metro to Sacre Cour. The Metro was very fast and filled with Parisians, old and young. The girls were wide eyed at some of the actions of the young couples they saw. Hugging and kissing did not seem to be frowned upon. Off at our stop and down the narrow cobbled streets and it started to rain hard. We gave up seeing the church and took the Metro back to the hotel where we slept like logs.

Saturday, July 16th
Up at 9:00. We all have basins and a bidet in our room but the toilet is in the hall and we must order our baths in the evening. Tea, hot chocolate and wonderful fresh croissants in the lobby. There were three small tables covered with red checked table cloths, and Madame did the cooking and serving. We ate with a Boston family named Pendleton, very nice people who were leaving that day. We took a taxi to Cars Overseas where we must get our Peugeot by noon or be without it until Monday. Elden had quite a time with French and the telephones trying to get in touch with the Jim Galehouses in Ariens. After several tries with the aid of Madame Pelloile, Monsieur Gellihoose answered with a French accent!

The girls and I sat in an outdoor cafe while Elden transacted the car details. We finally had our car. It ran like a Swiss watch but the tires were half flat. (Low pressure tires). The French garage workers were very industrious and we shot out of the garage at twelve noon in the gray Peugeot and into Paris traffic. I think we were all holding our breath. No gas coupons available on Saturday but perhaps we can find a station and pay extra. The tires are half flat and Elden wonders if there is oil in the engine! We find a park and that is checked. All is fine but we do need petrol! There are no gasoline pumps visible on the streets. Finally in a garage a mechanic brings out a long hose which reaches to our car and fills the tank! We are learning and grateful. We parked on the street and visited the Arc de Triomphe. Very handsome memorial and the eternal flame burned brightly surrounded by flower wreaths. Went to the top which gives a wonderful view of Paris and helped us become somewhat oriented in directions. We could readily see why it is called The Etoile. There were no sky scrapers in Paris. The highest buildings were ten stories. One is impressed by the lack of tall buildings, which allows you to have an uninterrupted view, over a huge area, and the beauty of the avenues—so wide and long—bordered by lovely trees. It was a sunny day and we snapped many pictures. Walked down Champs-Elysee and lunched at a sidewalk cafe. I loved these cafes. They are so relaxed, nobody in a hurry and you see the most fascinating sights. Drove to the Eiffel Tower and took the lift to the top. It was quite an experience as it ran on a slant and there were several different levels, it seemed as though we were entering and leaving many more lifts than we actually did. We were intrigued by the posted signs, "watch for pickpockets" and took precautions. Again we had a beautiful view of the city and could see the traffic going up and down the Seine River. Wonderful clouds and sun for pictures. We all enjoyed it.

Back to the Lenox to rest and then walked to dinner at a small French restaurant where I had a delicious omelet. No milk for the girls and they hate mineral water, but they don't want wine so I'm afraid they will be thirsty. Drove up Champs-Elysees afterward so we could see the night picture. The lighting was impressive, from the cars, fountains, and streets. Paris is exciting. Back to bed, but the Bongo-Bongo night club next door kept all awake and the noise from the cars and scooters on the street bothered me. It seems to me that the girls spend much time at their window when I think they are in bed but I forgive them because it is so different and fascinating.

Sunday July 17th
Awakened late. Madame & Marcel brought our breakfast to our room. We are going to the Louvre so must hurry as Jim Galehouse is meeting us here, with the children, at noon. Rainy and dull day, as we drove along the quay there are no book stalls open and few people on the streets. Parked on Place de Concord, a very impressive square, and walked through the Tuilleries Gardens. Very beautiful. If there was only more time to explore, but we have to hurry. Into the Louvre, a tremendous building, found our way to Winged Victory and Mona Lisa. There is gallery after gallery, I'm sure you could spend months and not see it all. I bought several prints and the girls bought etchings and postcards of paintings and statues. Back to the hotel. Jim and the children are there. It was quite a reunion. We all (11) lunched at Les Ministers, the Galehouse four chatting with the waiter in French. Wonderful soup and French bread here. We are on our way to the Flea Market and Jim pointed out de Gaulle's house and other points of interest. The Flea Market was quite a place! Such a conglomeration of beautiful old antiques, junk, odd people, open sewers, old clothes, dogs, but I did find a lovely piece of Pewter for the Grossmans. After tramping around an hour or so, we said goodbye to the Galehouses and they were on their way back to Amiens. We'll see them there in a couple of weeks. Found our way back to Arc de Triomphe, our landmark,

and I must say that Father is driving like a veteran. Mary wanted to see Les Invalides and after parking and walking all the way up, it was closed so we could only drive around it. She wanted to see Napoleon's tomb very much. They managed to look through the gates. Drove out on the Island but Notre Dame Cathedral was closed and could only look at the spire of St. Chappele. Still raining hard. Dark now so back to rest then walked to a charming bistro for supper. We were getting along fine with our French but when we asked for milk to drink, the waiter almost collapsed, but after a long wait it did appear. After a walk, to bed. We are leaving in the morning and thanks to the Peugeot and Elden's driving we have really seen a lot of Paris. I hope we can come back some day. I was intrigued by the architecture and antiquity of the city. Our hotel was a few blocks from the Sorbonne, which was interesting to Jane and Dad. We saw the building where Pasteur worked. The people on the streets were fascinating but a little shocking in their behavior and the urinals are behind partitions that do not go to the ground which was surprising, but normal in this country.

Monday, July 18th
Everybody packed and we are amazed at the room we have for luggage. Only two bags for the luggage rack. We finally get gas (benzine) coupons. You stop at the curb and they bring out a ten-foot hose as mentioned to fill the tank. Expensive ($8). Fond farewell to the Pelloiles and on our way at noon. Drove to Versailles and toured the palace gardens. They are vast and so beautiful and formal in their plantings. The sun was bright so all the cameras were out. We especially enjoyed seeing the tropical gardens. The trees are planted in boxes so they can be carried inside in winter. The pools and statuary were lovely but the fountains were not operating, disappointing. The Palace was huge and surrounded by an extensive cobblestone courtyard. The girls were intrigued with Louis XIV statutes, for he was on horseback. Had lunch in a wonderful restaurant, where we could see the palace and the girls had an orange for dessert. What a treat! Motored on, very fertile land, the fields are fenced and they are cutting wheat by hand. The whole family is working in the field. Through Orleans, a very pleasant, peaceful drive and into Glen, on the Loire River. Hotel clean and nice rooms on the third floor, no lifts. Pumpkin soup and fish from the river for dinner. Service and cleanliness outstanding. Walked through the town and along the river before bed. We have found the French people to be very helpful and courteous and they seem pleased that we are trying to speak their language. The girls are wonderful travelers, we have had no quarreling, even though we are somewhat cramped for space. Mrs. Barrow has given Jane a good French background in school and we are all benefitting from her historical comments.

Tuesday, July 19

Up at 8 A.M. after a good rest. Chocolate and rolls in the lobby. Drove to Chateau de Loire. High on a hill, with wonderful view of the town and river below. Had a quick look at the church and baronial hall of the chateau. On our way again, the countryside is beautiful and peaceful. Everything is cultivated and is so tidy. Stopped at Nevers and shopped for our lunch in the village market. Beautiful displays of fruit and vegetables, each stall with a country woman in charge. They do not have sacks to wrap for anything so we bought a string bag to carry our purchases. Nancy and Dad bought bread from the bakery, also unwrapped and a stop at the milk store makes us ready for lunch, which we ate at a camping stop down the road a short distance for the equivalence of 15 cents. A farm house there provided running water, toilet facilities, and plenty of room to stretch our legs. The roads are so narrow, with no place to pull off, we are delighted to find these sites. It has started to rain again, the roads are very winding with glimpses of the river and many beautiful chateaus. Stopped in a small village patisserie for eclairs and cookies. Jane said they were the best she had ever eaten. Short stop at Roanne for chocolate and a stretch of legs. On to La Tour de Pin. Parked on the square and into the hotel. It is a bit embarrassing to have the women carry the luggage and we sputter French to try to carry our own. A wonderful dinner with fresh fruit for dessert. This is always a treat. Everyone in the hotel were friendly, maid drew bathwater for us. After a walk around town, the girls were trying to lock their hotel door with a key as big as a wrench about four inches long. They kept pushing it all the way through the keyhole so Dad gave them quite a scare by holding it from the outside. Much consternation as they tried to look through the keyhole to see who was breaking in. He was looking back at them. Good sleep.

As we came through Lyon, an interesting large city on three levels, we tried to look up Tom Schaffer's friend. Walked up four flights to her apartment but no one home and we left a note. The Rhone River runs through the city and has many beautiful bridges over it. We are happy with the Peugeot but seem to be slowpokes on the road. The French drive like fiends, and we are all agreed the Citröen is the silliest looking car we have seen. They are predominant.

Wednesday, July 20th

Chocolate and croissants for breakfast. On the way at eight-thirty. This is known as the Gateway to the Alps so we are all excited. Sunny with low-hanging clouds. Countryside still lovely with many small farms under cultivation. There is no waste in this country. Stopped at a market town to buy bread, meat and cheese for an outdoor lunch. Our next stop is

Chaminoix and we see Mont Blanc in the distance. The Alpine meadows and mountains are indescribable in beauty. Into Chaminoix, a bustling resort town, with Mont Blanc towering overhead. Streets are full of people in all sorts of dress. Knickers, pants, skirts, Alpine shoes and hats, walking sticks, backpacks and climbing ropes. Very cheerful. Dad bought a French beret. Wrote postcards beside a roaring stream in the middle of town. On our way again, very narrow road full of hairpin turns, real mountain driving. There are many bicycles and scooters on the street, the latter going like the dickens. Into Visp, Switzerland at 6 P.M. We must leave our car here and take a train to the Matterhorn. No trouble crossing the border. The guards are polite and friendly. We are staying at a Swiss pension tonight. We have three rooms, all very clean and our first eiderdowns. They speak German here and Dad is getting along fine. Our room has a balcony and the village is very picturesque, heavy steep slate roofs on the houses with window boxes of gorgeous geraniums. We order dinner and she is making Swiss fondue for me. Simply delicious. After dinner we walked to the station and bought tickets for Zermatt. The shop windows are full of climbing boots and alpine clothing. There were strange smells during the night and we found our bedroom was above a stable necessitating closing the balcony doors but it was great. Wish we could take this pension with us, it is so clean and comfortable.

Thursday, July 21st
Awakened seven A.M. by the ringing of church bells and the distant sounds of a saw mill. From my window I can see a swallow feeding her young. The nest is wedged between the slate shingles. All slept well. Dad took us to the station and is storing the car in a garage. We are surrounded by luggage of the people taking the train. The electric train came into the station at nine and there is a mad scramble to get aboard. There are two cars and we are separated in the rush but we all get seats. Dad and Jane are in the car behind. They were helping an old porter get the bags on. The car is filled with mountain climbers and their equipment and as we start up the valley, maps come out so that all the peaks can be identified. The scenery is magnificent, and we cannot get our fill of looking. Stopped at two tiny stations, the train whistle sounds like a toy engine. many tunnels, rushing streams, tiny farms and meadows, snow-covered peaks and then Zermatt. It has taken one and a half hours for the trip. When we got off the other car was missing. We lost Jane and Dad! It arrives ten minutes later and we are glad to see them. The hotel porter was at the station to meet us and took our bags while we walked two blocks to the hotel. This is a colorful village. No cars. Horses with bells around their necks pull all the vehicles and go along at a good speed. The chalets have

balconies and more beautiful flower boxes. It is a riot of color. Our hotel rooms were a pleasant surprise. Very modern, big wash basins in the rooms and Elden and I have a lovely balcony overlooking the main street. More lovely window boxes. The girls are just down the hall and also very comfortable. Eiderdowns again! We look out at a snow-capped peak and can hardly believe we are really here. To the dining room for lunch, food is very good and the service superb. Serving is done from lovely copper dishes and warmers, snowy white napkins each in a case. Lots of milk to drink too!

Jane went out, bought corduroy knickers and disappeared, with her books, to explore. Dad and the girls hiked up a hill back of the hotel and I strolled the main street and out the village to Gorner Gorge, which is the path to the Matterhorn. This mountain is really impressive, dominates the village and always has a wreath of clouds around its top. The sun is bright and warm. Watched a family raking and bundling hay in their small hillside field. Women and children are working, using wooden rakes. The men hoist a huge load of hay onto their back and trudge down the hill to a barn, up a ladder and heave the whole thing into a loft. The farm buildings are all snug and built close to the ground. Very small chalet type houses, stained brown and lots of colorful flowers. The children are charming, aprons over their dresses and kerchiefs over their heads. Very shy. Back to the village and window shopped. Lovely handmade blouses and linens and wonderful hand-knitted sweaters and socks. Leisurely dinner and to bed early—under the eiderdown. This is an enchanted spot for all of us. Nancy has picked wild flowers wherever we stop and we are pressing them in our travel book. Bought a bunch of Eidelweiss from a small farm boy who was holding them in his hand. A velvety gray flower.

Friday, July 22

Up at eight-thirty. Clouds in the valley, and can only see glimpses of the mountains but the sun is beginning to peak through. Took the cog railway to Gonnergrat, a lovely ride lasting almost an hour. Zermatt is in the valley and we go up and up above the timber line and into the snow belt. It seems like the top of the world, surrounding peaks and the clouds drifting by. Weather clear over Monta Rosa but the Matterhorn is covered by clouds but we did get one wonderful view of it. Nancy, Betsy, Mary and Dad are off on a hike, carrying lunches and walking sticks. Jane is off to seek a spot to study and relax on her own. I stay at the hotel sitting on the terrace, getting my fill of beautiful scenery and all the people. The sun is terrifically hot and the air quite cold. The steam heat in the hotel feels wonderful. The hikers return. They had walked almost to Stockhorn and were full of excitement. Everyone fortified with hot tea and back down the cog railroad.

At the next to last stop, Dad and the girls get off to walk the remaining four or five miles down. It was so steep that it was strenuous. They passed the farmers at work in their fields. It took two hours and they are tired out. About six P.M. we heard a great jingling of bells and looked out to see a herd of about twenty-five goats, all with neck bells, coming down the main street. Two or three little boys were having a terrible time keeping them on the move. The goats were trying to eat the geraniums in the flowerbeds in front of the hotels and the packages people were carrying. This was a nightly occurrence as they were brought down from pasture. Community goats and community herding! Dreamless sleep tonight. Mary says it is "The top of the world."

Saturday, July 23rd

Awakened by sounds like the jingling of a winter sleigh but it is the goats going back to pasture. They have a great time nibbling at the window boxes of the hotels but each hotel stations boys out front to chase them back. Up at eight and after breakfast walked to the chair lift with Dad and the girls but don't go along. They have lunches and will hike down. I think the girls are natural Alpinists as they cannot get enough hiking. Nancy would like crampons for her shoes and if encouraged would attempt the Matterhorn. Took a sun bath on the balcony and had my hair washed. When the hikers returned we toured the village museum with an interesting retired mountain guide. He had climbed the Matterhorn one hundred times and was full of exciting stories and lore about the mountains and the town. Many interesting relics and pictures here. Beautiful sunny day, had outdoor tea in one of the hotel gardens with an orchestra playing. It's still hard to believe I am really here. Visited the English church and cemetery. There are rows of young men killed while climbing the Matterhorn. Many of the tombstones have ice picks and ropes on them. Also the natives have lovely beaded flowers marking their graves. After dinner a local band, in uniform, marched up and down the street, followed by the townspeople, very gay—everyone singing. Seems this is the custom every Saturday night. We have all truly enjoyed Zermatt. We have had marvelous weather and have done whatever we wished to. We found the Swiss very polite and helpful but somewhat reserved. The food has been superb, the places clean and the scenery magnificent!

Sunday, July 24th

Up early. Took pictures of the goats going to pasture, one with a huge red geranium in his mouth. Took the eight-twenty train back to Visp. A professor and his wife from Dennison University were on the train. First people we have met from Ohio. All back into the Peugeot for a day's travel through the Alps. Roads were narrow, twisting and lots of big sight-seeing busses. Many times the road is so narrow the traffic is one way and we back up. No barrier on the right side and it is a long way down. The weather is good so we see some breathtaking scenery. Through the Furka Pass and stopped to look at the Rhone glacier. An awesome sight. The ice is a beautiful color, very cold here with a strong wind blowing. We are now in German-speaking Switzerland and have made several unsuccessful stops for lodgings. Apparently they think we are asking for six rooms. Dad changes his request to rooms for six people. With this change in wording we find a pension at Murg. Dinner and hot baths and we are lulled to sleep by a swift rushing river beside the house. It's been a hard day's drive for Dad. We passed many large lakes today. Many campers, it makes a pretty sight as their tents are bright colors.

Monday, July 25th
Breakfast and off to an early start at eight. Countryside is still beautiful, many steep hills, flowers enormous and colorful. There are many huge espaliered trees and the houses are beginning to be decorated with wonderful paintings of cherubs, flowers and figures. Passed through the storybook kingdom of Liechtenstein, a monarchy only sixty-five square miles in area. The castle sits on top of a mountain overlooking the village. Long line in the post-office. Their stamps are very valued. Added quite a few to our collection. Crossed the border into Austria without difficulty into Innsbruck at three-thirty. Looked around the open market, all kinds of interesting foods and flowers. We stock up on fresh fruit for breakfast. The old part of the city really looks ancient. The streets are cobbled and very narrow. We did not have time to tour the palaces but they are handsome and one had a balcony covered with gold leaf. The shops look interesting but there are so many people in the streets it is hard to get around. When we got back to the car parked on the street, my passport case was sticking up on the luggage rack. My purse had been knocked out of the car and as the contents were picked up the most important case had been missed. We wished to thank our anonymous benefactor but could not. I don't like to think of the difficulty we would have had without it. Drove for another hour or so and found lodging in a private home in a small Austrian village. Ate our supper at the village inn. I ordered an omelet and it turned out to be pancake filled with jelly! The girls were afraid we were going to have to wash dishes as we did not have Austrian currency or enough German marks and the waitress was suspicious of Swiss money. Had the same trouble paying for our lodging and Dad gave her extra American dollars. Next morning as we were eating our breakfast, the lady of the house was

mixing the swill for the pigs and telling about World War II and about her brothers that were lost in the war. When the swill was mixed, she opened a trap door from her kitchen and poured it down a shoot to the pigs below while still talking to us. We will remember that breakfast for a long time. Stopped at an orchard for a basket of apricots. Delicious!

Tuesday, July 26th

On our way in the night rain. We will be driving most of the day. The countryside is still lovely, the mountains are giving away to hills and the land is becoming very fertile. Hay is drying in the fields, it is hung over long lines. Drove into Zurich about five P.M. The traffic is very heavy and droves of people are on bicycles on their way home. They seem reckless to us and manage a good rate of speed in the traffic. We are intrigued by the street cars that are very long and narrow, single seats with an aisle in the middle full of riders. Checked in at Hotel Triumph. We are on the fourth floor, in an annex and no lift. Up with the luggage and nice clean corner rooms. We are going to get our exercise on the stair. Walked to Cafe du Nord for delicious dinner and then strolled the Bannhoffstrasse, this street is supposed to have some of the loveliest shops in Europe. Took a two hour boat ride on the Zurichsee. Many swans on the water and the lights of the city were spectacular. The children enjoyed this very much and it was a tired group that walked back to the hotel at eleven-thirty.

Wednesday, July 27th

Slept late and had breakfast in our room. Fresh fruit and milk. Only twice did we have milk in a paper carton, somehow it seems much safer to drink. Found our car was obstructed in the parking lot. (An inconsiderate American we later found out.) Hemmed in, the police would not intervene on the private property, we had to walk. Spent considerable time in the Swiss Handcraft shop, beautiful woven material, linens and carvings. Sell all the native dresses of Swiss cantons. Lunched at a sidewalk cafe. Taxied back to the hotel and managed to get the car out. (Dad was greatly tempted to let the air out of the obstructing car's tires but repressed the desire!) Drove past Ken Newcombe's University and out to the Dolder, an Olympic sized swimming pool where they produce breakers mechanically which are quite real. The girls went swimming and said they were scared when the waves started to roll. On to the Zoo, a most interesting modern one with many unusual animals well displayed. Mary was feeding peanuts to the goats and before she could get them out of the sack, they were chewing her dress. Drove around town and through the park, dinner at a very nice restaurant and then to bed.

Thursday, July 28th

Off early. Countryside very fertile and well planted. All the land seems to be under cultivation and the villages are charming. Stopped at Basil, wonderful square with old church that had a magnificent blue and white tiled roof and an open air market on the square. We all went with Nancy to a jewelry store where she picked out a Swiss wrist watch. She chose a lovely one and was thrilled. On our way again and into Heidleberg at five P.M. This is a bustling town and we go right to Heidleberg Castle. This is beautiful and is high on a hill on the banks of the Neckar River overlooking the town. We could see the crews shelling on the river. The castle is huge and built of a lovely rosy hued brick. There are many interesting moats and passageways and they were beginning to lay out formal plantings. It was now dark and we did not see the huge wine cask as the room was closed. No accommodations in town so we stayed at a Gasthouse at the city limits. Very nice. Had dinner at a Hofbrau where they roasted chicken on a spit for us. Jane was happy with that. The beer was good and Dad was doing quite well with his German, at least making himself understood. Money was fun for Dad; I mean converting it from one country to another.

Friday, July 29th

Early start on the autobahn where traffic is very heavy. Both lanes are full of cars and trucks of every description. There are many places to pull off and we see truck drivers resting and others having picnic lunches. Left the autobahn north of Frankfurt and found the traffic exceedingly heavy through the small towns. This is rolling farm land and many of the houses and barns are connected. The farm animals were very well kept and healthy looking. Nancy and Mary were thrilled to see so many horses in the fields and also many oxen. The country roads are full of slow-moving farm vehicles, huge wagons loaded with hay and slow going.

Arrived Marburg about three P.M. The town is full of people and our reservation is not good. The University is having some special occasion. We are sent to the town of Allendorf a small village about five miles from Hatsbach. Arrived to find we are in a very modern hotel. Jane and Mary have single rooms and there is lots of hot water. Excellent venison for dinner.

This part of Germany has been marked as a "distress area" and the government is locating new industry here. The housing is not being finished as fast as the industry so accommodations are at a premium in this rural area. We met a Canadian lady with three small children whose husband is head of one of the new firms. She has had to live in this motel for the past and is a bit discouraged. Back of the motel is a huge government barracks for unmarried girls. This area has a rather tense, explosive kind

300

of atmosphere. After dinner we drove about nine kilometers to the dorf of Hatsbach to see where Grandfather Weckesser came from and visit the people there now. They do not know we are coming. We find it to be a small village, the houses with red tile roofs, along a creek called Hatsbach. Many years ago boars were hunted along this bach, hence the name. Next year they will celebrate its 700th year of existence. The village is very quaint. Four hundred and fifty people live here and they wear native Hessian dress: long dark woolen pleated skirts, white bodice or blouse and a dark bodice over that, a neckerchief and their hair pulled straight back and into a knot on the top of their head for the women. The men wore a dark green suit made of Loden cloth. The chief person in the village was Baron von Coblitz. We were not able to completely understand his political position but we understood that Heinrich Weckesser gave a percentage of each of his crops to him. The houses are tall, 3 stories, and the fronts are timbered and painted. The sides and back are shingled. A high stoop for both front and back doors, the houses being right on the street. The barn and out buildings are at the back along with a barnyard with a huge pile of manure in the middle. In Hatsbach as since medieval times the people live in the village where they keep themselves, their livestock, farm machinery, etc. They go and return from their fields each day and these are at different locations. We were told that the Weckesser fields were at many different locations. This may be where the Baron comes into the picture. It would have been a good question to ask. Was the village arrangement for protection or for the allocation of the productive land? We'll have to ask that on the next trip.

While inquiring which house was Weckesser, a young man came speeding on his bicycle and somehow seemed to know we were looking for his family and led the way. This was Hubert the fourteen-year-old Weckesser son. He spoke no English. We got out at the house and had a warm welcome from Frau W., a sweet pleasant woman about fifty-five years old, Christine, a daughter, eighteen years, a very pretty blond girl, long hair done up in a braid and a wonderful smile. Herr Weckesser, a very nice quiet person about sixty years, Heinrich, one of the sons, about twenty-two years, a tall quiet nice looking blond and Fraulein W., a maiden sister of Herr W. who lived with them. There was a son, Conrad, who did not live at home but worked in the city. Before we could get into the house we were joined by a cousin of Herr W., Frau Drescher, a very talkative alert eighty-year-old woman who spoke a few words of English. We went to the back steps and into a large hall, then into a combination dining and sitting room. Christine got lovely crystal glasses from the cupboard, Herr W. appeared with a long tall bottle of wine and Frau W. opened a door of the floor-to-ceiling black heating and cooking stove, and produced a lovely pound cake. We sat around the table and drank a toast to Weckessers, American and German. Communications were somewhat difficult but Dad did fairly well. A granddaughter of Frau D.'s came in who was in school at Marburg and spoke some English. Ingrid was about seventeen years and the young people were able to get along pretty well. They will be busy in the fields tomorrow so we will come back in the afternoon. We felt that they were genuinely glad to see us and we felt the same way about them. This has been a long dream for Elden for this village and this house is where his grandfather lived until he came to American in 1854. The girls seemed to truly enjoy this experience. Home to Allendorf at ten-thirty.

Saturday, July 30th
Slept late. Jane stayed at the motel to read and sunbathe. Left other girls at Schwim-Bad in the small village of Kirchain. On to Marburg to call on Frau Weckesser, widow of a doctor, a professor of dermatology, University of Marburg. Sweet old lady who spoke no English. Elden had corresponded with her and she knew who he was. Gave us some history of her husband's family and some family papers. Bought lederhosen for Mary and strolled around the University town. Back for the girls who had quite an experience for two and a half hours with a group of German boys and girls. The pool was clean and large and a master kept his eye on them. Back to Hatsbach at four P.M. Christine, father and two brothers just coming from the fields, riding in the wagon on top of sacks of grain. They had threshed barley today. They carried the sacks up a ladder in their barn and poured it into a bin. Three or four sacks were kept back for the Baron. Christine did not think the Baron was good and Herr W. quickly changed the subject.

We had a tour of the barn and out buildings. An ox, cows, quite a few pigs, three of four horses, and lots of ducks and chickens. Everything looked productive and the animals healthy but it seemed filthy to me. They were reinforcing one part of the basement for a bomb shelter on their own initiative. It seemed strange to have them doing this way out in the country but these people are very conscious of war.

We went inside for a glass of cool chocolate milk topped off with whipped cream and sipped through a long piece of macaroni. Frau Drescher had arrived and we now had a walking tour of the village. They opened the school house and the school mistress showed us through. Elden asked permission and photographed an aerial view of Hatsbach which hung on one of the walls. It was a one-story brick building with black-boards, globes and usual student seats. It seemed to be well equipped and modern.

As we walked along the streets, villagers put their heads out to look at us. This seems to be the village way of keeping up with things. I'm sure all knew who we were and what we were there for. We drove to the cemetery to see the family burial plot. Plain headstones with the edges planted with pine trees. We were introduced to villagers as we moved along. Saw a mother and father, tools over their shoulders, driving a cart pulled by two oxen and two little blond boys riding in the cart. They were returning home from their day's work. Herr W.'s land consisted of fourteen fields with different crops and widely separated. Even the kitchen garden was about a mile from the house and was the responsibility of the women. They work hard. The girls helped (?) to milk the cows and Nancy had a wild bareback ride on one of the horses, right down the street—what a commotion! Supper was served when the chores were done. We had German hot potato salad, homemade spicy sausage, cold sliced meat and brown bread. Nothing to drink. We talk (?) for an hour or so and then say good-bye as we must be on our way in the morning. We have had a wonderful visit and wish that this family or some of the children could come and visit us.

Above the front door of the house is this saying:

"Das Schoensta Wappen, auf der Welt
Das ist der Pflug in Ackerfeld."

"The Best Weapon, in the World
Is a Plow in a Fertile Field."

(With this touching thought we leave the Weckessers of Hatsbach with a better understanding of Grandfather's origins and background and his outlook on life dedicated to advancement, complete honesty and fairness for others, which he carried with him through danger and adversity and handed down to his descendants.—ECW)

Sunday, July 31st
Left the motel at nine A.M. This has been one of the best and we are a little reluctant to be on our way. Raining. The land is becoming quite flat and there is little traffic. We are beginning to see signs of industry. Ate lunch at a small conditeri and arrived in Telgate about four P.M. Visited with Dr. Woltering with whom EC had corresponded regarding Weckesser ancestors in Germany. One of his sons had married a Weckesser and he was knowledgeable about the different family groups of that name in Germany. We visited with the family for several hours. Frau W. was a charming lady who spoke some English. They had three sons, two were nose and throat doctors and the other had an extensive greenhouse on the estate. All sons served in the German army during World War II. One

was a little annoyed that we were driving a French Peugeot. The other asked where we were from and when we answered Cleveland on Lake Erie, he recited from memory, the ballad "John Maynard" by Horatio Alger. In that ballad, the helmsman of a crowded burning wooden ship, *The Ocean Queen,* on Lake Erie ("The Erie Sea") lost his life grounding the vessel saving the lives of the passengers. A moving ballad.

We toured the grounds with a lovely lake and tennis court and had coffee. They were warm and friendly and we enjoyed our stop very much. The grandchildren were sturdy little blonds, all dressed in lederhosen. It is still raining and we go on to Bochum, the steel center of Germany where EC had been in touch with a hand surgeon by the name of Hilgenfeld who had done some outstanding work on reconstruction of the seriously damaged thumb. In the rain we manage to find a comfortable hotel and put up for the night. Baths for everyone, garage for the car and a good night's sleep. The girls thought this was a "spooky" place. They rode the elevator from the dark basement to the third floor and thought someone was after them.

Monday, August 1st
Elden left early to contact Dr. Hilgenfeld at his hospital, Augusta Kranken-haus (Hospital) and watched him operated. Had some difficulty communicating but enjoyed seeing him work and having a tour of the hospital. The girls and I ate breakfast at the hotel and about eleven A.M. were called by Mrs. Adler, the young attractive wife of Dr. H.'s resident. She was an American girl who had met her husband while he was in training at a U.S. hospital. We were taken to Dr. Hilgenfeld's apartment and soon the doctor and EC arrived, much surprised to see us already there. (Some sort of magic, he said, Dr. H. had not told him what was happening!) We all enjoyed a lovely luncheon. Many German men return home at noon, have a large mid-day meal and return to their work about three. Both our host and hostess were charming and hospitable and it was interesting to see and hear about the life of a German doctor and his family. Their apartment was very modern and beautifully furnished, many beautiful paintings. They have two grown daughters who live away from home. Dr. H. returned us to the hotel and in an hour we were on our path north. We cross the border into Arnheim, Holland where we spend the night. Arnheim was almost completely destroyed by the Germans during World War II. There is still much evidence of bomb damage. Bochum also had severe bomb damage from English and American bombing since it was a heavily industrialized city. The ruins we saw made a deep impression on us all. Had a good dinner in the hotel but our rooms were noisy. We'll be glad to be on our way.

Tuesday, August 2nd

Up at seven-thirty. We are all looking forward to seeing Holland. The land is really "low." You sense this as you drive along. We seem to be on the same level as the water in the canals. Peaked roofs on stucco houses, occasional windmills, houses with thatched roofs, dikes and many, many people wearing wooden shoes. Almost everyone walks or rides a bicycle, the strangest sight is a woman in high heels, hatted and gloved, purse in the bicycle basket, peddling along like mad. On to Utrecht, a nice old town, the old church and a beautiful blue and white tiled roof. Stopped at fruit market and had lunch on the road.

Arrived Amsterdam at twelve-thirty. A large bustling city, not very clean. Took an hour-and-a-half boat ride on the canals, I understand why this city is called the "Venice of the North." Saw Rembrandt's house, "Weeping Towers," the busy ocean port and we all liked the steep, narrow houses built so close together, all with a hook at the top so furniture and pianos can be hoisted in. On through the peaceful countryside of Edam, a small town with many store houses for cheese. The windows on these cheese storehouses were open for ventilation and you can see tiers and tiers of cheese there ripening. On to Volendam, a picturesque fishing village where the townspeople wear native costume. Harbor filled with fishing boats that had striking red sails, and fresh and smoked fish were being sold in stalls along the waterfront. Bought a few trinkets and wooden shoes for three and five guilders each (80 cents = 1.50 dollars). On to the Island of Markhem, now connected to the mainland by a road built on top of a dike. Native costumes on villagers here and also at a fishing village. The women wore their hair in long curls, long black skirts and small white lace caps. The men wore baggy breeches and a small cap on their head. These two places were very interesting but we thought quite commercialized. On to Harlaam, the bulb center of Holland. Spent the night in a small, crowded hotel, all in one noisy room with sagging beds. Eight guilders apiece for this type of accommodation, motor cycles and scooters on the street all night long and they are much noisier, with their backfires, than autos. We have decided the Dutch speak English and charge American prices. The food has been good but the hotels are the poorest and prices highest of our trip so far. Dad says the men wear the baggy pants with deep pockets to carry their money.

Wednesday, August 3rd

Off to an early start past acres and acres of fields that are being readied for tulips, into Delft. It is a sweet little town, lovely church on the square where we heard the church bells ring. Bought some china. The shops are full of beautiful porcelain Delft Ware and handsome brass and copper

305

Dutch antiques. Meat, cheese and fruit for lunch, which we ate beside a canal with a huge windmill in the background. Ducks and boats on the canal and a strong cold wind blowing. On to Antwerp but did not stop to sightsee. The whole family is tired from not resting last night. Into Belgium after passing courteous border guards. The countryside is beautiful and we pass many lovely farms. Passed World War I towns with familiar names and many military cemeteries, English, German and American. Into Brussels at four P.M. A very large city, full of activity. Hotel very nice and they gave the children a warm welcome. Three rooms, lots of hot bath water and a superb dinner in the dining room. Spent the evening catching up on correspondence and washing clothes. To bed early.

Thursday, August 4th
Up early. Betsy and I went shopping. Spent an hour in a lovely lace store where we bought a wedding veil for Margie Mayher and for the Weckesser girls. They were most interested in explaining the history and patterns of Belgian lace and we learned many interesting things from the saleslady. Betsy has a good time modeling all the veils. Jane and Nancy had chosen to stay at the hotel. Mary and Elden looked up M. Louis Weckesser who turned out to be an important official in the Belgian National Bank. They had to pass several people to get to his office. He was a very large man who, speaking no English, greeted them cordially through an interpreter. Dad communicated about the family with interest. He was pleased that Mary could speak a little French and as they left sent out for a box of luscious Belgian chocolates which he gave to her.

Did not have time to explore the old city which was a disappointment. I would like to return. Left hotel shortly after noon. Lunched along roadside. Crossed the French border at a small village as we are going cross country to Ariens. No bank at this border so we take along Belgian francs and will take a loss when we exchange them for French francs. We again see many monuments to American soldiers of World War I and cemeteries in the small villages. In Ariens at 5 P.M. On inquiry as to where the Galehouses live the reply is, "Oh, the Americano, Gellihoos" and a small boy volunteers to lead the way on his bicycle. Shirley and the children are home and give us a warm welcome. We are glad to be there. Jim gets home about seven-thirty from the Goodyear, a new factory site at Amiens that is being built under his supervision. We have a wonderful dinner, talk and get to bed late.

Friday, August 5th
Breakfast late, we all enjoyed Shirley's "porridge," good coffee and tea. Baby Martha is a sweet little blond and just beginning to walk. Our girls

are anxious to help with her and they enjoy the Galehouse children very much. They are off to investigate the village, shops and ruins of a castle right back of the house. Shirley's French maid washed our clothes and I ironed so everyone is in order again. Shirley's house is very interesting and large but poorly planned as far as housekeeping efficiency is concerned, but she has a good maid. Our girls are very good about helping with meals, dishes and the baby. Jim doesn't get home until late, Amiens is nearly twenty-five miles south. The boys have firecrackers left from celebrating Bastille Day so we have a display in the evening. Elden and I walked to an old chateau and around the village. I seem to be getting a cold so to bed early.

Saturday, August 6th

I have a temperature and cough this morning so I stay in bed. The rest went to visit a cave, La Cite Souterraine de Naours, and were very impressed especially by the dungeon where there was a ball and chain and carvings on the walls made by prisoners. A real poke back into the middle ages. They also visited the Chateau at Picquigny and Shirley who speaks French well has shown them many points of interest. The children love wandering around Ariens and were fascinated with the abattoir where the local butchering is done. They enjoyed getting milk in a pail at the store and French bread of course with no wrapper. Jane is happy speaking French and says the best way to really know the people is to stay in a village like this.

Sunday, August 7th

Still have a temperature. Elden is giving me penicillin. Jim is home at noon. He really works long hard hours but seems to thrive on it. Quiet day, everyone is doing as they please. Temperature still 103. If it is still up in the morning we shall have to cancel our trip to England. Thank goodness we are here with Jim and Shirley. Everyone has been wonderful, climbing the stair with trays and going back and forth to the store for bottled water and other supplies.

Monday, August 8th

Still have fever and a bad cough so England is out. Elden has taken three of the girls and driven to Paris to cancel our channel crossing and try to make arrangements through the Paris Auto Club to get transportation home. They had a busy time in Paris running from one agency to another. We have seats on TWA leaving Paris on Wednesday, the Paris Auto Club was very helpful. Back by four P.M. Stopped at Amiens to see Jim's new factory and the Cathedral. The latter was very beautiful. This has been a wonderful visit for all of us which we shall long remember.

Tuesday, August 9th

Left Shirley's about eight-thirty after taking photos of the children and the house. The girls said regretful goodbye especially to Martha. Two and a half hour drive to Paris. The weather is cold and sunny. To the Auto Club, which is in Place Vendome, a very intriguing square full of exclusive shops. They get us rooms at Hotel Printemps, rather old but our suite must have been the best in the house. Very large and beautiful furnishings and a large bathroom. The girls are down the hall in a similar room. This is living it up. Lunch in the hotel. Nancy and Dad left to drive the car to Le Havre to ship it home to Cleveland. They got back on the "boat train" at ten-thirty P.M. Had a harrowing time finding the proper offices in Le Havre to ship the car and nearly missed the boat train back. They ate French bread on the boat train back and were happy. The girls and I went shopping. I did not feel as though I could leave Paris without seeing a few things. Walked to Rue Royal and bought Lalique glass, gloves and perfume. Heavy downpour of rain so we taxied back. Wonderful sole for dinner. We have all enjoyed French cooking. To our rooms early. It is exciting to think we are leaving for home tomorrow and I think we are ready to go.

Wednesday, August 10th

Up early, our last continental breakfast. Taxied to the air terminal; it is a beautiful warm sunny day. There were so many bags that only Betsy and I go in the cab. The others take the Metro and we meet at the Terminal. Customs checked us through. We get on a bus that delivers us to Orly Airport. Dad has changed his money not expecting additional charges. At the airport there is an un-anticipated airport tax of three dollars each so dear old Dad had to reconvert dollars back to Francs to get us by! This was a tax just to walk through but I guess all taxes are like that. A smaller bus takes us to our American TWA Jet and we are glad to get on board. We sit three and three again, and take off at one-thirty P.M. There are 136 passengers aboard, every seat taken. There is a holiday atmosphere aboard in contrast to our quiet takeoff when we left New York coming over. People are talking and exchanging experiences and visiting up and down the aisle. Perhaps the cocktails are helping but we detect more than that. This load of folks is returning to their country of choice and they are feeling good about it. Elden has set his watch to New York time and mine says five-thirty P.M. Paris time. The flight is smooth. We are able to see Goose Bay far below and have to change course because of air force maneuvers over Maine. After eight and a half hours we make a smooth landing at Idlewild Airport. Forty minutes to go through customs. When we get to the lobby and look outside, the sky is very dark and it is pouring rain. Elden, Jane and Nancy take a taxi to Long Island to pick up our car.

The rest wait with the luggage. It is several hours before they get back with the car but we load up and take off. Drove until ten P.M. and found a motel in New Jersey. A tired crew tonight.

Thursday, August 11th

Drove to Princeton, New Jersey for breakfast, a real American meal, then back on the road home. Weather dull, some car trouble with the fuel line causes a delay but we are back on the road again. Everyone is tired of looking at scenery and glad that we shall be home tonight. All agreed that we have had a wonderful trip but Nancy said it best, "America, U.S.A., the best place." Arrived at 2708 Coventry Road at nine P.M. to find our friend Helen Herbut there and Dutchess, our Labrador Retriever, delirious with happiness to have us back. We have a week end to catch up on mail and a chance to visit the cottage and pony, Apache, before Elden goes back on call.

Our trip has deepened our appreciation of our wonderful home and all that we have here. All the planning and expense has been worth while.

—Kathryn Tuttle Weckesser

Finis

Hand Surgery Meeting, 1961

Electrical injuries of the hand were presented by Dr. Snyder then of that city. He pointed out that the hand is frequently the point of entry in electrical injury since the hand is the organ of prehension. The current is transmitted particularly along blood vessels and nerves to an exit area of the body which has the least resistance. Extreme temperatures, up to 3,000 degrees fahrenheit can occur at areas of resistance along that route causing extreme destruction and frequently extensive loss of tissue. The demarcation between healthy remaining tissue and that which will not survive may be slow to develop. Adequate time should be allowed for that to occur. Electrical injuries are noted for slow healing. Sensation may be impaired after nerve injury. Dr. Snyder described a patient who could feel objects in the affected hand but could not describe the shape of the object.

In the nineteen-sixties clothes wringer injury was still prevalent when children's and women's hands in particular were accidentally drawn between the wringer rollers. Dr. Vinton Silver gave an interesting review of 444 patients, 320 of which had been followed during twenty years of treatment at the Cincinnati General Hospital. The majority of the patients were treated as outpatients. Nine percent of the patients required skin grafting. The results were good in 94 percent of his patients.

Some of these injuries are extremely severe. I had a terrible case of wringer injury sent to me. A five-year-old boy, the son of deaf parents, caught his hand between the rollers of a wringer in such a way that it rolled against his thumb and the rollers continued to turn producing much heat and destruction in his little palm. His screams were not heard by his deaf parents and the child was trapped there for an unknown interval of time. The tendons were visible in the center of his palm. This required pedicle skin and subcutaneous tissue to be brought into his palm from his abdomen with several operations, restoring most of his function.

Events of 1961*

In 1961 conditions were worsening with the Soviet Union. The "Cold War" was intensifying following the U-2 incident of 1960. This was manifest by the breaking of diplomatic relationships with Cuba before President Eisenhower left office.

On January 20, John F. Kennedy was inaugurated president. In his inauguration address he said, "Ask not what your country can do for you, ask what you can do for your country." Brother Robert Kennedy was made Attorney General.

April 17, an ill-planned, or at least poorly coordinated, attempt by Cuban nationals to invade Cuba was unsuccessful. The intended invasion of Cuba ended in a sad failure, the Bay of Pigs disaster, on the fifty-sixth day of his administration. Had the outgoing president adequately briefed the new young president on this venture?

In mid-summer, President Kennedy met with Soviet leader, Nikita Khrushchev in Vienna. They were able to talk and discuss disarmament and the problems of Laos and Germany, although tensions between USSR and the U.S. remained strained. The atmosphere was somewhat better than it had been between Khrushchev and President Eisenhower.

A Big Four meeting with Britain, France and Germany was held in Washington, D.C. to consider the problems of getting supplies into West Berlin in the face of the noncooperation of the Soviet Union.

The minimum wage was set at $1.25 an hour. A bill was passed by Congress to allow a National Debt of one billion dollars. Surgeon general of the United States, Dr. Terry found that smoking tobacco was related to the development of serious heart and lung disease (Carruth, 633).

May 5, an American astronaut, Alan Shepard, was rocketed into space—the first American to make this type of voyage (World Almanac, 524) which helped a little to lighten spirits and build confidence for Americans. We now had made definite progress in the space program. Yuri Gagarin, USSR, was the first on April 12, but we were catching up.

May 25, Kennedy's State of the Union message. He announced that the U.S. would continue taking a leading role in space exploration (Carruth, 632).

---

*This page was done from memory and Wenborn (317).

Bomb Shelters, Cuyahoga Countywide

On October 6, 1961 President Kennedy recommended the construction of shelters by individual families in the United States to protect against thermo-nuclear fallout in case of nuclear attack (Carruth, 633). This was followed by widespread construction of air raid shelters through out the country and a program of Civil Defense with widespread planning in all communities to deal with the effects of atomic bomb attack should it come.

In Cleveland, this was taken up by the Academy of Medicine. Other doctors and I took an active part in the planning for Civil Defense by the Academy of Medicine, Cleveland, coordinated with officials of Cuyahoga County. Many meetings were held with many different groups and with the thirty-one mayors of the county. It was a large undertaking taken seriously by all involved. We were living under the threat of nuclear attack by Inter-Continental Ballistic Missiles (ICBMs). On the light side, my good friend, Dr. Fred Mautz said, "Those are nothing new, the Eskimo's have had them for years!" A joke sometimes helps lighten a burden. We all took the problem very seriously holding meetings with the mayors and hospital groups in Cuyahoga County, arranging for construction and stocking of public shelters in preparation for the worst which everyone hoped and prayed would not happen. Fortunately it did not, although the tension lasted between the Free Countries and USSR from 1945 to 1992.

My medical associations were primarily with University Hospitals, Cleveland and Western Reserve University. (Case and Western Reserve became associated in 1967 into Case Western Reserve University).

There was some Town-Gown attitude in Cleveland at that time that I thought might be lightened by University participation. President of the university, John Schiff Willis, gave encouragement in the undertaking. The meetings for disaster planning were carried out by the Academy of Medicine coordinated with Civil Defense. I was chairman of the Disaster Planning Committee of the Academy. We had run out of town speakers and many of us traveled to other cities for their meetings to develop the best ideas. Possible nuclear attack added a new dimension to defense. No one was experienced in the undertaking. Football rivalry was forgotten. We even shared ideas with doctors of Pittsburgh! A fine relationship developed. It was for mutual understanding and the benefit of each in a most serious situation, which fortunately never materialized. The potential international adversaries each knew the advantage of the aggressor, a first strike, but also realized the probable annihilating consequences for all involved. The "Cold War" held for forty-seven years. My participation in those Academy activities led to my becoming president of that organization for the 1967–68 term, which was an interesting experience leading to meeting many fine people in the community just after the introduction of Medicare, which provided assistance for medical expenses for those age sixty-five years and older.

Events of 1962
Twenty-fifth Wedding Anniversary

The spring of 1962, March 17 was the twenty-fifth wedding anniversary for Katy and me. Somehow, Mrs. Spencer, a grateful patient, learned of this and offered us the use of her lovely resort home on Harbor Island, Bahamas for two weeks. It was a beautiful spot and we enjoyed it tremendously. Kathryn's mother, "Grandmother Tuttle" came from Lima to keep the home fires burning and take care of the children at 2708 Coventry Road. Jane, the eldest, was away at Albion College in Michigan. Betsy and Nancy were in Shaker Heights High School and youngest daughter Mary was in Woodbury Junior High. We felt comfortable with Grandmother Tuttle in charge and flew to Miami, Florida. There we changed planes and flew to Nassau, then in a much smaller plane northeastward to an airfield near Harbor Island, then in a boat to Harbor Island proper. The low flight from Miami over to Nassau was particularly beautiful with the blue ocean and islands with palm trees and beautiful sand beaches. Everyone was relaxed in the small plane, including the pilot on the last leg.

Suddenly en route there was a loud noise and a terrific draft in the cabin. A porthole of the plane had come open and air was noisily rushing, I think, in. At any rate it was very noisy. An elderly lady sitting nearest the porthole was naturally quite frightened. The hostess changed her seat and reported the condition to the pilot. He said, "Let her blow, we're almost there, that porthole has done it before."

About twenty minutes later we made a noisy but otherwise uneventful landing followed by a pleasant boat ride to small Harbor Island. Our spacious house was near the harbor in town. This was ours with an attentive housekeeper and a house on the beach about a five-minute walk away.

According to instructions we had ordered a supply of food from the mainland to be brought in by boat. A storm held up the supply boat so that it was a week late. With the aid of our good housekeeper, we managed very well, but when the late supplies finally arrived, it was overwhelming. We ate what we could, gave some to acquaintances and left the rest to our housekeeper, a very fine lady who had taken good care of us.

On the trip home we flew back to Miami, where we rented a car and drove over the Tamiami Trail to Naples, Florida. Sanibel Island and

Tampa, where we turned the car in and flew back to Cleveland. The Tamiami Trail had been completed in the mid-1920s when I was in high school. One of my schoolmates had bragged knowingly about it at the time of its construction and I had wanted to see it. It was a fine two-way traffic road at that time leading through the Everglade Swamp to Naples and then northward to Tampa where it connected with Route 301 north completing a north–south route from the west coast of Florida.

When we stopped at Sanibel Island we had to ferry from the mainland. The now existent bridge was being talked about with many pros and cons. The Island Inn had been a very popular place with doctors from Lakeside Hospital, Cleveland. I had heard it mentioned a great deal in the dining room at Lakeside Hospital and elsewhere. Katy and I found Sanibel Island quite beautiful with its tall Australian Pines and beautiful sand beaches with good shelling. In 1962, before the causeway, it had not been developed greatly. We visited a small shell shop not far from the ferry terminal run by a very nice elderly lady named Mary Cunningham. There had been a rather hard rain that morning with some high wind gusts shortly before our visit. We were at the front of her store, where she was showing us shells when, on looking out the window, she suddenly exclaimed, "Oh my snails!" The wind and rain had blown them to the ground from a small tree in front of her shop and she rushed out the door with much concern to place them back up on the branches of the tree, a most unusual and touching display of compassion of one living creature for others, in this case tree snails! On subsequent visits to Sanibel Island Katy and I were unable find her shop.

The whole two weeks were a great experience for both of us and a most generous gift for a patient to give her doctor. The children had a good time with Grandmother Tuttle while we were away.

Surgery, 1962

The seventeenth annual meeting of American Society for Surgery of the Hand was held at the Palmer House in Chicago, January 26 and 27. The problem of flexor tendon repair in the palm and digits was a subject of discussion. The problem has been worked out in subsequent years as follows.

This was a "No Man's Land" area in which the results of surgery were extremely disappointing due to adherence at the site of repair. There was no question that primary repair of tendons in this area was a special problem and needing to be handled by a surgeon skilled in techniques to prevent this complication.

The first method advocated was cleansing of the wound, doing soft tissue closure only, and referring the patient to a surgeon skilled in the techniques of tendon surgery who would then do a tendon graft as an elective operation. The joints of the finger were exercised to prevent joint stiffness. This was an advancement. Results were better.

As time went on a second method was developed that is the one most frequently used today. It was found that primary repair could be successfully delayed if the patient was referred immediately to a person skilled in the techniques of tendon repair. The primary physician with this method cleanses the wound, applies a sterile dressing, gives the patient an antibiotic, and makes the referral at the time of injury. This gets the patient to a skilled operator for the primary attempt. This delayed primary repair is carried out within the next twenty-four hours if possible, with a very gentle technique to prevent further injury to the delicate gliding mechanism of the tendon, the tendon sheath and surrounding tissues. Nonreactive suture material is used. Lastly, in order to prevent tendon adherence at the site of repair, early guarded passive, then active, movement is instituted under the supervision of a trained therapist. This technique of delayed primary repair has made "No Man's Land" a "Some Man's Land" or "Some Woman's Land" in regard to successful flexor tendon repair in the palm and finger. It has given great improvement in a very serious type of injury.

Other Events of 1962

There was some easing of tension over Berlin but the wall remained. The United States removed its tank force from the wall and several days later several Soviet tanks in the area were removed. On January 29 a three year nuclear test-ban conference between Britain, United States and USSR adjourned. The talks were deadlocked over a monitoring system for international control.

American troops were sent to Vietnam on training missions. They were instructed to fire to protect themselves.

January 12—The Pennsylvania and New York Central rail systems merged. American and Eastern Airlines merged.

February 20—John Glenn orbited the earth three times in a space capsule (Carruth, 638–39). Alexei Leonov of the USSR had done this earlier. The Atomic Energy Commission announced the first Atomic power plant in Antarctica.

In April the Defense Department ordered full integration in military reserve units.

April 21—"Century 21 Exposition" opened Seattle, Washington.

April 25—The U.S. resumed nuclear testing in the atmosphere after a three-year hiatus. President Kennedy announced that the USSR had already broken the moratorium (Carruth, 640).

June 4—122 Americans killed when French jet plane crashed in Paris.

Treasury Department announced U.S. expenditures for 1962 at $87 billion, revenues at $81 billion. The national debt exceeded $300 billion.

July 27—Marines were withdrawn from Thailand (Carruth, 642).

May 24—Scott Carpenter, orbited earth three times in *Aurora 7* (Carruth, 643).

September 24—President Kennedy activated 150,000 reserve soldiers for active duty.

President Kennedy and the Cuban Missile Crisis

On October 24, President Kennedy announced that photographs showed that Soviet Missile sites were being constructed in Cuba ninety miles off

317

our shore! The process was under way with more Soviet ships en route to Cuba bringing more equipment. President Kennedy placed an air and naval quarantine on Cuba allowing no more ships or planes with supplies to arrive. It was a very tense international situation in which the unthinkable could happen. It was the most critical incident in this regard; the possible exchange of nuclear weapons that had occurred since the end of World War II. The whole nation watched on television and I remember an announcer on the car radio saying, "Keep your car filled with gasoline." Where one would drive to was an unanswered question. Kennedy and Khrushchev negotiated for several days while supply ships were en route. President Kennedy was able to talk to Khrushchev and was more successful than President Eisenhower had been.

On October 28, agreement was finally reached. Khrushchev was to remove missile bases in Cuba under UN supervision. The United States would not invade Cuba and would withdraw missile sites from Turkey. On November 20, President Kennedy lifted the blockage of Cuba. The critical situation was resolved. There were no enemy missile launching sites built in Cuba. The mutual destruction of atomic attack was realized by both countries. Subsequently, the stand-off continued but communication between Washington and Moscow was improved.

Structure of DNA

The Nobel Prize for Medicine was awarded to Drs. James D. Watson, Harvard, Maurice H. F. Wilkins, Kings College, and Francis H. C. Crick, Cambridge, for their interpretation, and recognition, of the double helix molecular structure of deoxyribonucleic acid (DNA) which carries all of our individual characteristics in each nucleated cell of our body and is the basis of heredity (Carruth, 647). This was the culmination of the efforts of many people (Asimov, 579). It is *mind-boggling* that each of our physical characteristics is recorded in each of the trillions of nucleated cells of our body! The DNA of each nucleus carries this information in special sequences of amino acids. These sequences are different for each characteristic; the color of our eyes, our hair, the shape of our face, and so on. This amazing natural event is especially remarkable in view of the trillions of nucleated cells present in our body!

Surgery, 1963

Dupuytren's Contracture

My results in eight-one cases of Dupuytren's Contracture treated by excision of the palmar fascia over a period of fifteen years were presented at the meeting of the American Society for Surgery of the Hand on January 18, 1963, at the Americana Hotel, Bal Harbor, Florida. Among the cases that followed more than two years, 67 percent had a good to excellent result, 28 percent fair, and 5 percent had a poor result. Dupuytren's Contracture is an unusual condition, cause still unknown, more common in men and usually more severe in men, which causes the fingers to contract into the palm. The problem was thought to be in the flexor tendons in early days but this was not the case. In 1831 Baron Guillaume Dupuytren demonstrated at the City Hospital of Paris, Hotel Dieu, that the problem was in the palmar fascia, a layer of tough fibrous tissue beneath skin of the palm that normally gives the palm of the hand resistance to the strains and stresses of heavy manual use. A plaque in the courtyard of Hotel Dieu commemorates him today.

Dupuytren's Contracture is painless but interferes significantly with hand function. The patient is not able to straighten the fingers, put on gloves, open the hand completely for grasp or wash one's face normally, and can be embarrassing when shaking hands.

The typical contracted position of the ring and small fingers with the long and index fingers extended constitutes the Apostolic Posture of the hand given credence in theology. It is quite possible that an early theologian had the condition. It is more common in those of Anglo-Saxon descent and not common among those of southern Europe descent or the Black race. There is an increased association with heredity and alcoholism.

It is frequently bilateral. There was an increased incidence in our Diabetic Clinic. There is some indication that Vitamin E, an anti oxidant, taken by mouth is of some benefit and is worth trying in early cases. Once strong contraction bands have formed, which are frequently associated with contraction in the overlying skin, surgery is necessary by a surgeon well versed in caring for the problem. Z-plasties are very useful at the base of the digit and in the digit to gain more skin length to allow extension. The use of skin grafting is necessary in severe cases with guarded early motion to provide extension and to prevent further joint stiffening. Immobilization is good for wound healing but the small joints of the hand stiffen readily when immobilized. Proper hand function requires mobility of the digits. This is the dilemma that the experienced hand surgeon can best cope with and even then not in every patient.

Microsurgery

A very interesting paper by Drs. James Smith and Herbert Conway of New York described the use of the dissecting microscope to suture small nerves in the hand. This was Microsurgery of Peripheral Nerves. By means of a magnification of ten diameters it was possible to actually place very fine microscopic stitches accurately into the connective tissue covering the nerve fibers and give very accurate approximation to the nerve bundles. This was a great advancement. The microscopes would soon be available as well as the necessary fine instruments with which to do the work. Up to this time it was not known that one could operate under this degree of magnification. Microscopes were soon developed with multiple heads so that the surgeon, assistant and the scrub nurse could all focus their attention in the magnified field. The nurse or assistant would bring the fine needle and suture into the microscopic field under the microscope with a tiny instrument where the surgeon could pick it up with his tiny instrument and place it accurately where it should go. It was a new world, so to speak, within the magnified operative field.

This magnified technique would develop very rapidly in all sorts of other situations where magnification was needed. It was found especially useful to repair small blood vessels and make possible the reattachment of small severed parts, such as digits. It also led to the method of transferring tissues from one part of the body to another by reuniting small arteries and veins in the new location. The heart by-pass operations were a direct descendent of this technique. All sorts of magnification loops were soon available for use when the degree of magnification required was less than that supplied by the microscope. Microsurgery was to develop very rapidly with these new tools. In the case of the tiny blood vessels, which were prone to clot, thrombose—the use of coumarin and other anti coagulants—would be developed rapidly to greatly reduce this risk. The advances have been tremendous.

Events of 1963
John F. Kennedy President of U.S.,
Lyndon B. Johnson, President of U.S.

On June 8, the American Heart Association began a campaign against tobacco smoking (Wenborn, 323). It was publicly reported that habitual tobacco smoking is caused by the addiction to the nicotine in the cigarettes. This is still resisted by the tobacco industry in the 1990s.

Tobacco Smoking a Nicotine Addiction

The tobacco industry is large and very strong. Tobacco has been a very lucrative product, tied up in the economy of the entire country, especially in the southern States. According to a *Wall Street Journal* article on September 22, 1995, quoting from a recent article from the *Journal Science,* researchers at Columbia-Presbyterian Hospital in New York have known that nicotine can activate nerve cells, although nicotine is not a chemical that the body normally uses. Nicotine is similar to a very important chemical in the body, acetylcholine, which activates nerve cells and is involved in the transmission of nervous impulses. The nicotine is similar enough that it activates the same receptors on nerve cells that are activated by acetylcholine. It makes blood vessels constrict and the heart go faster.

In addition, the nicotine also turns on the Limbic system deep within our brain where "behaviors important to survival are reinforced." This makes the person more alert, improves attention and aids short term memory. The work done by Drs. Lorna W. Role and Daniel S. McGehee was carried out on brain cells of chicken embryos. They found that the small concentrations of nicotine in the blood of a smoker were sufficient to activate the chicken embryonic limbic cells. Their hope is that with this finding, drugs to counteract addiction can be developed.

It is the exhilaration of nicotine that causes people to continue to smoke. It is possible that some other substance can be found to give this exhilaration without ill effects on our lungs and blood vessels. Tobacco smoke causes degeneration of blood vessels throughout our body and severe changes in pulmonary function, emphysema and malignancy. The dangers of tobacco smoke are proven now and accepted by all those addicted and those in the tobacco industry. The number of people killed by the ill effects of tobacco smoke has been astronomical. I can count a large number of my own friends among this group. My wife Kathryn has had the upper lobe of her right lung removed and has had to have extensive irradiation, which has been successful and for which we are very thankful.

With the facts known at present, it is very unwise for people to continue to smoke. This is said in view of the numbers of my friends who have died from tobacco smoke and the difficulty that my wife Katy has had requiring the removal of her right lung. When I see people smoking, often outside the door as I enter an office building, I wish to and sometimes do call out "Four," similar to the "Fore" in golf, then say, "Each cigarette smoked costs four minutes of your life!" When I say that to a smoker, my message is usually not well received. The tobacco industry needs to find a harmless form of nicotine or a harmless substitute for acetylcholine. Until that time, willpower is the best solution with emphasis on avoiding the habit completely especially by our young people.

June 26, President Kennedy traveled abroad. He was especially well received in Berlin and the Soviet Union. A "hotline" was set up between Washington and Moscow. The civil rights movement gathered momentum. Martin Luther King, Jr. made his "I have a dream" speech at the Lincoln Memorial in Washington in which he said he saw the division between races melting away.

On September 24, Nuclear Test Ban was ratified by Senate.

Assassination of President Kennedy

President John F. Kennedy was shot by rifle bullets on November 22, 1963, in Dallas, Texas, while riding in an open touring car from the airport with the First Lady and Texas Governor John Connally and Mrs. Connally. This horrible event was seen on television by the entire nation and throughout the world. He was shot in the head by rifle bullets fired supposedly from a warehouse window along the parade route, according to the official investigation and report. There are still questions about what actually transpired and the entire truth is probably not known. There were factions with Cuban interests that did not like his successful handling of the Missile Crisis in Cuba in October one year earlier. The entire country was stunned.

The First Lady was not struck by bullets but was witness to the entire ordeal. Governor Connally was wounded but survived. The assassin, Lee Harvey Oswald, was himself assassinated a few days later by a nightclub owner, Jack Ruby, who was imprisoned and later died there. Questionable aspects of the assassination remain.

Vice President Johnson was sworn in as president of the United States in the plane that flew him back to Washington.

Vietnam War

President Johnson, the newly sworn in president of the United States, inherited the unpopular Vietnam War, an unsolved problem for him and the country. He decided to carry it on even though it had no specific objective that could readily be settled by force. Vietnam was a poor country. The natives were fighting on their own territory, so to speak, even though we were supporting the South Vietnamese attempting to prevent takeover by communist North Vietnamese. America had the high objective of supporting free people and help them elect their own leaders. There were many factions in the primitive country who for their own selfish interests did not want this to happen. After reverses, the French, who the U.S. was supporting, withdrew. The United States had intervened to help the French protect their possession and prevent the spread of communism. After the French withdrew, our objective was no longer clear. Our stated objective for being there became: "To bring Hanoi to the conference table" and then let South Vietnam set up its own free Democracy.

The local people in Vietnam did not fully understand this or at least some ruling factions there did not want it to happen and did not respond vigorously to the call for arms to prevent takeover by communist North Vietnam. We were fighting to protect the South Vietnamese from takeover but they did not show organized enthusiasm for the idea. Other factors, from a military standpoint, were that there were no identifiable concentrations of power or strength that could be taken or destroyed by modern war tactics. The war dragged on. There were analogies to the situation that existed between the American colonists and the British during the

323

War for Independence in the 1770s. This time, however, things were not in our favor. Finally, the necessary and wise decision was made to allow the South Vietnamese to fight for their own freedom. They had to decide their own fate.

By November 27, the national debt limit was raised to $315,000,000 (Carruth, 660).

On December 17 President Johnson addressed the UN calling for efforts to eliminate hunger, disease and poverty (Wenborn, 323). This was a high calling from which he and his First Lady ''Ladybird'' would be distracted by our involvement in the Vietnamese war that had been handed down.

Surgery, 1964

The Program Committee of the American Society for Surgery of the Hand this year was Weckesser, Western Reserve, Chairman, Henderson, Mayo Clinic, Stromberg, University Chicago and Goldner, Duke University.

We decided to hold the meeting in two parts. The first part at the Mayo Clinic January 15 and 16. Being winter and with the probability of bad weather, and the uncertainty of some air flights at that time, it was decided to use the train between Chicago and Rochester, Minnesota for reliability.

The second part of the meeting was at the Palmer House in Chicago January 17 and 18, 1964. The evening train from nearby Winona Junction, Minnesota, was scheduled to arrive in Chicago at 8:30 P.M. the evening before, which would give enough time to get to our hotel in preparation for the morning meeting January 17.

We arrived in Rochester on schedule about noon on January 15 and were put up at the Kahler Hotel, which serves as the living quarters for patients before admission to the hospital. We were welcomed and given a tour of the Mayo Clinic, which was very nice. In the evening we met in the Heritage Hall for a social gathering and dinner.

On Thursday, January 16 we met at 7:45 at Mann Hall of the Medical Sciences Building and were welcomed by the chairman of the board of governors of the Mayo Clinic, Dr. L. E. Ward. Clinical presentations were then given by our hosts, Drs. P. R. Lipscomb, E. D. Henderson and R. L. Linscheid.

The presentations included electromyography as an aid to diagnosis in diseases and conditions of the hand such as nerve entrapments. The sensory conduction time was shown to be the earliest detectable alteration in Carpal Tunnel Syndrome, useful in the diagnosis of that condition.

Numerous other cases, including Claw Hand following gunshot injury, quadriplegia from motor accidents and falls from a tree, and severe fractures provided much discussion among the group.

At noon we had lunch at the Mayo Foundation House, which was very nice, followed by an afternoon clinical session again at Mann Hall, which covered Dupuytren's Contracture, congenital anomalies, and the arthritic hand. It was a very pleasant and instructive meeting. Our hosts made our stay very pleasant and made our meeting very worthwhile.

Winona Junction

At about 5:00 P.M. we left the Kahler Hotel by bus for a short trip to Winona Junction to catch the Burlington Zephyr for Chicago, due at 6:00 P.M. This train was to whisk us to Chicago quickly for our main meeting early next morning at the Palmer House Hotel. That was the plan.

The train did not come and several hours went by while we waited and worried in the cold station. It finally arrived about three hours late, clanking along at a very slow speed due to a burned out bearing in one of the cars!

The condition of the car with the bad bearing did not allow rapid travel and we clanked slowly to Chicago arriving there well after midnight! With just a couple of hours sleep, on checking on our meeting room at the Palmer House found that it had not been set up for our meeting. This took additional time and our meeting started late.

Papers presented at the Palmer House included early excision of electrical burns by Rex Peterson, to diminish disability time. The conclusion drawn was that this idea was sound if it was certain at operation that the vessels to the remaining structures were intact and uninjured. The electrical current travels in the blood vessels and can seriously damage the linings of those vessels. Early repair and shortened immobilization periods are highly desirable but it is necessary that further closure of blood vessels does not occur. In this regard anticoagulation can be helpful.

Freeze-dried flexor tendons were transplanted in dogs with a study of the healing process within the tendon sheath by Austin Potenza. This was a worthwhile observation. The tendon can heal within the tendon sheath and early, gentle, protected movement can also diminish adhesion formation during the healing period.

Julian Bruner of Des Moines, Iowa advocated the use of a magnifying optical loupe to be worn with a headband on the forehead of the operating surgeon during tendon repair. This was a good suggestion and was rapidly adopted. His motto was, "See More in '64." It did not give the magnification of the microscope but was less cumbersome and helpful in making accurate approximation of tendon ends.

J. William Littler recommended rotation of the index finger for children with absent or rudimentary thumb. The index finger is rotated into thumb position at the age of three to five years. It is well to have this

326

done before school age as it is for deformities in general so that ridicule by other students can be kept at a minimum.

The meeting wound up with a panel discussion on mobilization of the stiffened interphalangeal joint (middle joint) of the finger. This is an important because a stiffened finger not only does not function properly but gets in the way of other digits, diminishing their function. The panel consisted of Elden Weckesser, Moderator, J. William Littler, J. Leonard Goldner, Raymond Curtiss, Robert Carroll and Mr. A. R. Wakefield of Melbourne, Australia and Mr. H. Graham Stack of England.

Dr. Littler reviewed the anatomy of the middle finger joint. Mr. Stack reviewed the facial layers, and Dr. Carroll emphasized that the articular structure must be intact for any chance of success. This is shown by pre-operative X-ray. Dr. Goldner also emphasized this point choosing ankylosis in severe deformity. (Now joint replacement is also possible.) Dr. Curtis considered that the best indications for removing the tight capsular ligaments was in stiff joints in which the bone contour was normal. He considered post-operative flexion of 80 degrees to be a good result.

Mr. Wakefield favored early post-operative motion with which the moderator agreed heartily and added that local injection of triamcinolone had value along with the early movement. The panel agreed that the final result depended greatly on post-operative care best given by a trained therapist with the surgeon following progress closely.

The 1964 trip to Rochester, Minnesota, and the fine meeting there, the bumpy late trip back to Chicago on the train and the two days of meetings there is remembered by all who made the trip. I can report that no further transportation problems occurred on the way home. Arthur Barsky did not take the train from Chicago to Rochester, he went by air instead and had no difficulty getting back to Chicago in time to have a good night's rest before the second part of the meeting.

327

Events of 1964
Lyndon Johnson President of U.S.

January 8—President Johnson delivers the State of the Union address announcing his "War Against Poverty" (Wenborn, 323).

January 11—Surgeon General announces proof that tobacco smoke severely injures human lungs (Wenborn, 393).

March 16—President Johnson requests Congress to appropriate $962 million for "War Against Poverty."

April 5—Gen. Douglas MacArthur dies.

May 19—Bugging of U.S. embassy in Moscow announced by State Department.

May 27—Major earthquake in Alaska kills 117 people (Wenborn, 327).

June 24—FTC announces requirement of health warnings on cigarette packages.

July 23—Senate passes Anti-Poverty Bill supplying $947 million for same.

August 2–5—Two U.S. destroyers attacked by North Vietnamese PT boats in Gulf of Tonkin.

August 7—Gulf of Tonkin Resolution gives president power to defend U.S. forces (Wenborn, 327).

August 24—Lyndon Johnson, for president, and Hubert Humphrey, for vice president, nominated by Democratic Convention.

August 28–30—Race riots in Philadelphia.

September 24—Warren Commission concludes that Lee Harvey Oswald acted alone in assassination of President Kennedy.

October 20—President Herbert Hoover dies.

Khrushchev deposed in Russia.

China explodes an atomic bomb and declares an open breach with USSR.

November 3—Lyndon Johnson and Hubert Humphrey elected by large majority (Wenborn, 327).

Surgery 1965

The twentieth annual meeting of the American Society for Surgery of the Hand was held at the Americana Hotel in New York City on January 8 and 9, 1965 with Robert McCormack of Rochester, New York as president.

There was a preliminary Clinical Meeting on Thursday, January 7 at the New York Academy of Medicine. Local men presented patient histories of interesting patient problems as well as actual patients. Robert Carroll, Arthur Barsky, J. William Littler, L. R. Straub, Herbert Conway and William Metcalf made these presentations, following which there was much interesting discussion by members.

On Friday and Saturday, January 8 and 9, the meeting was at the Americana Hotel. (Only some of the many subjects covered can be referred to.)

Dr. James Smith gave a report of his studies on the blood supply of tendons in animals. He reported that the most important blood supply is segmental through the mesotenon and that few vessels come from the bone insertion of the tendon. New vessels, the first part of any healing or regenerative process, are produced from the divided ends accompanied by cellular proliferation from the divided tendon ends. The new cells need nourishment, which is supplied by this early regeneration of blood vessels. The mesotenon allows the tendon to move and also supplies nourishment to the tendon.

James Hunter gave his experiences with artificial tendon implantation. Silicone rubber prostheses were left in place about which a gliding mechanism was formed. Passive movement was maintained to prevent joint stiffness. These prostheses were replaced by tendon grafts three to six months later in the majority of patients. This technique is recommended only for "tendon salvage situations." The concept of producing new gliding surfaces for the tendon was an interesting attempt at salvage in severe situations.

Ritchey, Shaw and Nahigian of Cleveland presented results of delayed flexor tendon repair. This was recommended for division of the deep plexor tendon of the distal joint of the digit. Thirty out of thirty-three cases flexed their fingertips to within one centimeter of the base of the digit. These were good results, much better than lacerations of both tendons at the base of the digit.

329

Tendon transfers to overcome paralysis of the small muscles within the hand, which provide delicate movement, were presented and discussed by Frank Clippinger and Leonard Goldner.

The Founders Lecture was a scholarly address by Professor J. M. Landsmeer of Leiden, Holland. He analyzed the fine motions of the hand identifying the many small intrinsic muscles within the hand responsible for these movements. (The coordination of all these fine movements is a truly marvelous thing.) His lecture was very well received by this group of hand surgeons.

George Phalen of Cleveland gave his experiences with Carpal Tunnel Syndrome over the previous seventeen years. He discussed the methods of diagnosis, including the wrist flexion test presented by him fourteen years earlier. He had operated on 654 hands and had followed 439 of them. Results following Carpal Tunnel release were good, with improvement even in those who presented atrophy of the muscles of the base of the thumb, a sign present in advanced cases.

The Presidential Address was given by Robert M. McCormack of Rochester, New York, who gave a review of the history of the organization. Its inception was in 1946 and 1947 just after the close of World War II. The formation of the organization followed the army development of Hand Surgery Centers in 1944–45 for the care and reconstruction of the upper extremity injuries of war. At the end of the war, the men in these centers were largely responsible for the formation of the organization.

He pointed out that the organization had held post-graduate courses and symposia throughout the country that had been very valuable in teaching proper methods of hand care and had been very influential in raising the level of hand care in the country. He thought the greatest value was in providing properly trained people opportunities to practice throughout the country. "Born of World War II, the society has had strong international influence throughout other countries including Mr. Wakefield of Australia and Professor Landsmeer of the Netherlands on this year's program."

Rotational Osteotomy of the Metacarpal for Phalangeal Malunion

When the bones of the finger, metacarpals or phalanges are fractured it is very important that these bones be accurately realigned to regain proper function and relationship of the fingers as they converge on flexion toward the center of the base of the palm. To gain this end it is frequently best to do open reduction and internal fixation. The proper alignment of these small bones is nearly as important as maintaining motion to prevent joint stiffening. If not properly carried out, the fingers may overlap when they are flexed. This produces discomfort and weakens the grip.

Rotation at a fracture site may be difficult to see on X-ray but becomes very apparent when the fingers are brought into flexion. This can be avoided by treating fractures of the phalanges and metacarpal bones in flexion primarily, if open reduction is not done.

I reported at this meeting a method of treating patients with overlapping fingers from rotational malunion of phalanges or metacarpal bones. On my first patient, rotational deformity had not been recognized on X-ray by the primary doctor treating the patient. A splint had been applied with the finger straight instead of in flexion. The fracture of the proximal phalanx had healed in a rotated position. On attempted closure of the hand, the fingers severely overlapped. The flexor tendons had also become adherent at the site of fracture. It had been a spiral fracture. Rather than take down the healed fracture, the base of the metacarpal was transected and the digit rotated to bring the finger into alignment. It was then securely stabilized in its new position with transverse Kirschner wires. The adherent tendons were also freed at the same operation. Movement was started immediately, post-operatively. The Kirschner wires were removed a month after the operation and a good result was obtained. This procedure was used for malunited phalangeal and metacarpal fractures with good results.

Many fine papers were presented at the 1965 meeting at the Americana Hotel in New York City. It was a very successful twentieth anniversary meeting.

331

Events of 1965
Lyndon Johnson President of U.S.

February 18—Defense Secretary McNamara calls for nationwide building of bomb shelters.

April 28—Marines sent to Dominican Republic to protect U.S. citizens.

May 17—Mass bombing in Vietnam.

June 26—Additional 21,000 U.S. soldiers deployed in Vietnam.

July 14—Death of Adlai Stevenson.

July 30—Medicare began providing limited health care for those over sixty-five years of age or disabled. Becomes law.

August 4—President Johnson requests Congress to appropriate $1.4 million for Vietnam War effort.

August 11–16—Severe race riot in Watts section of Los Angeles, thirty-five dead and great numbers injured (Wenborn, 329).

October 1—Antipollution bill empowers Secretary of HEW to set emission standards for toxic air pollutants.

November 9–10—Severe New England power blackout which puts NYC in darkness.

December 4—*Gemini 7* launched at Cape Kennedy to rendezvous in space with *Gemini 6* (Wenborn, 329).

Missiles and Future Wars

Technical advances will alter how future wars are fought but to what extent cannot be accurately predicted because of the great variation in tactical situations, which change continually. In the Buna Campaign of World War II in New Guinea, August of 1942, things were at a standstill with the enemy entrenched in very effective coastal tunnels and fortifications. Finally flame throwers were brought in to effectively dislodge them from their entrenchments and the campaign then progressed. Technical advances applied properly in any situation can mean the difference between success and failure. The musket in Colonial times was a great and decisive advancement over the bow and arrow.

In general, the side with the most suitable and adaptable methods has the advantage. Radar, for example, developed early in World War II by the United States, gave a great advantage by providing effective scanning in darkness, clouds, fog and other situations where vision was limited. Wonderful as it is, to my understanding, it is not equal to 20/20 vision.

Guided and homing missiles that zero in on a specific target have great potential when they are properly controlled. The use of satellite guidance is changing this tremendously.

The goal is to do as much as possible by remote control and keep personnel protected. The fact has been that the human brain, the greatest of all computers, is needed to make quick decisions at the scene of action. Do new developments change this? Can radar surveillance, possibly by small unmanned aircraft sensors, be developed to supply sufficient information and awareness at the scene of action to allow complete remote control? This is the unanswered question (Stix, 92). Unmanned craft are highly desirable but can they do the job? The answers lie in the future. In the meantime we still need aircraft carriers and the ability to get them through the Panama Canal rapidly in case of need.

Summary of Advances of Nineteenth and Twentieth Centuries

In summary, the number of developments of the nineteenth and the twentieth century related to the development and use of energy is striking. In physics, energy is defined as the capacity to do work, to overcome resistance. Being invisible, in many ways it seems like magic but follows the laws of nature. We cannot see energy but are able to see its effects and what it does for us. Early humans must have soon appreciated that it was easier to walk downhill than uphill, even though they did not understand just why. They did not know what is now common knowledge: when we are at a higher level, we have additional potential energy due to the forces of gravity. They surely took advantage of the fact although it was not understood. Let us first consider the peaceful use of energy.

The Peaceful Use of Energy

In the beginning of the world, the energy of sunlight supplied early man with light, warmth and food. This was followed by manmade, controlled fire some five hundred thousand years ago (Asimov, 5). With fire, the ancestors of the human race had an extraneous source of heat and light, which allowed them to exist in lower temperatures. They soon put it to work for cooking, heating and probably more, and the pace of developments accelerated with time.

Let us look further at these developments from a constructive peaceful standpoint, ever mindful that energy, power, has been used traditionally to establish leadership and control. It has been used destructively by those seeking domination by war, an ever-present, unsolved threat, demanding continued special attention and a continued strong defense. The following is a list of types of energy that we humans have used peacefully.

Human Muscular Effort
Sunlight
Fire
Wind
Tide

334

Beasts of Burden
Falling Water
Steam
Gasoline
Internal Combustion
Gas
Oil
Atomic Energy

Gas is usually piped to consumers for home and factory use. Internal combustion engines usually run on gasoline electrically ignited and controlled. Diesel engines ignite fuel by high compression but have electrical controls.

With large amounts of energy, converted to convenient electricity and readily available, multitudes of applications followed. Some of the amazing things electrical power has made possible are-

In the Home:
Heating
Cleaning
Washing
Cooking
Refrigeration
Radio
Television
Travel:
On roads:
Motorcycles
automobiles, etc.
On Rails:
High speed trains
On Water:
Many types of sail, propeller and jet methods
In Air:
Airplane, sub and supersonic planes
Space:
Travel, limits to be established

Electronic

(use of electrons): Radio, television, radar, laser, transistor (leading to computers and automation—events detected electrically and response made usually now electrically without immediate supervision) and ever greater developments constantly.

The developments shown above are due to increased knowledge and understanding of physics and chemistry. Similar effects are evident in the practice of medicine to the same or even greater degree. Many of the complicated functions of our bodies are becoming better understood and the process is expanding at a rapid pace. This includes a much better understanding of the functioning of each of the trillions of cells that make up our body. Indications are that life itself depends on electrical charges within our individual cells.

In earlier days doctors did not have the knowledge available today and were restricted in many instances to treating symptoms of disease rather than curing the disease itself, as is often possible today. This is no reflection of them. They were doing the best they could under the circumstances that existed and with the knowledge and methods they had. Actually, that is what we are still doing today with better understanding, methods, medications and procedures. It has been said that doctors in earlier times, with their limited knowledge, were not able to do much. Comparatively speaking, that may be so. However, they were able to give comfort and relief of pain to their patients and give psychological support, which was as important then as it is today. The practice of medicine is now based on science and facts. In spite of this, the art of medicine is still needed as much as ever, to give comfort and psychological support, emotional control, in time of stress as well as relief of pain. This needs to be remembered in this age of rapid scientific development. It is still a valuable part of medicine that patients need.

Medical Advances of the 1800s

Control of Infections

Our skin protects us from most outside invaders and prevents evaporation of our internal body fluids. Our bodies are 60 to 70 percent water.

Microorganisms were first observed in 1676 by Leeuwenhoek with his excellent hand-ground lenses. This man showed that these tiny microorganisms existed in rain water much to everyone's astonishment at that time. Pasteur, in 1956, showed that tiny organisms were involved in the fermentation of wine.

Nine years later, in 1865, the year our War between the States ended, Joseph Lister published a paper "On the Antiseptic Principle in the Practice of Surgery." In this publication he advocated the use of carbolic acid spray in the operating room to deter the growth of germs. This related wound suppuration to the growth of microbes in the wound for the first time. There was much delay in accepting Lister's method and in accepting the idea that small organisms not visible to the naked eye were the cause of wound suppuration.

Eleven years after Lister's publication, Koch, in 1876, proved that microorganisms caused disease by culturing them outside the body, injecting the cultured organisms into animals producing disease, then once again recovering the same organisms from the diseased animals. This idea was sound. Fulfilling those postulates in 1876, Koch proved that microorganisms caused suppuration and disease. The next and last remaining step, following Lister's antiseptic methods, was to go to asepsis by sterilizing all things before they came in contact with the wound to prevent the introduction of microorganisms. With the latter the truly modern method of preventing wound infection was attained. With refinements, it is the method used today.

The work of Lister, Pasteur and Koch established that microorganisms caused certain diseases. Note the time required. Two hundred years. It seems long now with hindsight but the relationship of new facts is slow to evolve.

Control of infectious disease was thought to be effective, with the advent of asepsis. Holmes and Semmelweiss, especially the latter, independently advocated cleanliness in obstetrical delivery rooms in 1846–47 with much reduction of Puerperal Fever (Asimov, 317).

Antibiotics, after World War II, became the great boon for the treatment and prevention of infection making many more operations and the use of fabricated replacement parts safe to use in our bodies. This allowed the use of artificial heart valves and artificial joints without the great threat of destructive infection that existed previously.

The introduction of antibiotics in the late 1940s, was the final step forward leading to the opinion by some doctors that the problems of infection had been solved. Now, fifty years later, we know better. All living things, including microorganisms, are able to make adjustments in their metabolism to overcome unfavorable conditions in their environment. Microorganisms have done just that. They have become resistant to many antibiotics and now live with them instead of being destroyed by them. This is a serious problem now confronting modern research. Adjustments in antibiotics are being made but the final answer is not clear. One thing is certain. We should not use antibiotics unless they are truly needed and then only for a limited time to prevent the development of resistance. Each doctor and patient must make this judgment.

Viruses are very tiny bits of nucleic acid inside a protein shell that have the ability to enter our cells. They are one two hundredth the size of the smallest bacteria (Asimov, 105). They enter our cells, particularly our lymphocytes, as parasites and reproduce themselves there with the mechanisms of the host cell. "Nervy" in the extreme, robbers! They break out in great numbers, weakening or destroying the host cell to enter other lymphocytes and repeat the process.

A great unsolved problem at present is HIV (Human Immunodeficiency Virus), a virus that destroys immune cells in our body so that we cannot fight off even simply infections. Much effort is being applied to this baffling problem and it is hoped that a solution will be found. Life here on Earth continues to encounter one serious problem after another.

Relief of Pain

Medications for relief of pain were pioneered by Paracelsus (1493–1541), a Swiss physician using opium extracts, tinctures of laudanum. In 1805 a German chemist, Serturner, isolated the active ingredient, which was named morphine (from the Greek word sleep) (Asimov, 258). Morphine and other alkaloids have been used for pain relief since then with proper attention to the dosage necessary to avoid addiction to the substance.

The inhalation of ether was first used as general anesthesia to allay pain during an operation to remove a tumor of the neck by Crawford W. Long in 1842 (Asimov, 313). He continued to use ether but did not report his accomplishments. His work was verified by others in his community (Garrison, 505).

In September 1846, a dentist, William Morton, who had extracted a tooth painlessly, gave a demonstration of the use of ether at the Massachusetts General Hospital in which the patient was made unconscious by inhaling ether vapor while Dr. John Collins Warren painlessly removed a tumor from the left side of the patient's neck. At the end of the procedure, Dr. Warren turned to the audience saying, ''Gentlemen, this is no humbug'' (Garrison, 505). Dr. William Morton is generally given credit for the discovery although Dr. Crawford Long had used it four years earlier with out so reporting. Chloroform was introduced soon after ether. Now many other substances and techniques, a long list of them, are used by those in anesthesiology. The substance is chosen to best fit the surgical procedure being carried out.

Control of Hemorrhage

After pain, loss of blood was the next problem for surgeons when they incised tissues of the body or treated injuries that had severed or injured blood vessels. Application of local pressure, the method still used today in emergency situations, was and is useful. Small vessels soon seal off by coagulation when pressure is applied to a wound. This was followed by visual identification of larger arteries and veins in the wound, clamping with the use of special clamps aptly called hemostats, then litigation when necessary to do so. A French army surgeon, Ambroise Pare, usually is given credit for reintroducing the ligature for control of hemorrhage during amputation of severely wounded extremities in the 1530s. Experience and judgement is required when larger vessels are ligated.

Vessels are now rejoined by suture or staples, which has led to the development of vascular surgery and explains the great salvage of extremities and lives especially in recent wars.

The tourniquet, originally an emergency tight constriction about an extremity to prevent serious loss of blood, now is a broad pneumatic cuff with controlled air pressure also used for operating on extremities, especially the arm and hand, for limited periods of time.

Advances of Twentieth Century

Improved Medical and Surgical Training of All Medical Personnel

Science, with its emphasis on accuracy and facts rather than opinions, was developing in the nineteenth century, becoming ever more present with time. Europe and the British Isles, with earlier beginnings and greater background, were the leaders during the American Colonial period and some time after. According to Garrison, modern science attained full stride well after the mid-nineteenth century (Garrison, 408).

It was common for American students to take some of their training abroad well into the twentieth century. As our country developed this became less common, although a healthy exchange of ideas on the postgraduate level has continued. As American universities developed, the exchange of knowledge here and abroad, including all countries of the world, has had much mutual benefit. The universities on our East coast developed first because this section was settled first. As the country developed, fine universities developed throughout.

The first medical school in America was established in Philadelphia in 1765, in the College of Philadelphia, which later became the University of the State of Pennsylvania. Philadelphia was the largest city in the country at that time with a population of 25,000 people. The second medical school in America was Kings College in 1768, in the city of New York, and is now called the College of Physicians and Surgeons of Columbia University. The third medical school in America was Harvard College in September, 1782. After this, there was an hiatus in the formation of new medical schools in America. This hiatus was ended by the opening of the Johns Hopkins University School of Medicine in 1893, called by some the most significant event of the 1890s.

Johns Hopkins, a Baltimore banker and largest stock holder in the Baltimore and Ohio Railroad, provided the funds for the university in 1873 just before his death (Kaufman, 149). The Johns Hopkins Hospital, with a separate board, was planned to operate as an integral part of the medical complex. It was staffed and operating in 1889, four years before the Johns Hopkins Medical School opened in 1893 with a four-year graded curriculum. The staff of the hospital was very well known. Welsh, pathology; Halsted, surgery; Osler, medicine; and Kelly, gynecology, known as the four horsemen, each a leader in his field. The hospital training program included planned training program for interns and residents, a very foresighted provision, becoming the fourth excellent medical training center in America. This was then followed by Yale and other great universities of inland cities: Pittsburgh, Ann Arbor, Cincinnati, Cleveland, Chicago, to name only a few, extending eventually to the West Coast.

In the early part of the twentieth century, before and during the development of these medical centers of our East coast, the training for doctors was largely tutorial in America. Cleveland Medical College, the forerunner of what is now the School of Medicine of Case Western Reserve University was formed in 1843. The affiliation became complete in 1884 when Western Reserve University was incorporated, becoming Case Western Reserve University in 1967. Advanced training on the British Isles and in Europe was popular in the nineteenth and much of the twentieth century.

In Ohio this tutorial system was in vogue in 1843 when Cleveland Medical College, now the School of Medicine of Case Western Reserve University was founded. This was forty years after Ohio had been admitted to the union.

To practice medicine, a candidate then studied under, observed, helped and "rode with" a medical practitioner for a fee. After three years, when all requirements were fulfilled, the candidate received a certificate that legally provided the right to practice medicine. Many candidates began practice with this certificate. The quality of training given under the tutor depended upon many factors. How busy he was, how interested in teaching and his effort to instruct his protege.

By 1886, there were seven medical schools in the United States with four-year courses and twenty-three with a three-year curriculum. The number of four-year curriculums then increased rapidly, and was given a tremendous boost later by the Abraham Flexnor study and report referred to below.

In order to obtain a medical degree in the 1840s, it was necessary to attend at least two additional sixteen-week sessions at a medical college, following which, after successfully passing examinations, a medical degree was bestowed by the associated university (Weckesser, 1986, 3).

The place of the hospital in the community was changing quite rapidly in the latter part of the nineteenth century. First it was being separated from the "Poor House" and the "Old Folks Home." Secondly, brought about by better understanding of the cause of illness and understanding of the physiological functions of the body, the new well-equipped hospital became the center of advanced medical care. Many of the complicated modern methods of treatment were and are no longer possible at home. In response to this need, the modern well-equipped hospital fortunately developed. In America this first took place in the large universities on our East coast, as mentioned above, leading to the house staff residency programs for the further training of doctors after the completion of medical school. This was associated with the development of nursing programs for the training of nurses, both leading to the present training programs at medical centers throughout our country.

Flexnor Report, 1910

The 1909 study of medical education in the U.S. by Dr. Abraham Flexnor led to his 1910 "Flexnor Report." In this he recommended that medical education be given in medical colleges with a close association with a university. Western Reserve Medical School was praised by him for its university association.

This association with the university placed emphasis on academic study and the scientific method, which emphasized factual reasoning and understanding. The latter have had a tremendous beneficial effect in understanding the cause of disease. With an understanding of cause, logical forms of treatment could be and were worked out for many illnesses.

The Flexnor Report of 1910 and its recommendations had great influence in placing emphasis on scientific methods, resulting in upgrading medical education as well as medical practice in the United States. The value of properly supervised medical education in improving the quality of medical care in America and the world cannot be overemphasized. In the years following the report, the weaker, proprietary schools, the main object of the effort, were either upgraded or closed.

Better Understanding of Physiology of Shock

With the discovery of anesthesia, pain was no longer a strictly limiting problem. Antisepsis and asepsis, which followed two decades later, was shown to greatly reduce, nearly preventing, postoperative infection. Two great restraints were removed from the advancement of surgery. More extensive procedures were possible. What would the physiological effects of extensive surgery be on the patient? It was known that extensive injury had in the past been associated with a condition known as "shock," in which the blood pressure dropped, the pulse rate accelerated, and death frequently occurred.

342

Physiology, the study of organ function, carried out by surgeons and physiologists, provided answers. It was shown that blood loss caused the blood pressure to drop because of a diminished volume of blood in the patient's circulatory system. This diminished blood pressure caused a diminished oxygen supply for the cells of internal organs, which augmented the low blood pressure and other sequela. Shock could be prevented by administration of blood or crystalloid solutions (saline and sugar solutions particularly). These replacements during operations increased the time in which surgeons could operate safely, and hence greater procedures could be performed.

New anesthetic agents were developed that were better tolerated, also making surgery safer and extending its scope.

Pulmonary Emboli

Slow blood flow in the lower extremities after an operation is conducive to clot formation in the veins. These clots are in danger of breaking free and traveling to the lungs, where they seriously obstruct the blood flow and can cause death.

Venous return circulation is increased by elevation, which hastens circulation due to the effect of gravity, and by muscular contraction. Early ambulation after surgery is a good prophylactic procedure to prevent slow circulation in the lower extremities, where clots are apt to form when a patient is resting in bed or sitting in a cramped position. Muscular exercise is a strong aid to circulation. It should be remembered not only in bed but on long airplane flights. Flexing and extending the ankles is a very worthwhile preventive.

Anticoagulants are frequently used now postoperatively to prevent clot formation when the risk is high. The development of anticoagulants to control blood clotting has made surgery even safer and is particularly useful in long procedures and after vascular repair or replacement.

Controlled Respiration (Positive Pressure Breathing)

When our chest wall muscles and diaphragm contract it enlarges the size of our thoracic cavity, thus lowering the internal pressure, and we say that we inhale a breath of air. Actually, the air rushes into our lungs due to the outside atmospheric pressure of approximately fifteen pounds per square inch until the lungs are filled and the pressure is equalized.

We exhale by letting our chest wall muscles and diaphragm relax, causing our chest wall to spring back to its original shape and position, causing the excess air that had entered our lungs to be pushed back out, ready for our next breath.

Antibiotics

The control and prevention of infection have played a very important role in surgery. This was not only in the treatment of infection but in the prevention of it. Antibiotics have made it safe to insert prefabricated materials into wounds. Heart valves and prefabricated blood vessels are outstanding examples of this. Both have been of very great value.

Anesthesia and Surgery

During World War II, in the field and military hospitals anesthesia consisted of local injection, spinal injection, and regional block anesthesia done by the surgeon. Nurse anesthetists did an excellent job with inhalation anesthesia, GOE, oxygen, gas and ether. I remember an emergency appendectomy done on shipboard on the *USS Barry* in convoy in mid–Pacific Ocean with several generals looking over my shoulder. This was under spinal anesthesia personally administered. That was an anesthetic of choice at that time for abdominal work. It was effective for the patient and gave good relaxation of the abdominal muscles so that the surgeon could visualize the organs he was working on.

With advancements in surgery after World War II leading to extended and protracted procedures by specialists on all parts of the body, new anesthetic methods and agents were required, leading to specialists in anesthesia: anesthesiologists. This was natural as the field developed and became more complicated. Advancements since that time have been very great, with many new drugs administered by different routes and monitored constantly during operations.

Chest Surgery

Breathing is vital for life, and because opening the chest cavity interfered with or stopped the process of breathing, chest surgery was slow developing. Methods of maintaining respiratory exchange with the chest open were not developed until the late 1930s. This was accomplished with positive pressure breathing. Respirators were finally devised to deliver air and other gases under pressure slightly above atmospheric pressure just enough to inflate the lungs, controlled so as not to injure the delicate alveoli in the lung, which transfer oxygen to the hemoglobin of the blood. (Once the oxygen is taken up by the hemoglobin of the blood it travels rapidly to all parts of the body.)

Dr. Frederick Mautz of Western Reserve University perfected such a respirator, which he described in 1939 and again on page 544 of the *Journal of Thoracic Surgery* (June 1941). The slightly increased pressure that the respirator supplies with the chest open is just enough to inflate the lungs and give an adequate oxygen supply without causing damage. Actually, the slight elevation of pressure at which the air or gas is applied through the respirator has the same effect as lowering the pressure within our thoracic cavity when our respiratory muscles contract and expand the chest. This respirator gas pressure is slightly more than the pressure in the lungs, and because of that the lungs are inflated and normal gas exchange can occur in the lung. Mouth-to-mouth respiration is based on the same principle and has the same effect in emergencies.

Heart Surgery

With the advent of safe positive pressure breathing, organs of the thoracic cavity, including the heart, were open to surgical repair. The barrier had been broken. Previously stab wounds of the heart only had been treated. In the treatment of this injury the surgeon did not have the responsibility of an elective operation. It was a bloody procedure for the surgeon, who, with a finger over the wound to diminish the squirting blood, sutured the heart muscle back together. The walls of the operating room frequently needed to be washed. Now elective procedures could be undertaken with reasonable risk.

Heart valve procedures for mitral stenosis to open the mitral valve orifice by finger fracture or incision have been done by Elliott Cutler and Claude Beck, operating through the sternum, in the early 1920s. Now with positive pressure breathing new fabricated valve replacement operating through the chest is possible. This is made even safer by the use of antibiotics. Prior to antibiotic usage foreign bodies frequently became infected.

Endoscopic Surgery

More recently endoscopic surgery has been gaining a place for many areas of the body, and accordingly many surgeons think it has a promising future. Extensive training and experience are necessary with this new technique. One drawback is that the sense of touch is lost. It is all done with metal instruments in the body cavities, with the surgeon viewing an electronic screen. The small size of the incision required is one of endoscopic surgery's greatest virtues, with less postoperative pain for the patient. Time will be required for full evaluation of this new technique. It is now possible, as I understand, for the surgeon to operate electronically from a remote location! That I have difficulty accepting. Unexpected things happen, and the person in charge should be there.

Final Thoughts—Better Understanding of Ourselves and Others Here and Abroad

With our ever-increasing population and all the conflicts in the world it seems that our greatest problems collectively lie within ourselves, regarding our personal relationships with those about us. We must get along with each other as nations as well as individuals. As citizens we must recognize the necessity of helping others less fortunate, curbing selfishness and greed. It is a personal responsibility. The more this is done, the less legal restriction on our activities is required and the more we can enjoy the freedom upon which our great nation was founded 222 years ago. It requires individual effort and regard for others from all of us.

Bibliography

Allen, Tony, editor. 1990. *Time Frame A.D. 1950–1990.* Time-Life.

Archives of Case Western Reserve University, Cleveland.

Archives of University Hospitals, Cleveland.

Asimov, Isaac. 1989. *Asimov's Chronology of Science and Discovery.* New York: Harper and Row.

Beecher, Henry K. and Mark D. Altschule. *Medicine at Harvard the First Three Hundred Years.* University Press of New England.

Beschloss, Michael R., and Strobe Talbot. 1993. *At Highest Levels: The Inside Story of the End of the Cold War.* Boston: Little, Brown.

Blades, Brian, M.D. August 1944. *Journal of Thoracic Surgery* 13:104–306.

Bridgewater, William, editor-in-chief. 1953. *Columbia Viking Desk Encyclopedia.* New York.

Brown, Kent, ed. 1977. *Medicine in Cleveland and Cuyahoga Counties 1810–1976.* Cleveland: Academy of Medicine.

Carrel, Alexis. *Man the Unknown.* New York: Harper, 1935.

Carruth, Groton, and Associates. 1956. *An Encyclopedia of American Facts and Dates.* New York: Thos. Crowell.

Churchill, Winston. 1949. *Their Finest Hour.* Boston: Houghton Mifflin.

Daniel, Clifton, ed. 1989. *Chronicle of America.* Mount Kisko: Chronicle.

DeGregorio, William A. 1991. The Complete Book of U.S. Presidents. New York: Barricade.

Donovan, Hedley, chief ed. 1970. *This Fabulous Century.* New York: Time-Life Books.

Edwards, W. Sterling, M.D., and Peter D. Edwards. *Alexis Carrel.* 1974.

Egeberg, Roger Olaf. 1983. *The General: MacArthur and the Man He called Doc.* New York: Hippocrene.

Encyclopedia Americana. 1920.

Encyclopedia Britannica. 1955.

Flaherty, Thomas H., ed. *Encyclopedia America.* 1992. *Time Frame A.D. 1950–1990.* New York: Time-Life Books.

Freidel, Frank. 1968. *Our Country's Presidents.* Washington, DC: Geographic Society.

Garrison, Fielding H. 1966. *An Introduction to the History of Medicine.* 4th ed. W. B. Saunders.

Gorbachev, Mikhail. 1987. *Perestroika: New Thinking for Our Country and for the World.* New York: Harper and Row.

Gimble, Ian. *Scottish Clans and Tartans.* New York: Harmony.

Gordon, Lois and Alan. *The American Chronicle.*

Hoffman, Mark S., ed. 1993. *The World Almanac 1993.* World Almanac.

Howell, W. H. and Emitt Holt. 1918. "Heparin and Proantithrombin, Two New Factors." *American Journal of Physiology* 47:328–341.

Kirk, John, and Robert Young. 1990. *Great Weapons of WW II*. Walker, 120–127.

Kaufman, Martin. 1976. *American Medical Education*. Westport, CT: Greenwood.

Malinin, Theodore I. 1979. *Surgery and Life: The Extraordinary Career of Alexis Carrel*. Harcourt Brace Jovanovich.

Manchester, William. 1974. *The Glory and the Dream 1932–1972*. Boston, Toronto: Little Brown.

Manchester, William. 1978. *American Caesar: Douglas MacArthur*. 1880–1964. Boston: Little Brown.

Mautz, Fred R. October 1939. "Mechanical Respirator as Adjunct to Closed System Anesthesia." *Proceedings Society Experimental Biology and Medicine 42:190*. Also *Journal of Thoracic Surgery*. (June 1941). 10:544.

Miller, Nathan. 1991. *The Naval Air War 1939–1945*. Annapolis, MO: Naval Institute Press.

Nelson, C. F. November 12–13, 1930. "Hypoxemia." Read at meeting of Southern Association of Anesthetists, Louisville, Kentucky.

Nelson, C. F., and Parke Woodward. 1925. "The Relief of Experimental Arterial Anoxaemia by Compressed Air. *Journal of Pathology and Bacteriology, 28:507–13*.

O'Malley, C. D., ed. 1970. History of Medical Education. UCLA Forum in Medical Sciences, no. 12. U. of California Press.

Sharnik, John. 1987. *The Cold War*. Arbor House.

Spector, Ronald. *Eagle vs. Sun.*

Steinberg, Rafael, and Editors of Time-Life. 1978. *Island Fighting WW II.*

Stix, Gary. December 1995. "Future Wars?" *Scientific American.*

Trimble, Vance H. 1974. *The Uncertain Miracle*. Garden City, NY: Doubleday.

Weckesser, Elden C. 1977. *"The Lakeside Unit of WW II."* Chapter 39 in Brown, *Medicine in Cleveland and Cuyahoga Counties,* 570–578.

Weckesser, Elden C. 1986. *The Department of Surgery, Case Western Reserve University 1843–1986.*

Weir, David R., and Lewis H. Bronson. March 1946. "History of the Fourth General Hospital." *Clinical Bulletin of School of Medicine of WRU and Associated Hospitals* Vol. No. 2:17–27.

Wenborn, Neil. 1991. *The USA: A Chronicle of Pictures*. New York: Smith Mark.

World Almanac. 1993. *World Almanac and Book of Facts*. New York: Scripps Howard.